Jean-Baptiste Morin

Astrologia Gallica

Book Twenty-Three

Revolutions

Translated from the Latin

By

James Herschel Holden, M.A.

Fellow of the American Federation of Astrologers

2nd Edition, revised

Copyright 2002, 2003 by James Herschel Holden

All rights reserved.

No part of this book may be reproduced or transcribed in any form or by any means, electronic or mechanical, including photocopying or recording, or by any information storage and retrieval system without written permission from the author and publisher, except in the case of brief quotations embodied in critical reviews and articles. Requests and inquiries may be mailed to: American Federation of Astrologers, Inc., 6535 S. Rural Road, Tempe, AZ 85283.

First Printed in a limited edition in 2002

Revised and reprinted 2004

ISBN: 0-86690-515-4

Published by:
American Federation of Astrologers, Inc.
Tempe, AZ 85283

Printed in the United States of America

This book

is for

my friend

Susan Horton

**Jean Baptiste Morin of Villefranche
Regius Professor of Mathematics at Paris**

**Who he was, What Kind of Person, and How Great
Can be Known from his Writings, his Horoscope and his Portrait.**

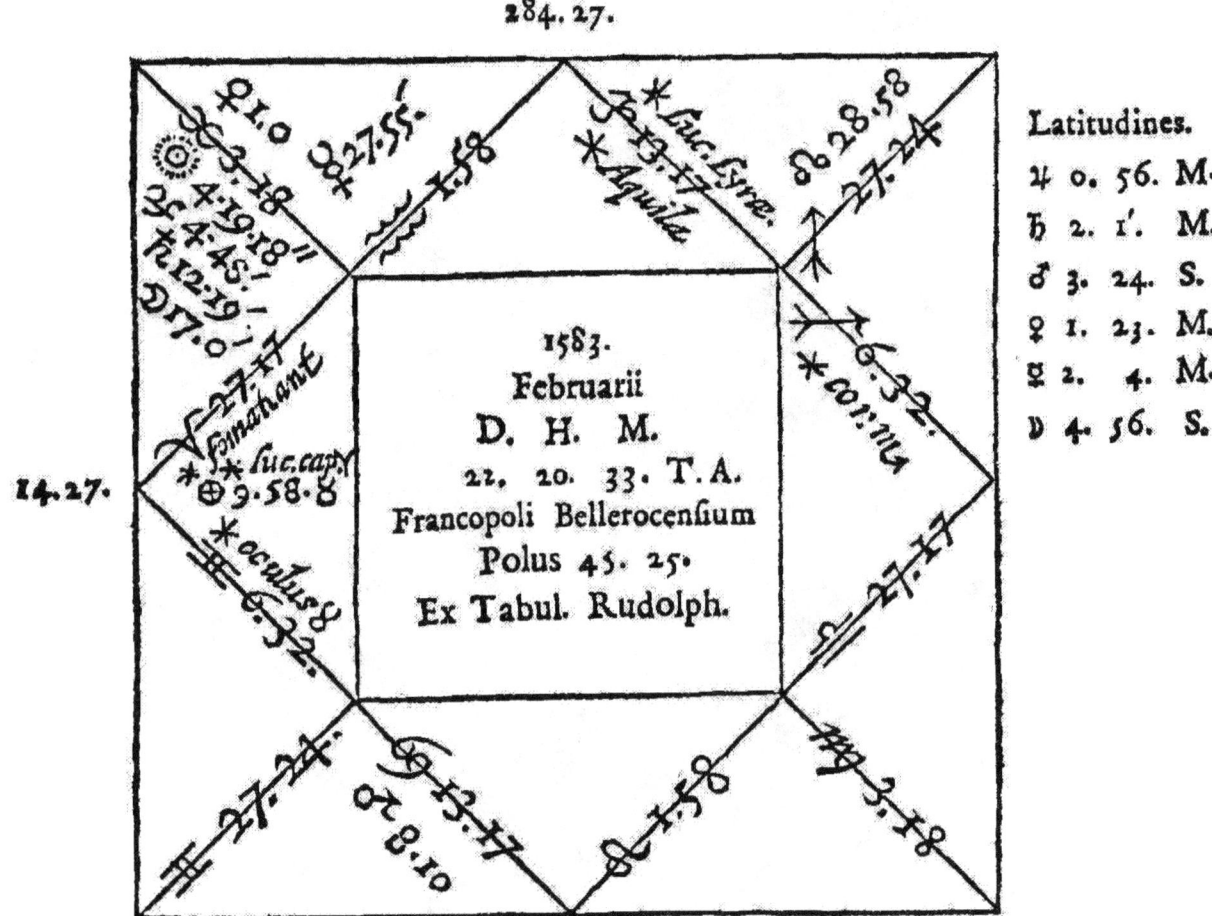

Jean Baptiste Morin
Villefranche-sur-Saône 45 N 25
23 February 1583 8:33 AM
from the Rudolphine Tables

Translator's Note:

The true longitude of the Moon was 16♓47. The longitudes of the outer planets were Uranus 23♒47 (conjunct Mercury), Neptune 17♋52, and Pluto 28♓51.

Table of Contents

Translator's Preface   ix

Book Twenty-Three

Preface   3

Chapter 1. What Astrologers Consider to be a Revolution, and How
Many Kinds of Them There Are   3

Chapter 2. The Mundane Revolutions of the Planets   5

Chapter 3. The Genethliacal Revolutions of the Planets, their Force and Utility   6

Chapter 4. For What Place Should the Figure of a Revolution be Erected   9

Chapter 5. How a Genethliacal Figure of a Revolution of the Sun May be Erected   11

Chapter 6. Whether the Celestial Bodies are Again Determined to
the Native, and by How Much   20

Chapter 7. Whether the Figure of a Solar Revolution can Prevail Against or Over the
Figure of the Geniture or Anything not Signified by the Nativity. A Doctrine
Set Forth with Reasons and 25 Figures   23

Chapter 8. Whether the Annual Status of the Native can be Sufficiently Known from
the Revolution of the Sun Alone if the Revolutions of the Other Planets are Omitted   66

Chapter 9. How the Figure of the Revolution of the Moon should be Erected   69

Chapter 10. In Which the Force of the Revolutions of the Moon is Shown Through
Their Effects in Several Genitures   70

Chapter 11. Whether the Genethliacal Revolutions of the Sun and the Moon Should be
Distributed in Quarters, and Whether Their Figures Should be Inspected for
Accidents Signified by those Revolutions   88

Chapter 12. Whether Revolutions Without the Concurrence of Directions can
Have any Effect on the Native   91

Chapter 13. In Which the Accompaniment of Radical Directions by Revolutions
of the Sun is Proved by Many Examples   93

Chapter 14. In What Way Revolutions Act; and What Must be Noted both
Generally and in Particular about the Times of Their Actions   103

Chapter 15. Whether Their Own Directions Should be Assigned to Revolutions
of the Sun and the Moon, and in What Way and the Measure of Time   106

Chapter 16. In Which the Verity of Revolutionary Directions is Proved by
Many Examples in Revolutions of the Sun and the Moon   114

Chapter 17. The Ruler of the Revolution   125

Chapter 18. The Universal Laws of Judgments on Solar and Lunar Revolutions of Nativities   129

Chapter 19. Compendiously Embracing General Things that must be Looked at in
Revolutions, with a Directory of Judgment   137

Chapter 20. A Caution of no Small Importance that Must Be Observed in Judging Revolutions   138

Appendix 1. The Equation of Time   141

Index of Persons   143

Bibliography   146

Translator's Preface

Those who have not yet read Richard S. Baldwin's translation of the *Astrologia Gallica*, Book Twenty-One, which is on Determinations, and my own translation of Book Twenty-Two, which is on Primary Directions, should do so before reading the present work. In particular, my preface to the translation of Book Twenty-Two contains information about Morin, his masterwork the *Astrologia Gallica*, and my methods of translation. It would be superfluous to repeat all of that here. I will simply say here that Jean-Baptiste Morin, M.D. (1583-1656) was perhaps the greatest French astrologer of all time. He specialized in what is now called "event-oriented" astrology, i.e. the prediction of definite events at specific times in a person's life, rather than the vague psychological pronouncements and mystical maunderings that are characteristic of much of today's astrology. His main tools were Primary Directions, Solar Returns, and Lunar Returns. He takes some note of Transits, but he considers them to be subsidiary influences. And he does not mention Secondary Directions, which were invented by his younger contemporary Placidus (1603-1668) and had not yet come into general use (and would not do so until the twentieth century).

The present book begins with a philosophical discussion of planetary influences with special reference to what we call "Solar Returns" today, but which Morin calls, in the language of his day, "Revolutions." This discussion may seem tedious and unrewarding to the modern astrologer who is mainly intent on learning the fine details of the Morin method of interpreting Solar Returns, but if he will have the patience to read these early chapters, he will gain a valuable insight into the theory behind Solar Returns. After explaining the theory, Morin goes into his method of calculating Solar Returns and finally, into what is of most interest today—his method of interpreting them. He draws many examples from his own life, and some from the lives of others, among them Gustavus Adolphus (1594-1632), King of Sweden; Albert of Wallenstein (1583-1634), the Duke of Friedland; the famous Cardinal Richelieu (1585-1642); and a popular preacher of his day, Father Charles de Condren (1588-1641). He gives a considerable number of Solar and Lunar Return charts, and discusses each chart in light of the events that occurred in the life of the person in the year or month for which it was set, thereby illustrating his method of interpretation by many actual examples. This is followed by a chapter on Primary Directions of the Solar Return charts, again with numerous examples.

Finally, in Chapters 18 to 20 at the end of the book, Morin gives condensed rules for the judgment of Revolutions. These three chapters were translated previously and were included as an appendix to my translation of Book 22 (published by the A.F.A. at Tempe, Arizona, in 1994); they are repeated here with only a few slight changes.

The translation is fairly literal. I have avoided paraphrase where possible. The original text is complicated, so the translation is also complicated. In it I have retained some obsolete or now seldom used technical terms, such as "Revolutions" (for 'Returns'), "figure" (for 'chart'), "geniture" (for 'horoscope'), "genethliacal" ('relating to the natal chart'), "apheta" (now more often called "hyleg"), and "anaereta" (less accurately spelled "anareta"—the point in the chart that indicates death when the apheta moves to it by direction). I have also kept the useful terms "constitution" and "virtue": "constitution" refers to the overall makeup of a chart—the sign and house positions of the planets; "virtue" refers to the active force of a celestial factor—its strength or ability to act in a characteristic manner. Those who have read the translations of Books 21 and 22 will already be familiar with the terms peculiar to Morin—"determinations," "celestial state," and "terrestrial state." I have also decided to translate the Latin word *morbus* as 'illness' rather than 'sickness', as I translated it in Book 22, since Morin usually refers to serious and prolonged maladies rather than short-term and less severe ones. Here and there I have added a few needful words in square brackets and footnotes to clarify some obscure points. I have also written out the names of planets, signs, aspects, etc., although in the *Astrologia Gallica* they are usually indicated by symbols.

Those astrologers who favor Solar and Lunar Returns and Primary Directions as predictive tools will find that a careful reading of this treatise of Morin's will provide an outstanding guide to their interpretation. However, they should always bear in mind Morin's oft repeated dictum that the birth chart forecasts the native's entire life, while the Solar and Lunar returns, considered in relation to the Primary Directions, are useful to indicate the approximate time when events signified by the nativity will happen and to add some precision to the exact nature of the events, while transits can indicate the very day of their occurrence. But, and Morin stresses this point repeatedly, the Returns, the Primary Directions, and the Transits are all subordinate to the birth chart — they must be interpreted within the framework set at birth; they cannot overrule it! He also points out that some events can occur that are not indicated in the birth chart, and he explains the reasons for this.

I have chosen to reproduce the horoscopes and the Solar and Lunar Return charts directly from Book 23 rather than redraw them in the modern round form. Thus, the reader will see them exactly as Morin drew them. They may look odd at first, but the reader will soon become accustomed to the square form. The chart data is given in the center of each chart in Latin and a translation is given underneath the chart. The times are LAT (counted from the previous noon, in the center of the chart). If the reader wishes to recalculate a chart, he should apply the Equation of Time from the table in Appendix 1 to the time shown in order to convert it from LAT to LMT. The result of the recalculation can then be checked by comparing the calculated RAMC with the RAMC of the original chart; it should be within half a degree or less. There are numerous small errors in these charts, most of them insignificant. Where I have noticed an error in a chart, I have mentioned it in a footnote, but I have not checked each chart in detail.

However, in the case of the Lunar Revolutions, there are frequent errors in the **time** of the chart. The reason is two-fold: (1) the longitude of the Moon in the natal chart may be in error by as much as half a degree; and (2) the calculated longitude of the Moon at the time of the Lunar Return may also be in error by as much as half a degree. These errors are due to the inherent inadequacy of the lunar theory of the *Rudolphine Tables* with which they were calculated. The average error will therefore be a half degree in the Moon's longitude at the time of the return, which will cause an average error of nearly 1 hour in the calculated time of the Revolution. In a worst case, the error could be as much as two hours.[1] Morin was evidently unaware of this possibility of error, since he assumed that the lunar longitudes calculated from the tables were correct. I have recalculated the true time of each Lunar Revolution (with an accu-

---

[1] In his calculation of the Lunar Revolution preceding the demise of Father Charles de Condren, Morin inadvertently calculated the return of the Moon to 25 Scorpio 10 rather than 28 Scorpio 10 (as he had calculated it for the natal chart). This caused an error in the calculated time of the Lunar Return of 5 hours and 3 minutes!

racy of plus or minus 2 or 3 minutes) and given it in a footnote.

And I have not checked the calculations of the Primary Directions in Chapter 13. Those who wish to do so can find the necessary formulae and instructions in Appendix 5 of my translation of Book 22 of the *Astrologia Gallica*.

The reader may also wish to recalculate those Lunar Revolutions whose true times produce significant changes in the corresponding charts. This would be a good exercise for the student astrologer.

James Herschel Holden
Spring 2000

Note 1. This translation was circulated privately after its completion in the year 2000. The present version has been reformatted for publication and slightly revised—the principal changes being the correction of typographical errors and the addition of a few more footnotes.

James Herschel Holden
28 December 2001

Note 2. A few dozen copies of this book were published and distributed in the summer of 2002. But in the following November I acquired a copy of Kepler's *Rudolphine Tables*, and from the information there I have now revised Note 1 on Page 2 of the translation to correct my previous erroneous surmise that Kepler had adopted a fixed value of the Obliquity of the Ecliptic.

J.H.H.
10 December 2002

Note 3. This second edition adds the portion of Chapter 5 that was omitted in the first edition and also adds a few notes and one Bibliography entry. The Index of Persons is revised to reflect the new page numbers. And I want to express my special thanks to my friend Kris Brandt Riske who edited both the first and second editions of this translation.

J.H.H.
5 September 2003

ASTROLOGIA GALLICA

BOOK TWENTY-THREE

THE REVOLUTIONS OF NATIVITIES

Preface

Judicial astrology is especially destined for mankind; it is particularly concerned with two kinds of Celestial Charts that pertain to mankind: namely, Natal Charts and the Charts of Revolutions. We have spoken at length about the former in Books 21 & 22; but that which remains for us is to treat of the Revolutions of Nativities.[1] Moreover, many astrologers, Stadius among them, have believed this doctrine to be vain and false; which is not surprising; because, due to the erroneous Tables of the motion of the Sun available in their time, the hour of the Chart of the Solar Revolution sometimes differed from the truth by more than 6 hours: and so a Celestial Chart resulted that was absolutely erroneous, from which they could predict nothing other than falsities[2]. But others, even at the present time in which Tables of the Sun are available that are sufficiently accurate for this purpose, persist in that same belief without any reason whatsoever, but because of their stupid ignorance they should only be hissed off stage. On the other hand, others have asserted this doctrine to be true and in conformity with experience; but, being unaware of its principles, they have written about it in a diverse manner, and one swarming with notable errors; and in truth, they have handed it down to us incompletely. Since, therefore, this doctrine is almost a half part of genethliacal Astrology, we have tried with all our strength to leave it to Posterity, not only whole and complete, but also based upon true foundations and experiences. As to which, whether we have done what we wanted to do, the Reader initiated into these sacred things will easily judge.

Chapter I.

What Astrologers Consider to be a Revolution, and How Many Kinds of Them There Are.

Among astrologers, a revolution is the restoration of a planet to the same celestial longitude by its traversal of its whole orbit. It is said to be to the same longitude because although there are several kinds

---

[1] "Revolutions of Nativities" = "Solar Returns." In this translation I have retained the older term "Revolution" rather than substitute "Return." A related term is "Revolution of Years," which can be qualified by the addition of "of the World," in which case it = "Aries Ingress," or by the addition of "of the nativity," where it is simply a lengthier way of *saying* "Revolution of the Nativity."

[2] This statement is false. And it is surprising that Morin, who was the Royal Mathematician of France, made it. He was thinking about the fact that the older tables of the Sun had errors of 15' of arc or more in the Sun's longitude. But what he failed to consider was that the error mainly consisted of a constant part and a cyclic part with a period of one year. Hence, if the natal solar longitude was 15' too great, the solar longitude at each of the solar returns would also be very nearly 15' too great. Consequently, the calculated *times* of the Solar Returns would have been very nearly correct, even though the Sun's *longitude* was somewhat in error. Hence, if the older astrologers found Solar Returns ineffective, it was not because the charts were wrong.

of revolutions of a planet, yet only two modes of them occur here that are worthy of our consideration. The first is that in which the planet revolves to the same point of the *caelum* according to its latitude and longitude; and this mode only pertains to the Sun, which moves perpetually in the ecliptic, not varying on either side, but fixed, as Kepler rightly judged in his *Rudolphine Tables*, which [ecliptic] is perpetually of the same inclination to the equator,[1] the sectional points of which are also fixed, whatever the champions of terrestrial motion chatter about without any demonstration to the contrary.[2] Hence, it follows that the Sun comes in a year's time to the same point in the *caelum*, drawn through the whole ecliptic, according to its longitude and latitude (which is zero in the ecliptic) and also its declination. The second mode is that in which a planet returns for instance to the same point in the sky in longitude, but not in latitude. And this mode is proper to the rest of the planets from the Sun, which, since they have their own orbits that are inclined to the ecliptic, they are therefore subject to [having] latitude. And because their nodes move in the ecliptic, it happens that, with the exception of the Moon, whose nodes revolve to the same point in the ecliptic in about 19 years, scarcely ever is any one of the rest of the planets restored to the same point in the *caelum* both in longitude and latitude, on account of the very slow motion of their own nodes. Whence, it is evident that the revolutions of the Sun are much simpler and more preeminent than the revolutions of the other planets, and also more efficacious.

It is also said about the travel of a planet's whole orbit, on account of the regressions of Saturn, Jupiter, Mars, Venus, and Mercury, which also restore the planet to the same point in the *caelum* in longitude, but without its having traveled through its whole orbit. So in fact a planet is not said to be revolved.

But since the revolutions of no planet are infinite, because, except for God, neither is unlimited action given nor can it be given, it is therefore necessary that there shall have been something primal, and some beginning of this too; that is, a place in the *caelum* in which a planet was placed by God at the beginning of the World. Whence it ought to be considered that the revolution of a planet occurs in two ways. First, with respect to the beginning of the World, by which the planet is restored to the same place in the *caelum*, at least in longitude, at which its motion begins from the beginning of the World. And this is for the whole World and universal for all the nations of the Earth, and it is called *mundane*. The second is with respect to the beginning or to the generation of any living thing susceptible to influences; by which a planet also returns to the same place in the sky in longitude in which it was [posited] at the moment of its generation or birth; and this is particular, and it is designated "from birth"; for instance, it is said by Cardan[3] to be the first, the second, or the twentieth, or some other revolution of the nativity from the moment of the geniture.

---

[1] This seems to imply that Kepler thought the Obliquity of the Ecliptic had a fixed value. But he didn't. Its actual variation is only about -46.8″ of arc per century. And this is too little to have been detected in the carefully recorded observations of Tycho Brahe, from which Kepler worked. However, on p. 103 of his *Rudolphine Tables*, Kepler proposes a curious cyclic motion of the Obliquity, varying from a minimum of 23°28′28″ to a maximum of 23°53′16″ and back again in 2664 years. Its value in 1627 was 23°31′16″. He was perhaps led to this erroneous theory by the fact that Ptolemy had adopted the value of 23°51′20″ (although its true value then was only 13).

[2] Morin, following Tycho's lead, maintained that the Sun revolved about the Earth, but that all the other planets revolved about the Sun. This theory, wrong as it was, permitted an accurate computation of observed motions, while at the same time avoiding conflict with the doctrines of the Church, which preferred to believe that the Earth was fixed in the center of the universe.

[3] Jerome Cardan, M.D. (1501-1576), the famous physician, mathematician, astrologer, and miscellaneous writer.

Chapter II.

The Mundane Revolutions of the Planets.

Since the mundane revolution of a planet is its restitution to the same place in longitude from which its motion began at the beginning of the World, as was said in the preceding chapter, but since those initial places are unknown, at least for Saturn, Jupiter, Mars, Venus, Mercury, and the Moon, it is plain that the mundane revolutions of these planets are also unknown. In the case of the Sun, there is also a difference of opinion as to what point of the ecliptic it was made to be in on the 4th day of creation[1]; for some want it to have been in the beginning of Libra, others in the beginning of Cancer, since all agree that it was placed in some cardinal point. But I, from the demonstrated futility of the reasons adduced by both of them, and on account of reasons of much greater weight, have declared in Book 2, Chapter 4, that the Sun was placed [initially] in the beginning of Aries; therefore, we can erect its mundane revolutions, but [they are] of obscure and only incomplete signification; namely, because although the time of the Solar ingress into Aries can be known for any particular place on Earth, at least with the tables made according to the laws of our restored astronomy,[2] and consequently the figure of the revolution can be erected, by which there will appear at that moment what is the celestial state both of the Sun and of the other planets and their determination for the place on Earth for which the figure was erected. But because it is not known at what hour in that place the Sun was placed at the beginning of the World and what were then the places of the other planets in the sky, consequently that initial figure cannot be known in which the Sun with the other planets began to influence these inferior [regions], especially that particular place on the Earth, so that this [chart] can be compared with that, for only from this comparison of figures and their radical directions can a clear and complete signification be brought forth, as can be done from the revolutions of nativities, concerning which if anyone shall have made a judgment without having considered the natal figure and its directions, he will greatly err in his predicting. For he will predict great and favorable things if he sees the Sun in the ASC or the MC of the revolution, although unfavorable things should be predicted if in the genethliacal figure the Sun is badly afflicted in the eighth or twelfth [house]; and the same logic applies in other instances. Therefore, from mundane revolutions of the Sun, we can scarcely hope for any certitude of prediction by reason of the house of the figure or the influences according as they are generally referred to that same place on Earth, unless perhaps insofar as they are consulted together with particular revolutions of nativities, because the particular always depends to some degree on the general—although by reason of the constitution of the air those revolutions always have much virtue—[i.e.] from that initial figure to those independent of it. But about these [we shall speak] more fully elsewhere; and here this will suffice: that it is evident how much the annual revolutions of the World can be useful in [the understanding of] the annual revolutions of nativities. For if the annual mundane revolution shall have been very lucky and favorable in itself, this will be good for all those individuals living in the place of the figure, especially for those whose genethliacal revolutions agree with that revolution of the World; but it will be necessary to say the contrary if both the mundane and the genethliacal revolutions agree in evil and misfortune; for in fact the celestial constitution, general as well as particular, can always act as much as is in accordance with its own proper force, unless in acting it depends on something prior.[3]

---

[1] According to Genesis 1:14-17, God created the luminaries on the fourth day.

[2] He refers to the theory underlying the *Rudolphine Tables*.

[3] The point of this discussion is that it is not sufficient to compare the solar return with the natal chart, but the Aries In-

Chapter III.

The Genethliacal Revolutions of the Planets, their Force and Utility.

Since in the figure of a nativity we take the true place not only of the Sun but also of the other planets, and, having run through their own particular orbits and returned to their own radical places with respect to the nativity, they renew their own force with regard to the nativity itself, by reason of their own determination in the genethliacal figure, it would certainly seem to be necessary to erect and inspect the revolutions of the individual planets, so that it might be established to what degree from the state of the rest of the sky and the annual determination they are then helped or hindered in their action according to their radical determination; for that of the Sun is accustomed to become useful, although Ptolemy [2nd century], in the *Quadripartite,* Book 2, Chapters 9 and 11,[1] indeed handed down the doctrine of erecting an annual universal revolution of the Sun at the 4 cardinal points of the zodiac, but not of erecting particular figures for nativities, which in fact he didn't mention; whence it would be permissible to doubt whether genethliacal revolutions of the Sun were in use in Ptolemy's time.[2]

But Cardan seems to have given an inkling in his *Book of the Judgments of Genitures*, Chapter 6,[3] that revolutions, not only of the Sun but also of the planets, are useful, when he speaks of the reversions of the individual planets to their radical places, but he errs in many places. First, when he says that the reversion of the Sun to its place signifies nothing because it may be presupposed. For if the revolution of the primary and principal planet would signify nothing, why would its figure be erected for judgment? And what would the revolutions of the satellites of the Sun signify, about which it could also be said that they are presupposed, when their figures are erected? Secondly, when he says that the reversion of Mercury to its own place does not signify very much, because it happens frequently. For then it follows that the reversion of the Sun to its own place signifies more, because it happens more rarely than the reversion of Mercury: On the contrary, it follows that the reversion of the Moon will signify the least of all, against the opinion of Cardan, who gives it a moderate signification among the revolutions of Mercury, Venus, and Mars, Jupiter, and Saturn, against the truth of the matter, as will be shown below.

It will be said by the majority that hitherto the precise places of the planets at the moment of the na-

---

Ingress for that location must also be considered, since it predicts what in general will happen to everyone resident to that location.

[1] Book 2, Chapter 10, "Concerning the New Moon of the Year" in Robbins's edition of the *Tetrabiblos*. However, as Morin realized, Ptolemy does not prescribe setting up ingress charts, but rather he says to look at [a chart set for the time of] the new or full Moon that most closely precedes the four cardinal points.

[2] Apparently they weren't. The classical Greek astrologers had symbolic schemes for determining the ruler of the year, but they were not based on calculating a chart for the moment when a planet returned to a particular place. The earliest treatises on Aries Ingresses and solar returns as Morin and we understand them are those of the Arabian astrologers, not earlier than the 8th century. Thus, they appear to be an invention of the medieval astrologers.

[3] See pp. 440-443 of vol. V of the 1563 opera omnia edition. The chapter title is "The Significations of Revolutions, and the Method of Judging According to our own Opinion." It is illustrated with the 44th solar return of Cardan's own horoscope. The passage cited by Morin runs: "You should know thirdly that the Sun's return to its own place signifies nothing because it is presupposed. And Mercury little, because it happens frequently. Venus, more, but still not much. The Moon, a moderate amount, but not so much as the superior [planets] on account of the swiftness of its motion. Mars does more, then Jupiter, and most of all Saturn."

tivity were not known due to the deficiency of the astronomical tables, and for that reason it cannot be known at what moment of time [the planets] return to their own radical places, especially Jupiter and Saturn which are very slow in their motion; and, with the hour of their return unknown, the figure of revolution can hardly be erected.

Truly, this objection gives a definite reason why this cannot have been done, but it does not follow that it is impossible or useless. And therefore if accurate tables of the planets are available, revolutions of all the planets can also be erected accurately, certainly with great praise and utility for astrology. When moreover, after the greatest labors of the astronomers, and especially of the most noble Tycho Brahe [1546-1601], it has finally come about in this age for the Sun, that its motion has become sufficiently well known to establish its annual revolution[1]; it is at least proper to use the revolutions of this principal planet, especially since it is proved most evidently by experience that they are of the greatest utility for knowing in advance the state of the year; and it cannot be said more amply than that in his own time Stadius [1527-1579] used to say that he had not ever detected any force or verity in revolutions, which was of course because the *Alphonsine* and *Prutenic Tables*[2] were then in error in the place of the Sun by more than 20 or 30 minutes of arc, and so the figures of the revolutions are erected with an error of more than a quarter of the sky. Despite this, the laws of the revolutions certainly in fact remained true in themselves and with respect to a true figure; but because in place of this a very erroneous figure was given, who could have perceived any truth in that?[3]

Furthermore, nowhere can it be better shown in how much regard the genethliacal revolutions of the Sun were held among the old astrologers, than [in the statement by] by Hermes the Philosopher[4] in his *The Revolutions of Nativities*,[5] Book 1, Chapter 4, all of which I have thought proper to insert here:

---

[1] Unfortunately this was not the case. The *Rudolphine Tables* had less than a quarter of the error in the solar longitudes that the best of the older tables had. But they still had a cyclic error of a little more than 7 minutes of arc, and to make matters worse, the error reached its maximum near the Aries Ingress and the Libra Ingress. Hence, even when using the *Rudolphine Tables*, astrologers calculated Aries (and Libra) Ingresses that were about 3 hours off, thus vitiating the house positions and the accidental rulers. But Morin did not know this.

[2] The *Alphonsine Tables* were prepared under the direction of King Alphonso X of Spain (1226-1284) and were printed in 1483. The *Prutenic Tables* were those of Erasmus Reinhold (1511-1553), based on the theory of Copernicus (1473-1543) but with some minor revisions; they were printed at Tübingen in 1551. Most of the 16th and early 17th century ephemerides were based at least to some extent on one or the other of them.

[3] Here again it should be noted that errors in the solar longitudes have little effect on the accuracy of solar returns, but they do introduce large errors into solar ingresses, because there it is a question of the absolute accuracy of the solar longitude rather than merely a return to a previously calculated longitude, and Morin's "error of more than a quarter of the sky" was actually the case. In short, errors in the old solar tables caused all the house positions to be wrong for calculated solar ingresses, but did not essentially affect the accuracy of solar returns (contrary to what Morin evidently believed).

[4] What Morin had no way of knowing, and what in fact did not become known until the twentieth century, is that the book in question was not written by "Hermes the Philosopher" but rather by the great Arabian astrologer Albumasar (Abū Maʿshar) in the ninth century. Although the book in question is a good treatise on solar returns, Morin, who detested the Arabs, would probably not have cited it had he known its true author.

[5] Morin has cited this passage from the edition by Hieronymus Wolf, *Hermetis philosophi de Revolutionibus Nativitatum* (Basel, 1559). The same passage caught the eye of Auguste Bouché-Leclercq, who translated it into French in his *L'Astrologie grecque* (Paris, 1899), pp. 507-508. Bouché-Leclerq rightly observed in a footnote "The author is evidently an Arab..." The Latin version was made from a Greek translation of an Arabic original. The Arabic is extent in MSS but has not been edited. David Pingree has published an edition of the Greek version as *Albumasaris De revolutione nattvitatum* (Leipzig: B.G. Teubner, 1968).

The utility (he says) *of the understanding of things and their effects on men from the revolution of years is manifest. For all the Babylonians and Persians and Indians and Egyptians, kings as well as laymen, did not try to take in hand anything in any year unless they had first inspected their own revolutions of years. And if they found the year to have been good, they took the work in hand; but if the contrary, they declined it. And the kings were accustomed to inspect the nativities of those in charge of the army, and they observed their revolutions of years; and if they found the revolution of any one of them to signify power and victory, they sent them forth against the enemy; but if the contrary, they dismissed [them]. And they were not accustomed just to observe their nativities, but also those of the commanders, to see whether their revolutions of years indicated a fortunate outcome. Because if it was signifying a fortunate outcome, they would send them forth; but if less than that, they would bring forward others, whose revolutions of the year were indicating a fortunate success. Similarly too, when the kings would see a hindrance for some action in any year of their own nativities, they would scarcely take that action in hand. In similar fashion, both those kings and laymen were accustomed to observe, from the revolution of years, medicines useful to them, foods and drink also, selling and buying, and all of their initiatives, and they used them, dismissing what was going to be harmful in that year. They were also accustomed to make their determinations both from their own nativities and also from those of others: for men wishing to procreate children were accustomed to observe not only their own [revolution for the] year, but also [that of] the woman; and if either of the figures was signifying procreation, they would lie with them. Otherwise, they would look for others whose nativities were signifying the birth of children. Wherefore, the revolution of years is very useful and expedient.*

There is, therefore, a force inherent in the revolutions of the planets, and it is outstanding, and especially in the revolutions of the Sun. And that force very likely consists of this: that a planet, having accomplished the circuit [of its own orbit], returning to its own radical location, renews its own radical force with regard to the native, by reason of its own determination in the genthliacal figure, insofar as it first affected that one being born from that place in the *caelum*, and it rouses up the seeds of its own influence projected upon the one being born, to produce its own effects, and [it does] that by reason [of its being] similar or dissimilar to the geniture according to the similitude or dissimiltude of the *caelum* at the moment of the revolution, as well as by the celestial and the terrestrial state of the planet whose revolution is being noted. And because in the periodical revolution of any planet to its own radical place, such a similitude or dissimilitude should be noticed, and also the celestial or terrestrial state of that same planet; therefore, in any periodical revolution, the celestial figure must be erected, and the true places of all the planets must be placed in it. And the reason is because, when the planets are moving, they are continually determined with respect to us, as is established from their transits. When, therefore, some revolution of a planet takes place, the places of the others in the *caelum* should also be looked at, because they are pertinent to the celestial and terrestrial state of the planet which is making the revolution; but for perceiving that force by manifest experience, it is absolutely necessary that the revolutionary figure be had accurately.

Chapter IV.

For What Place Should the Figure of a Revolution be Erected.

About this matter, the old astrologers settled absolutely nothing; but, in common with them, the moderns by tradition only, always erect the figure of the revolution for the latitude of the natal place; but I erect it for the latitude of the place in which the native is found at the very moment of the revolution. And this difficulty, since it is one of the greatest importance in astrology, on account of the travels of a man, by which now and then he is transferred to places distant from his natal place by a sixth or a fourth, or even by a whole half of the circle of the Earth, and in which places he is found at the time of the revolution, or he may even spend the rest of his life there. Therefore, the reason why we may dissent from the others in this matter ought to be given by us here—the reason that has already been communicated in part to many astrologers, our familiars in Paris, and that has drawn them forcibly and instantly to our opinion. And afterwards, having been published in our abbreviated *Rudolphine Tables*, it has been approved by everyone.

It is therefore certain that in constructing a natal horoscope the longitude and latitude of the place in which the nativity occurs is exactly sought out, so that the exact placement of the *caelum* may be had, not primarily and per se with respect to that place itself, but with respect to the one who is born in that place; then it may be known what influences emanate from such a placement, embracing the native's fate; therefore, a chart is in fact erected for the place of the nativity, not by reason of the place, but by reason of [the birth of] the native. And because the placement of the *caelum* is not inquired into primarily and per se with respect to the place, but with respect to the native, it is plain then that either the celestial influx is imprinted only on the place itself, or only on the native, or on both. But the first of these cannot be said to be the case because the place of the nativity is merely a surface of the body surrounding the location of the birth, or a part of the mundane space enclosed by that surface, consequently it is a mere occurrence, because it cannot be subject to the virtue brought down from the *caelum*, nor can it experience anything like that virtue. And although the place of the nativity is not such a surface, but [rather] the house or the city in which the infant is born might be said to be by someone; nevertheless, the celestial influx of the natal constitution is not imprinted on them; from which it is plain that it is not on them but on the native that the natal influence bestows its effects. And it is not Paris that undergoes the fates of all those who are born in Paris; otherwise, what mutation of the city would there be from individuals born in Paris at individual hours? Add the fact that the house and the city are artifacts, very little susceptible to the celestial influx, as we have said in Book 20, Section 4, Chapter 2. But if you would allow the celestial influx to be imprinted on both, or if the influx can fulfill its effects on either of these separate entities (which we have already refuted in the place cited) or on both, or only on the other, namely the native, since these are existing together, then for the native himself it will be very easy by his departure from his natal place to avoid whatever effects are going to come forth from that celestial influence, [a matter] that experience struggles with—indeed it adds to the confusion, seeing that those travels from the natal place are found to be due to the celestial influx. The fact therefore remains that the celestial influx on the genethliacal constitution is imprinted on the native alone, who carries it with him wherever he will have taken himself. And especially when we may see many people born to lengthy or almost continuous travels, who spend almost their whole lives in a place very distant from their natal place under the compulsion of the fates arising from the natal influx. Therefore, the placement of the sky is noticed primarily and per se with respect to the native, on whom the place per se confers nothing in this regard, but only by accident.

But, having considered these things, it is clearly deduced that if the natal constitution of the sky pertains not to the natal place but to the native per se, the same thing should be judged about the revolutionary constitution, which would be investigated in vain with respect to the natal place from which the native is absent, since the influx of that constitution (as was said about the nativity) is not imprinted upon that place; and a revolution erected for the place of the nativity with the native absent has its effects only in that place and not where the native is. The reason for this is obvious, because the influxes of the stars are determined by their relation to the horizon, and they are active according to that location; therefore, when they are determined to a horizon where the native is not, they act in that place and not where the native is. But on what do they act? On that which is born there then or is living there, whether it is a plant, a brute beast, or a man, and not on a native then existing somewhere else! Therefore, the revolutionary constitution must be investigated primarily and per se with respect to the native in whatever place he is at the moment of the return of the Sun to its radical place, and it must be compared with the natal constitution, which, impressed upon the native, accompanies him perpetually.

Moreover, this doctrine is also confirmed by the annual revolutions of the World constructed for the whole circuit of the Earth. For, as in the annual return of the Sun to the beginning of Aries, whatever part of the Earth or whatever nation that is in that part notices the disposition of the sky with respect to itself—just as a man does in the annual return of the Sun to its own radical place. But this may be proven more effectively from the fact that anyone can discover, just as I have done, that this agrees with experience for natives who are very distant from their natal place.

But to this, the following objection could be raised: the native, by his change of location, is going to avoid his natal fate, and all the certitude of this science will be destroyed.

First, it may be said that this follows much more evidently and certainly if you have tied the influx of the natal constitution to the natal place, but not to the native, as was stated above. Second, the virtue of the revolution can extend itself to a certain degree to advance or hinder the radical influx by the influx of the revolution at whatever place, either natal or extraneous, that the native shall have received it—concerning which we shall speak below. And in this the infinite goodness of God shines forth, in that He will have allowed a man to be free to avoid or to mitigate, by a suitable change of location, those malign acts that are going to happen after his birth because of their natal impression, when in the natal place a bad revolution will have occurred agreeing with a bad direction; just as it can happen that a revolution not agreeing with a bad direction in the natal place may be made to agree with it if the native, at the beginning[1] of a revolution, shall have been found in a place distant from the natal place, where the stars with respect to it are allotted a worse placement. Truly from this the certitude of the science is more confirmed than refuted, since thereby the virtue of the stars is evident in nativities as well as in revolutions.

And it should not also be objected that this doctrine overturns all certitude of the prediction of events from the figure of the geniture by means of directions, since the significations of these are confirmed or refuted by the revolutions, the charts of which will not be known [in advance], since the place in which the native will be is unknown at the beginning of the individual revolutions. For the signification of a direction cannot be confirmed from a false chart of a revolution, but only from a true one, namely one

---

1 Reading simply *initio* 'at the beginning' instead of *initio sive* 'at the beginning or'.

erected with respect to [the actual location of] the native. And the astrologer can predict from the figure of the nativity alone all the events that are going to be from the directions in accordance with their virtue, but under the condition that they will be confirmed by true charts of the revolutions. For whoever has done otherwise will be in error. And if the native is an astrologer, he will easily set the chart of his own revolution for the location in which he is situated at the beginning of his own revolution. but if he is not an astrologer, he should take care that the chart is constructed by an experienced astrologer of that place and judged with respect to the radical figure and its directions. And nothing else can be done, at least nothing on which one can rely. Those men known to me as most judicious have been compelled to concede this to me, but others wanted the revolutions always to be looked at at the place of the nativity, even though they confessed that those are more uncertain than the others. From which, while I was looking for what these false revolutions would produce, with the true ones available, they remained silent.[1]

Moreover, as for radical directions, these are bound to the natal figure that is imprinted upon the native, in which the potential determination of the significators is reduced to action as in Book 22, Section 3, Chapter 2, and which the native carries with him always, wherever he goes. And therefore the artificial directions are always made with respect to the longitude and latitude of the natal place, because they are merely expressive of the natural directions that Nature herself made on the first day of the nativity and impressed upon the native at that same longitude and latitude, as we have said in Book 22, Section 3, Chapter 2.

Chapter V.

How a Genethliacal Figure of a Revolution of the Sun may be Erected.

Two principal ways [of doing] this occur to us. First, by ephemerides or fundamental tables of of the motion of the Sun, from which the true place of the Sun is taken at the moment of the nativity; but some ephemerides or tables bring in an error. Second, by special tables of the annual revolutions of the Sun.

For the first method, the place of the radical Sun must be taken accurately to minutes and seconds [of arc]. For since the mean hourly motion of the Sun is only 2′28″, an error of 30″ in the place of the Sun would cause 3 degrees of error in the RAMC and the OA of the ASC of the revolution; and a larger error would cause an error of more degrees. But the procedure is like this.

Let there be taken two places of the Sun at the hour of noon in the ephemerides; one greater and the other less than the radical place of the Sun; and having subtracted the lesser from the greater, there will remain the true diurnal motion of the Sun in 24 hours. Furthermore, let that lesser place be subtracted from the radical place of the Sun, so that the difference in hours is apparent. Then it is stated by the golden rule. If the diurnal [motion] of the Sun is [so much] in 24 hours, what will be the the value of the said difference? And the hours and minutes corresponding to that difference will be produced; and it

---

[1] In other words, they were unable to explain what the revolutions calculated for the birthplace might signify.

must be counted from the noon of the day corresponding to the lesser place of the Sun taken from the ephemeris. And thus the mean time of the solar revolution at its own radical place will be had [measured] from the noon time of the ephemeris,[1] [which is useful] for getting the places of the planets. And yet this will not be absolutely accurate, since the motion of the Sun in indiviual hours is not [entirely] equal, as the golden rule assumes. And in addition, the time thus found requires a double correction for erecting the figure. The first is called the Equation of Time due to the solar eccentricity and the obliquity of the ecliptic, which we have accurately set forth in Book 7 or our *Astronomy Restored* (badly in fact, by Longomontanus[2] in Book 1 of his *Theor.*, p. 42, and Maginus[3] in his *Supplement*, Can. 5; they have thought that the inequality of the Sun due to its eccentricity should be rejected in [dealing] with revolutions of the Sun), and thus the mean time that is found is turned into apparent or true time.[4] The second [correction] is called the correction of time for the difference in meridians, which is necessary when the place of the nativity does not lie on the meridian of the ephemeris, which, having been made by tables suitable for this [purpose], the true time of the revolution of the Sun at the place of the nativity is had, with which the figure of that revolution will be erected if the Native is [still] in that location, at the beginning of the revolution; but if he was in another place on a different meridian the time found for the place of the nativity will have to be reduced and the figure erected for the latitude and longitude of the place in which the Native is found at the beginning of the revolution, according to Chapter 4 [above]. And these [considerations] must be accurately observed; but in [calculating] the places of the planets and the cusps of the figure, I am not accustomed to be so scrupulous—I only put the whole degrees, because I would think [the minutes] to be superfluous.

But if the ephemeris from which the place of the Sun is taken is not continued up to the year of the revolution, then from the fundamental tables from which that ephemeris is deduced, there would have to be found those two places of the Sun mentioned above for the month and the year of the revolution, and they would be worked with just as [was said] above. But if these fundamental tables are not at hand, but others are; then, from these the true place of the Sun at the moment of the nativity must be taken, and then the places for the year and month and day of the revolution, and it must be worked out as above.

Moreover, Kepler, in his *Rudolphine Tables*, put a subsidiary table of the motions of the Sun,[5] by the use of which the time in which the Sun in the given year of the revolution comes to its apogee, and also the place of that apogee; and then, having subtracted the place of the apogee from the radical place of the Sun, or the other way around, the preceding namely from the following, not distant more than a semicircle, there remains the mean anomaly of the Sun,[6] which having been sought out in the aforementioned table, and having applied the rule of proportions by means of logarithms for the minutes and seconds, and having added them to that anomaly, there is ascertained how much mean time the beginning of the revolution precedes or follows the mean time of the apogee of the Sun on the meridian of the ta-

---

[1] In Morin's time, different ephemerides used different meridians for their time standard, unlike today when most ephemerides use the Greenwich meridian for their standard.

[2] Christian Severin (1562-1647), Danish astronomer. He assisted Tycho Brahe for nearly a decade and was later professor of mathematics at the university of Copenhagen.

[3] Giovanni Antonio Magini (1555-1617), professor of astronomy, astrology, and mathematics at the University of Bologna.

[4] That is, the Mean Time is converted into Apparent time.

[5] These tables are on pp. 91-92 of Kepler's *Rudolphine Tables*.

[6] Actually, it is the *true* anomaly that is determined by subtracting the apogee from the true longitude of the Sun.

bles; thus indeed the discovered time of the revolution requires the preceding double correction; and the [place of] the radical Sun must also be taken to minutes and seconds from the *Rudolphine Tables*, or from ephemerides based on them.

But for the second method, Cardan in his Book on the *Restoration of Times and the Motions of the Wandering Planets*,[1] Chapter 5, gave a double table of the revolutions of years, namely one in which for the elapsed years of the nativity either hours and minutes are added to the time of the nativity or degrees of the equator are added to the radical RAMC, so that either the true time may be had or the RAMC of the revolution. But this table is doubly erroneous. First, because the mean excess of the year above 365 days is only 5 hours and 48 minutes and 41 seconds, since it is 4″ greater according to Tycho, *Progymnasmata*,[2] p. 53. Second, because Cardan took no account of the Sun's sign in [calculating] revolutions of the Sun; and he always made the tropical year equal, when nevertheless it is unequal because of the diversity of the sign that the Sun occupies and the one from which it is revolved. Which, when Tycho discovered it, he set forth another Table of the Revolutions of the Sun at the beginnings of the individual signs in Book 1 of his *Progymnasmata*, p. 108, the use of which he teaches on p. 112. But there still appears a double deficiency increasing with the passage of time. First, because it is only constructed at the beginnings of the signs. Second, because it makes the mean longitude of the year still truly less. And consequently, having found the time of the revolution by that table, the true place of the radical Sun to minutes and seconds from the fundamental tables or ephemerides is not had by that; therefore, in [determining] the time of the revolution, an error of several minutes occurs. Which, since I discovered it many times, and also the greater precision in Kepler's subsidiary table of the motions of the Sun, leaving that [other table] aside, I have refined the use of it even further. Since it is of especial importance for revolutions, that their time may be had most precisely; and because it at least shows the true ascensions of the ASC and the MC at the entrance of the Sun into its own radical place for the determinations of the planets in the houses of the figure and the directions of the revolutions, concerning which [we will speak] below. Therefore, in place of these, we have put here the following tables, already set forth by us in our abbreviated *Rudolphine Tables*, published in the year 1650. The [reasons for the] choice of these, if indeed they are compared with the rest, are manifold. First, because the use of these is a necessary not a scrupulous observation of the minutes and indeed of the seconds of the radical place of the Sun. Second, because they are accomodated to whatever degree of the zodiac the Sun occupies in the radix; and from these, but especially from the second, the true excess of the year above 365 days appears, from whatever degree of the zodiac the year begins. Third, because having found the moment of the time of the revolution of the Sun from these tables, and for that same time having sought out the place of the Sun in the radical tables from which the radical place of the Sun was taken to the minutes and seconds and thirds; that same place of the Sun to minutes, seconds, and thirds, is always discovered if the work was done accurately. Fourth, because the use of these [tables] is the easiest of all others, as it will appear below.

Translator's Note: Morin gives instructions for the use of the tables and an example on pp. 18 and 19 following the tables. However, it may not be amiss to give another example in our own words. The tables on p. 15 enable the Reader to determine the longitude of the Solar Apogee in accordance with the motions given in the *Rudolphine Tables*. The small table at the top gives the longitude of the Apogee at

---

[1] Omnibus edition (Lyons: Huguetan & Ravaud, 1663), vol. 5, pp. 1-14.

[2] The full title is *Astronomiae Instauratae Progymnasmata* 'Preparatory Actions for the Renewal of Astronomy'. The first part was published in 1588.

the end of each hundred year period, and the large table at the bottom gives the motion for individual years. To find the longitude of the Apogee for, say 1646, it is only necessary to add the figures given for 1600 in the upper table to those for 46 in the lower table, and we have 3.05.44 + 0.0.47 = 3.06.31, which is 3 signs 6 degrees and 31 minutes or 96°31′.

The two tables on pp. 16 and 17 contain times in hours, minutes, and seconds as a double function of the True Anomaly of the Sun as shown in the left-hand column of each table and the Completed Years after the starting year. The purpose of this table is to show how much time must be added to the starting time to give the time of the solar return after a certain number of years. Thus, for a natal horoscope, the birth time is known; to find the time when the Sun will return to its natal longitude after, say 45 years, the first thing to do is to subtract the longitude of the Solar Apogee for the year of birth from the natal longitude of the Sun. That gives the number with which to enter the left hand column of the tables. Then go across to the vertical columns containing the completed years and take out the times shown there. Add these to the birth time, subtracting 24 hours if necessary, and you will have the time of the solar return for that number of elapsed years.

We will use the *Rudolphine Tables*, and let us say, for example that the birth took place at Paris at 10:50 AM on 12 August 1646 and that the longitude of the Sun at that moment was 19°32′ Leo, which is equivalent to 139°32′. From that we subtract the 96°31′ that we found for the longitude of the Solar Apogee in 1646, and we have 43°01′ for the True Anomaly of the Sun at that moment. That value lies between 40° and 50° in the left hand column of the tables, so we must interpolate by taking 3/10 of the difference of the numbers shown in the vertical columns for 5 years and 40 years, and we will have for 5 years 5.01.26 + (3/10) x .26 or .08; adding that to the 5.01.26, we have 5.01.34. Next we do the same thing for the numbers in the 40 column, and we have 16.10.05 + (3/10) x 4.49, which is 1.27, and adding that to 16.10.05, we will have for 40 years 16.11.32. Then we add the 5.01.34 to the 16.11.32, remembering that this is equivalent to 5:01:34 + 16:11:32 hours in our notation, and we will have 21:13:06 for the increment to be added to the birth date and time to find the date and time when the Sun will return to the natal position in the year 1691. We have 10:50:00 on 12 August + 21:13:06 = 12 August 32:03:06 or, subtracting 24 hours from the time, we have 12 August 08:03:06 in the year 1691. And if we calculate the longitude of the Sun at that time, we find that it is 19°31′ Leo in exact agreement with the natal solar longitude. So we have found the time of the solar return in 1691 to be 8:03 AM at Paris.

Thus we can see the utility of these tables for finding the time of a solar return. If ephemerides were not available for the future year, the use of these tables would give the astrologer the exact time for which to calculate the longitudes of the Sun, Moon, and planets.

The Use of the Tables.

The first table gives the place of the apogee of the Sun[1] at intervals of years after the birth of Christ, which years are understood to be completed years.

---

[1] According to modern theory, the longitude of the apogee on 1 January 1601, which corresponds to 1600 elapsed years, was 96°05′, rather than 95°44′, as shown in the *Rudolphine Tables*. Not a large error, but one that could cause a maximum error of about 45″ in the Sun's longitude near apogee or perigee. And Kepler (and following him, Morin) put the centennial motion of the apogee at +1°43′, which is very close to the true value of +1°42′57″ for 1600. On the whole, these figures are a tribute to Tycho's careful observations and Kepler's reduction of them to a theory and tables.

Tabula motus Apogæi Solis ex Tabulis Rudolphinis.

Anni A Christo	Sig.Gr.M.	Anni A.C.	S. G. M.	Anni A.C.	S. G. M.	Anni A.C.	S. G. M.
1000	2.25.28	1300	3. 0.36	1600	3. 5.44	1900	3.10.52
1100	2.27.11	1400	3. 2.19	1700	3. 7.27	2000	3.12.35
1200	2.28.53	1500	3. 4. 1	1800	3. 9.10	3000	3.29.42

Anni expansi.

An.	G.M.	An.	G.M.	An.	G.M.	An.	G.M.	Anni	G.M.
1	0. 1	23	0.24	45	0.46	67	1. 9	89	1.31
2	2	24	25	46	47	68	10	90	32
3	3	25	26	47	48	69	11	91	33
4	4	26	27	48	49	70	12	92	34
5	5	27	28	49	50	71	13	93	36
6	6	28	29	50	51	72	14	94	37
7	7	29	30	51	52	73	15	95	38
8	8	30	31	52	53	74	16	96	39
9	9	31	32	53	54	75	17	97	40
10	10	32	33	54	55	76	18	98	41
11	11	33	34	55	56	77	19	99	42
12	12	34	35	56	58	78	20	100	43
13	13	35	36	57	59	79	21	200	3.25
14	14	36	37	58	1. 0	80	22	300	5. 8
15	15	37	38	59	2	81	23	400	6.51
16	16	38	39	60	3	82	24	500	8.34
17	17	39	40	61	4	83	25	600	10.16
18	18	40	41	62	5	84	26	700	11.59
19	20	41	42	63	6	85	27	800	13.42
20	21	42	43	64	7	86	28	900	15.24
21	22	43	44	65	8	87	29	1000	17. 7
22	23	44	45	66	9	88	30	2000	34.14

Tabula Revolutionis Solis perpetua accommodata Apogæo

Anni completi.

Anomalia vera Solis	1	2	3	4	5	6	7	8	9
	H.M.S.	H.M.S.	H.M.S.	H.M.S.	H.M.S.	H.M.S.	H.M.S.	H.M.S.	H.M.S.
0	5.48. 2	11.36. 5	17.24. 7	23.12.10	5. 0.12	10.48.15	16.36.17	22.24.20	4.12.22
10	5.48. 4	11.36. 7	17.24.11	23.12.14	5. 0.18	10.48.22	16.36.25	22.24.29	4.12.33
20	5.48. 6	36.12	24.18	12.24	0.30	48.36	36.43	24.49	12.55
30	5.48.10	36.20	24.30	12.40	0.50	49. 0	37.10	25.20	13.30
40	5.48.15	36.30	24.45	13. 1	1.16	49.31	37.46	26. 1	14. 6
50	48.22	36.45	25. 7	13.29	1.52	50.14	38.36	26.59	15.21
60	48.31	37. 1	25.32	14. 3	2.34	51. 4	39.35	28. 6	16.37
70	48.39	37.18	25.57	14.36	3.15	51.54	40.33	29.13	17.52
80	48.49	37.37	26.26	15.14	4. 3	52.52	41.40	30.29	19.17
90	48.58	37.55	26.53	15.51	4.48	53.46	42.43	31.41	20.39
100	49. 7	38.13	27.20	16.26	5.33	54.40	43.46	32.53	22. 0
110	49.16	38.32	27.48	17. 4	6.20	55.36	44.52	34. 9	23.25
120	49.25	38.49	28.14	17.38	7. 3	56.27	45.52	35.16	24.11
130	49.31	39. 3	28.34	18. 6	7.37	57. 9	46.40	36.12	25.43
140	49.38	39.16	28.54	18.32	8.10	57.49	47.27	37.15	26.43
150	49.43	39.26	29. 9	18.52	8.35	58.18	48. 2	37.45	27.28
160	49.47	39.34	29.21	19. 8	8.54	58.41	48.28	38.15	28. 2
170	49.49	39.39	29.28	19.18	9. 7	58.57	48.46	38.36	28.25
180	49.51	39.41	29.32	19.23	9.13	59. 4	48.55	38.45	28.36
190	49.50	39.39	29.29	19.19	9. 9	58.58	48.48	38.38	28.27
200	49.48	39.35	29.23	19.10	8.58	58.45	48.33	38.20	28. 8
210	49.44	39.28	29.12	18.56	8.40	58.24	48. 8	37.52	27.36
220	49.39	39.18	28.57	18.36	8.15	57.55	47.34	37.13	26.52
230	49.33	39. 6	28.39	18.12	7.44	57.17	46.50	36.23	25.56
240	49.26	38.52	28.17	17.43	7. 9	56.35	46. 0	35.26	24.52
250	49.18	38.35	27.53	17.11	6.28	55.46	45. 3	34.21	23.39
260	49. 9	38.17	27.26	16.34	5.43	54.52	44. 0	33. 9	22.17
270	48.59	37.59	26.58	15.57	4.57	53.56	42.56	31.55	20.54
280	48.50	37.41	26.31	15.22	4.12	53. 2	41.53	30.43	19.34
290	48.41	37.21	26. 2	14.43	3.23	52. 4	40.45	29.25	18. 6
300	48.32	37. 3	25.35	14. 7	2.38	51.10	39.42	28.13	16.45
310	48.24	36.47	25.11	13.35	1.59	50.22	38.46	27.10	15.33
320	48.17	36.34	24.50	13. 7	1.24	49.43	37.58	26.14	14.31
330	48.11	36.22	24.32	12.43	0.54	49. 5	37.15	25.26	13.37
340	48. 7	36.13	24.20	12.26	0.33	48.39	36.46	24.52	12.59
350	48. 4	36. 8	24.11	12.15	0.19	48.23	36.26	24.30	12.34
360	48. 2	36. 5	24. 7	12.10	0.12	48.15	36.17	24.20	12.22

mobili, juxta Tychones hypotheses & Rudolphinas Tabulas.

Anni completi.

Anomalia vera Solis	10 H. M. S.	20 H. M. S.	30 H. M. S.	40 H. M. S.	50 H. M. S.	60 H. M. S.	70 H. M. S.	80 H. M. S.	90 H. M. S.
0	10. 0.24	20. 0.49	6. 1.13	16. 1.38	2. 2. 2	12. 2.27	22. 2.51	8. 3.15	18. 3.40
10	10. 0.36	20. 1.12	6. 1.49	16. 2.25	2. 3. 1	12. 3.37	22. 4.13	8. 4.49	18. 5.26
20	1. 1	2. 2	3. 2	4. 3	5. 4	6. 5	7. 5	8. 6	9. 7
30	1.40	3.21	5. 1	6.41	8.21	10. 2	11.46	13.22	15. 3
40	2.31	5. 3	7.34	10. 5	12.36	15. 8	17.39	20.20	22.42
50	3.43	7.27	11.10	14.54	18.37	22.21	26. 4	29.48	33.31
60	5. 7	10.15	15.22	20.30	25.37	30.45	35.52	41. 0	46. 7
70	6.30	13. 1	19.31	26. 1	32.32	39. 2	45.32	52. 3	58.33
80	8. 6	16.12	24.18	32.23	40.29	4.35	56.41	9. 4.47	19.12.53
90	9.36	19.13	28.49	38.25	48. 1	57.38	23. 7.14	16.50	26.27
100	11. 6	22.12	33.18	44.25	55.31	13. 6.37	17.43	28.49	39.55
110	12.41	25.22	38. 2	50.43	3. 3.24	16. 5	28.46	41.27	54. 7
120	14. 5	28.10	42.15	56.20	10.25	24.30	38.36	52.41	20. 6.46
130	15.15	30.30	45.44	17. 0.59	16.14	31.29	46.44	10. 1.58	17.13
140	16.21	32.42	49. 3	5.24	21.45	38. 6	54.26	10.47	27. 8
150	17.11	34.21	51.32	8.43	25.54	43. 4	0. 0.15	17.26	34.37
160	17.49	35.38	53.27	11.16	29. 5	46.54	4.43	22.32	40.21
170	18.15	36.30	54.44	12.59	31.14	49.29	7.43	25.58	44.13
180	18.26	36.53	55.19	13.46	32.12	50.39	9. 5	27.32	45.58
190	18.17	36.34	54.52	13. 9	31.26	49.43	8. 0	26.17	44.35
200	17.55	35.51	53.46	11.42	29.37	47.33	5.28	23.24	41.19
210	17.20	34.40	51.59	9.19	26.39	43.59	1.19	18.38	35.58
220	16.31	33. 2	49.33	6. 4	22.35	39. 5	23.55.36	12. 7	28.38
230	15.29	30.58	46.27	1.56	17.24	32.53	48.22	3.51	19.20
240	14.18	28.35	42.53	16.57.11	11.28	25.46	40. 4	54.21	8.39
250	12.56	25.53	38.49	51.45	4.42	17.38	30.34	43.30	19.56.27
260	11.26	22.52	34.18	45.44	2.57.10	8.36	20. 2	31.29	42.55
270	9.54	19.47	29.41	39.35	49.28	12.59.22	9.16	19. 9	29. 3
280	8.24	16.48	25.12	33.36	42. 0	50.24	22.58.48	7.12	15.36
290	6.47	13.33	20.20	22. 7	33.53	40.40	47. 6	8.54.1	0. 0
300	5.17	10.33	15.50	21. 6	26.23	31.39	36.36	42.12	18.47.29
310	3.57	7.54	11.51	15.48	19.45	23.42	27.40	31.37	35.34
320	2.48	5.36	8.24	11.11	13.59	16.47	19.35	22.23	25.11
330	1.48	3.35	5.23	7.10	8.58	10.46	12.33	14.21	16. 8
340	1. 6	2. 1	3.17	4.22	5.28	6.33	7.39	8.44	9.50
350	0.38	1.16	1.53	2.31	3. 9	3.47	4.24	5. 2	5.40
360	0.24	0.49	1.13	1.38	2. 2	2.27	2.51	3.15	3.40

And so let the place of the apogee of the Sun be found at the completed year 1582 A.D. First, for the years 1500, there are taken in the Table of Collected Years to the right of the year 1500, 3 signs 4 degrees and 1 minute. Then, in the Table of Individual Years, to the right of 82 years, there are taken 1°24′; these are added; and they make 3 signs 5 degrees and 25 minutes for the place of the apogee of the Sun at the aforesaid time. But if the apogee of the Sun is sought for a completed year and some [additional] months, the radical tables will have to be used, or there will have to be taken a proportional part of the annual motion of the apogee, which is 1 minute and 2 seconds; and so, the place of the apogee on the day 22 February 1583 at 20 hours and 34 minutes, for my nativity, is 3 signs 5 degrees 25′ 45″.[1] And so with others.

But the second table gives hours, minutes, and seconds to be added to the hour of the nativity in individual years, so that in this manner the exact time may be had when the Sun returns to its own radical place.

Subtract the current year of the radix or the nativity from the current year of the revolution, and so there will remain the completed years from the nativity. Then, from the true place of the radical Sun, subtract the radical apogee of the Sun; and there will remain the true anomaly of the Sun in the radix; it must be saved [for calculating] the individual revolutions, which you will look for in the left part of the table, and you will look for the completed years from the nativity at the top, having made a double entry both for the anomaly and for the years if it is needed. And in the common angle you will find the hours, minutes, and seconds which should be added to the time of the radix, and it will make the time of the revolution—the true time if in fact the time of the radix was true, but the approximate [time] if it was approximate.[2] But the testing of this table is certain, because if with the found mean time of the revolution, the place of the Sun is calculated from the tables which gave the radical place of the Sun, the same place of the Sun will be found to the minute and down to the second, which is a most certain judgment of the precision of the table.

However, if the sum of the hours exceeds 24, that number must be taken away, and only the excess will be retained counting from the noon of the day of the nativity, unless the year of the revolution was the first after leap-year; for then one day will have to be subtracted from the radical days; and thus the day, the hour, and the minute of the beginning of the revolution will be had. Moreover, the reason for the subtraction is this: because in leap-year one day was added, which in the following year would be an excessive number unless it is subtracted.

In order to find the accurate time of the revolution of my nativity beginning in the year 1645, I wrote these [numbers].

From the year 1645, I subtract 1583 the year of my nativity, and there remain 62 completed years.

Then, from the true place of the Sun in the radix, 11 signs 4 degrees 19 minutes, I subtract the radical apogee of the Sun, 3 signs 5 degrees 25.45 seconds. And there remains the true anomaly of the Sun in the radix, 7 signs 28 degrees 54.25 seconds, which you look for on the left side of the table, and the years completed 60 and 2 at the top, having made a double entry for that same anomaly on the right be-

---

[1] That is 95°26′. The true value was 95°47′.

[2] The Latin has *aequale verò, si aequale* 'but equal [if it was] equal', i.e. of an accuracy equal to that of the radix.

tween 230 and 240°. And having taken the proportional part for 8°54'25", as is the custom, the table will give in the common angle 25 hours 5 minutes and 28 seconds; that is, with 24 hours taken away, 1 hour 5 minutes and 28 seconds.[1] But now let this time of 1 hour 5 minutes and 28 seconds be added to the true time of the radix 20 hours and 34 minutes, and they will make 21 hours 39 minutes and 28 seconds for the true time of the beginning of the revolution at Villefranche, the place of the nativity. But because I was at Paris at the beginning of this revolution, and Paris is 12 minutes of an hour west of Villefranche, I therefore subtract 12 minutes from the 21 hours 39 minutes and 28 seconds, and there would remain 21 hours 27 minutes and 28 seconds for the true time of the beginning of the revolution at Paris, with which [time] you erect the figure for Paris, as is customary for the figures of nativities; and you will have the true degree ascending at the moment of that revolution, and it will be the figure as shown below.

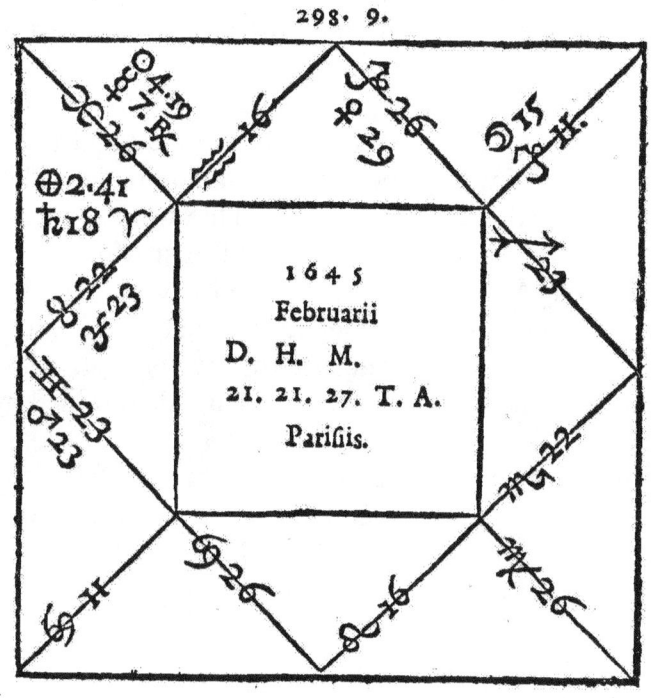

Morin's Solar Return
22 February 1645 9:27 AM LAT
Paris, France

But if you would like to have certain proof of such precision, since the true place of the radical Sun was taken from the *Rudolphine Tables*, constructed for the meridian of Uraniborg, 40 minutes of an hour more easterly than the meridian of Paris; therefore, to the 21 hours 7 minutes and 28 seconds, add

---

[1] The procedure is as follows. In the left hand column, find the numbers 230 and 240. Go across to the right to the column headed 2 Completed Years and write down the numbers 11:39:06 and 11:38:52; then go to the next page and again find the numbers 230 and 240 in the left hand column. Go across to the column headed 62 Completed Years and write down the numbers 13:32:53 and 13:25:46. Add these numbers to the previous pair of numbers to get the change in time for 2 + 60 = 62 Completed Years and subtract 24 hours from each number. You will have then for 230° 1:11:59 and for 240° 1:04:38. Next, you take the proportion 8°54'23" / 10°00'00" = 0.8906, and you multiply that times the difference in the two numbers 1:11:59 and 1:04:38, which is 0:07:21, and you get 0:06:33. Finally, you subtract that from 1:11:59, and you have 1:05:26. this is close to what Morin got, namely 1:05:28.

40 minutes of an hour, and they will make 22 hours 7 minutes and 28 seconds true time at Uraniborg; which again you reduce to mean [time] by our equation of days, which in the abovesaid place of the Sun is 14 minutes 40 seconds of an hour, to be added to the apparent time, and they will make at Uraniborg 22 hours 22 minutes and 8 seconds of mean time; for which, having taken the place of the Sun from the *Rudolphine Tables*, there will be found 11 signs 4 degrees 19 minutes and 10 seconds, in short [the same] as in the nativity. And the logic is the same in other cases.

But in fact let us look at placing the Part of Fortune in the figure of the revolution. Origanus,[1] Part 3, *Introduction*, p. 779, subtracts the place of the Sun in the radix from the radical place of the Moon and adds the remainder to the ASC of the revolution in signs, degrees, and minutes; and that sum determines the place of the Part of Fortune in the revolution. By having done this, the Part of Fortune in the individual revolutions is almost always in the same house of the figure that it occupies in the nativity. Origanus offers no rationale for this new method for [finding] the place of the Part of Fortune in a revolution.

Moreover, Origanus is wrong. For if all the planets and especially the lights change their house in the figure in the individual revolutions, why will the Part of Fortune stand always in the same house; especially, since in nativities it is moved with respect to the rising horizon as the Moon is with repect to the Sun; and therefore there is always the same distance from the ASC as the Moon is from the Sun or vice versa? For this reason, the Part of Fortune is said to be the Lunar ASC, to which the Moon is in the ratio of distance as the Sun is to the ASC of the figure, or vice versa; but that cannot be [the case] by Origanus's method. Third, it is proved by experience that the Part of Fortune calculated in Origanus's way is not effective, as it is when taken in the accustomed way in nativities. therefore, the Part of Fortune in both a nativity and in a revolution must be found and determined by the same method.

Besides, having found the moment of the revolution by these tables, if to that [time] you add 5 hours and 49 minutes, you will have the accurate time of the next following revolution on the same meridian; or if to the RAMC of the preceding revolution you add 87°15′, the RAMC of the next following revolution will result, without any sensible error, up to 3 or 4 subsequent revolutions.

Chapter VI.

Whether the Celestial Bodies are Again Determined to the Native, and By How Much.

That in revolutions the celestial bodies are again determined to the native is proven by reason and by experience. By reason indeed, because not only are we subjected to those bodies at the moment of the nativity, but also throughout the whole course of life, as is established from the [action of the] transits of the planets through the places of the geniture. Moreover, they always act upon us and these sublunar universals by reason of their own nature, celestial state, and placement with respect to the horizon, because it is determined to act with respect to us; and consequently both the Primum Mobile and the plan-

---

[1] David Origanus (1558-1628), professor of mathematics and Greek at Frankfurt-an-der Oder and the author of several volumes of Ephemerides and *Astrologia Naturalis* 'Natural Astrology' (Marseilles, 1645).

ets are determined anew with respect to us in a revolution, not differently than in a nativity. But if anyone shall have said then that it is only proven that they are always determined, but not indeed more at the moment of the revolution than at any other moment preceding or following, I reply that they are not in fact more determined at one moment than at another, since they are always determined, and yet they are determined more *effectively* at one moment than at another, as for example when they revolve to their own radical locations, or when they transit through the places of the geniture, or when they act in the revolutions of the luminaries. Therefore, at the time of that more efficacious determination the celestial constitution confers much; and consequently its inspection is useful for making predictions. But experience entirely confirms the same thing, whereby it is established that individual revolutions do act upon the native by reason of the determination of the celestial bodies in that revolution, as will be evident from the examples that will be given below.

Moreover, how they are determined is going to be understood thus. In a genthliacal constitution, the whole sky through its parts and all the planets are absolutely determined to all the native's accidents,[1] present as well as future, not individually but collectively. That is, no one part of the sky and no one planet is determined to all the native's accidents, but all the planets and all the parts of the sky together are determined to all the native's fates, to which the radical figure itself equates and corresponds; which fates it comprises by its own virtue, and it signifies those primarily. Nevertheless, the determination of each radical planet is still universal and potential for the entire life of the native because of all those things that can happen from the directions of a planet, or from revolutions and transits.

But in the annual revolution of the Sun, the whole sky and all the planets are determined only to those future accidents of the native during [the effective time span of] that revolution whose figure equates to those accidents. And they are not determined absolutely as they are in the nativity, but only with respect to the figure of the nativity, and most effectively for significant effects; since even if both the parts of the sky and the planets are determined anew towards the native in the revolution, by reason of the signification of the houses in which they are found, or which they rule, or which they aspect, they still retain their radical determination always; and according to that they operate in the revolution. As, for example, if Mars were in the eighth [house] of the radix, not only its radical place, but also [the planet] itself, ought always to be looked at in individual revolutions as the *anaereta* or radical significator of death; and this radical determination of it should always be combined in revolutions with the new determination that it is allotted in the revolution, either by reason of the houses of the figure, or by reason of its celestial state, since in fact the determination in the revolution, which is special for that year, brings about and actuates by itself the radical determination, which we have said above is universal for the native's entire life. As, for example, if in a revolution Mars shall have come from the eighth of the radix to the ASC of the radix, death must be feared for the native, or a illness, or some danger to his life; and if besides this it shall have been in the seventh of the revolution, [then] lawsuits, dangers to his life, or death from open enemies or from his spouse must be feared. And illness or danger to his life will also be signified if Mars has come from the eighth of the radix to the ASC of the revolution, and much more so if that ASC was the place of the radical Mars, and Mars itself was in the ASC. And the reasoning is the same for the [other] parts of the sky. As, for example, if the ASC of the radix shall have come to the eighth of the revolution, or the cusp of the eighth of the radix to the ASC of the revolution; either way, illness or dangers to his life are portended. And so with the others.

---

[1] Here, as elsewhere, the astrological term "accident" (from the Latin *accidere* 'to happen') refers to any significant occurrence, good or bad, in the life of the native.

But it can be asked, which new determination is prior and more efficacious in revolutions—is it the radical place of Mars, or Mars itself [in the revolution] viewed also with its own signification or with its radical determination, since both the radical place of Mars, which is fixed in the same point of the sky, and that of the Mars that is continuously mobile in the sky are allotted diverse determinations in a revolution by reason of [the difference in] the figures.

But I reply: the determination of the radical place of Mars is prior and more effective; consequently, it ought to be looked at first in revolutions, taking into account the state of both places in the revolution—both their celestial state and their terrestrial state—and the aspects between them. And if Mars shall have returned to its own radical place, their determination will be very strong in the revolution on account of the unity of place and also of state. And the same reasoning applies to the other planets and significators. And this is evident from the place of the radical Sun in its revolutions, where its determination is the same as it is with the place of the mobile Sun, and the same with both states in the revolution—both celestial and terrestrial—by reason of the sign and house of the figure, for both places are one and the same place.

Furthermore, with the exception that the planets in a revolution are determined anew to the native by reason of the signification of the houses in which they are found, these also determine the parts of the sky that they occupy, no differently than they did in the nativity; and if these shall already have been determined by the radix, either to the cusps of the figure, or to the places of the planets, or to their aspects, such a determination in the revolution will be strong and effective by reason of the nature and strength of the place; but if they were not determined by the radix, but rather by the determinations of another [planet], or of one widely disjunct, such a determination will be weak unless the determining planet is fortified either by its own place in the figure or by its connection with other [planets]. If, for example, Mars shall have come in the revolution from being in the eighth of the radix or being its ruler to the place of the ruler of the radix ASC or to its square, even if the aspect is platic, dangers to the life or illnesses are signified; but if it is not connected even platically to any place in the radical figure, it will only weakly determine that part of the sky that it occupies, and it will operate weakly; unless Mars shall have fallen in the ASC or the twelfth or the eight of the revolution, or is square or conjunct or opposite the ruler of the ASC of the revolution, for in these cases Mars is allotted a determination conformable or akin to its radical [determination], and therefore an efficacious one.

On which account, the determination of the celestial bodies in a revolution should always be noted with respect to their radical determination, which is fundamental and universal for the entire course of life, conferring the force of action on the revolution as a first cause [acting upon] a second, which nevertheless determines the first as to the *kind* [of action]. So, therefore, the determination of a planet in a revolution draws to another kind [of action] the general signification of that same planet from its radical determination. And if the revolutions should act absolutely and notably even without such a respect to the native, the natal fate would be overturned every year by the revolutions, and these would have power over and be contrary to the natal figure, in which, as a result, no faith could be had, contrary to the most evident experience.

Besides this, it should be noted that the radical determination lasts throughout the native's entire life,[1] because during his entire life effects occur from the transits of planets over the ASC, the MC, the

---

[1] Reading vitâ 'life' instead of viâ 'way'.

Sun, the Moon, and the other places of the geniture; but the determination of a revolution lasts only so long as that revolution, that is one year for a solar revolution, and the transits of the planets through the places of the revolution have no force beyond the time of that revolution. But this does not keep the revolution from producing effects that are going to last all the rest of his life, because the force and the effect of that revolution will be such that it surely will produce something notable or lasting.

Finally, in the case of solar revolutions, the Sun itself should be looked at primarily, along with its own system or satellites, and secondarily the Moon. But the Sun is not determined unless by reason of the house of the figure, because it is in its own radical place; but its state is attended to by its own satellites and the Moon, which are [themselves] determined by reason of their sign, house, and state.

Chapter VII.

Whether the Figure of a Solar Revolution can Prevail Against or Over the Figure of the Geniture or Anything not Signified by the Nativity. A Doctrine Set Forth with Reasons and 25 Figures.

This question is of very great moment, lest anything more than is proper be attributed to revolutions; and therefore, what we may think [to be true] about it, not only from reason, but also from many experiments, ought to be disclosed.

We have indeed asserted that a revolution per se cannot produce an effect that the figure of the geniture has not signified. For, since the celestial influx, imprinted upon the native at the hour of his nativity and seen concretely in him, is by that act the cause of whatever is *inherent* in the native when he is born, by reason of the constitution of his body, his temperament, health, character, and mental qualities; but, by its *potential* [it is the cause of] whatever is naturally going to happen to that same native, at least insofar as noticeable changes in body, mind, and fortune, it follows rightly that nothing of any moment is going to happen to the native in those things that the genethliacal constitution shall not have had in potential. Therefore, a revolution per se will effect nothing, at least nothing notable, that the genethliacal constitution has not presignified. Moreover, the fact that the nativity contains in potential whatever of any moment is going to occur to the native with regard to his body, mind, and fortune, is most evidently proven by the revolutions and directions that explain the fates of the native; for without any direction or revolution corresponding to the natal figure, there can be no change, at least no significant one; and notable individual changes have their own directions or revolutions corresponding to the natal figure by which they are invoked. But directions imprint their own strengths upon the native on the day of his nativity, as we have said in Book 22, Section 3, Chapter 2,. And therefore they pertain to that same geniture, which consequently contained that same change *in potential*.

This doctrine is confirmed, moreover, since otherwise no faith could be had in the geniture; [for] if with the geniture denying matrimony, offspring, or dignities, such things of contrary significations could be conferred by subsequent revolutions, then there is no man indeed who is wretched and unfortunate from the genethliacal constitution of the sky, or for whom good revolutions and accidents conformable to them will not occur if he lives to old age. That which is in fact contrary to experience!

Cardan himself agrees with this in his *Book on Revolutions*, Chapter 3, when he says, "But if in any geniture there are no significations of marriage, [then] no revolution will be able to cause that to happen." And he said no less afterwards in the *Book on the Judgment of Genitures*, Chapter 6, "The nature of revolutions follows the nature of genitures, insofar as judgment"; [but] then in Chapter 7, he judges two of his own revolutions, Nos. 34 and 35, and the things signified by all the houses, entirely as if they were two figures of his nativity, without having considered his own natal figure or its directions. Which, to be sure is foreign to reason, because of the natural dependency of the revolution on the geniture and its directions; indeed it is that way, since there is no force in revolutions [alone], at least for any notable effect. Because, if his revolution No. 34 were erected according to the rational mode, and judged in accordance with our method for the determinations of the planets from a consideration of their bodily location and their rulers, it was more closely in agreement with the accidents that Cardan said happened to him in that year than when judged by Cardan's method; lest anyone, therefore, follow Cardan in that regard more confidently than is proper, we ought to say here that revolutions should be judged like genitures, that is by the determinations of the signs and the planets in the figure, with regard to their bodily location, ruler, and aspect. And yet it is rash and erroneous to judge the figure of a revolution without any consideration of the natal figure, since the revolution is subordinated to it in its force, significations, and effects, and since it depends upon it. Consequently, a revolution may in fact cause whatever it signifies that is conformable to the genethliacal figure, to which directions also pertain, but it cannot signify anything contrary to it. As, for example, if it signifies matrimony, and the geniture signifies celibacy, there will be no matrimony, although there will be some talk about it, and some inclinations to it will come forth. For with the revolution not agreeing with the radix, it will indeed begin or there will be some action in that direction because it will be strongly signified, but it will not be brought to completion—either considered respectively to the nativity or absolutely. And this doctrine is especially true in those things that do not depend solely on the will of the native, but also on the will of others. See the objection at the end of the adjoining chapter!

And because this doctrine is of the greatest and most particular moment, it seems necessary to illustrate and confirm it with some examples and experiences. First, therefore, we shall take that 34th revolution of Cardan's, in which by the preceding table[1] 5 degrees of Taurus ascends, and not the seventh degree as Cardan found by his own table,[2] and we shall judge it according to our own method. See the genethliacal chart in Book 17, Section 2, chapter 2.[3]

He says, therefore, that in that year he had perfect health, but with some fear. The reason is that Jupiter in his radix was in the ASC on account of its latitude,[4] and both the revolution and the radix have the same ASC [sign], which the Moon occupies in the revolution, made fortunate by a trine to Venus,

---

[1] The tables in Chapter V above.

[2] This slight difference should have indicated to Morin that errors in the solar tables had little effect on the accuracy of solar returns.

[3] Although Morin does not repeat Cardan's horoscope here, and he puts the chart for Cardan's 34th revolution on the next page, I have chosen to insert them both here. Cardan's chart appears in his own *Book of Twelve Genitures* (p. 517 of the omnibus edition) as he calculated it (with Alchabitius cusps). Morin's chart for Cardan is on p. 396 of the AG, recalculated with the *Rudolphine Tables*, so that the positions of the planets are more accurately given. Morin has also drawn the chart with Regiomontanus cusps for the intermediate houses, although he has kept the exact ASC and MC originally computed by Cardan.

[4] That is, its mundane position was in the 1st house.

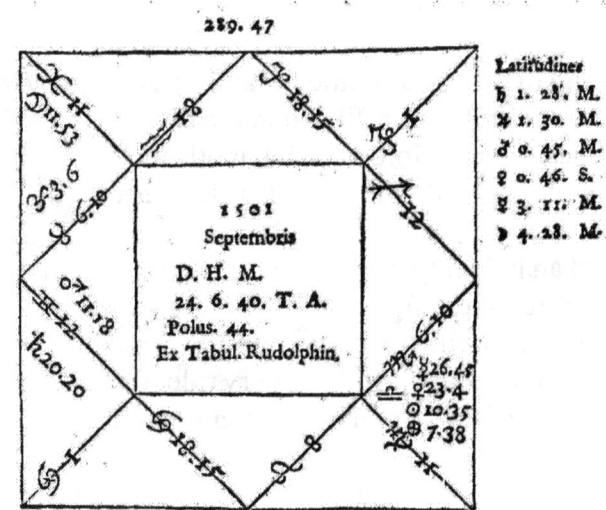
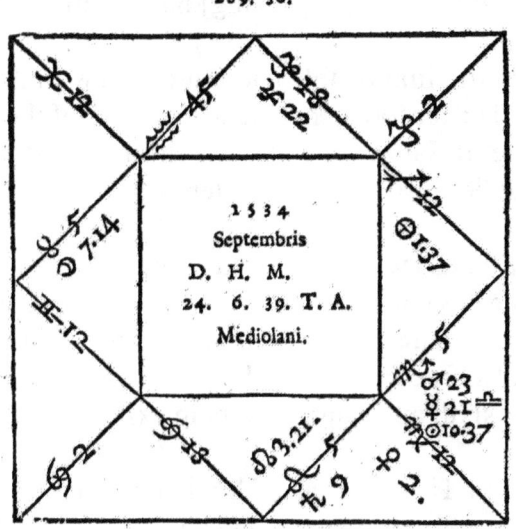

Jerome Cardan
[Pavia] 44N00
24 Sept 1501 6:40 PM

Cardan's 34th Revolution
Milano
24 Sept 1534 6:39 PM

which is the Moon's ruler and which is free from the malefics. Cardan should, therefore, have been healthy in that year, although the Moon was in the twelfth [house] of the radix, because it was of course under the rulership of Jupiter, to whose radical location it comes in the ASC of the revolution and to the trine of Venus. And the fear was from the square of Saturn to the Moon in the ASC, which also threw a square in the radix; and there was a direction of the ASC to the place of Saturn in the ecliptic.

Second. He underwent a dissipation of his assets due to his seeking a dignity, yet he also gained extraordinarily from [his practice of] astrology and medicine. The reason for the first of these is that in his radix he had Jupiter in the ASC and Mars on the cusp of the second, significator of the dissipation of riches; but in the revolution Jupiter is in its fall in the tenth and Mars in its exile[1] in the sixth, square Jupiter and conjunct Mercury ruler of the second. Therefore, since Jupiter was in the first [house] of the radix and was translated to the tenth in the revolution, it presaged an ambition for honors and dignities in that year; but because it was in its fall and square Mars in its exile, which planet was on the cusp of the second in the radix and is conjunct Mercury ruler of the second in the sixth [house] of the revolution, he tried in vain; and it portends the dissipation of assets because of [his striving for] dignity. The reason for the second of these is that Mars, in the radix and in the revolution, by its exaltation [in Capricorn] rules the MC and Jupiter in the revolution; but Mercury ruler of the second applies to Mars, which is in square aspect to Jupiter and trine the second house of the radix and the revolution; this, therefore, was able to bring profit from [the exercise of his] art.

Third. One of his blood relations intervened on behalf of Cardan and his [aim for] dignity; the reason is that the Moon ruler of the third of the radix and the revolution was in the revolution in the radical place of Jupiter and in its own exaltation in trine to Venus; and Jupiter, which has its exaltation in that same third, was in the tenth of the revolution. By these [positions], therefore, efforts by blood relations

---

[1] Now more commonly called 'detriment' (when a planet is in the sign opposite the one it rules).

directed towards [improving] his dignities were signified for the native.

Fourth. Immovable goods are kept with difficulty, and there was too little for any part of them to be sold. The reason is that the Moon ruler of the fourth in both figures is afflicted in the revolution by the square of Saturn in exile, which in the radix was in the second. Moreover, his mother was safe and sound because the Moon ruler of the fourth was exalted in the ASC and trine its ruler Venus.

Fifth. His wife conceived a daughter, who contracted an infirmity in the womb. The reason is that in the radix Venus ruler of the ASC was conjunct the Sun ruler of the fifth in the sixth. But in the revolution, that same Venus ruler of the ASC and the Moon was in the fifth in trine to the ASC, and the Moon was also free from the malefics, which signified offspring for Cardan. And Mercury ruler of Venus was in the sixth applying to Mars in exile, which presaged that infirmity of his daughter.

Sixth. He experienced hindrances and changes among his servants and animals. The reason is that Mercury, ruler of the second and the sixth of the radix, was in the sixth of the radix in a mobile sign and aspected by Saturn from the second. But in the revolution Mercury is again ruler of the second and the sixth, and it is in the sixth in that same mobile sign applying to Mars ruler of the twelfth.

Seventh. Something harmful happened to his wife because Mars and Jupiter rulers of the seventh in the radix and in the revolution are badly afflicted in this revolution; and the Moon too, significator of the wife because of its opposition to the seventh,[1] is afflicted by a square to a badly afflicted Saturn. Besides, open enemies are suppressed by fear of the prince and hindered by just men so that they cannot do harm. The reason is that Mars ruler of the cusp of the seventh is in exile in the sixth and square Jupiter in the tenth, where it signifies princes and magistracy.

Eighth. He had several dignities in that year, but they were vitiated and with little glory, and rather with hindrance from both open and secret enemies. The reason for the several dignities is that Jupiter, which was in the ASC of the radix, is found in the tenth of the revolution in aspect with the conjunction of Sun and Mercury and Mars, with Venus ruler of these and of the Moon and the ASC being oriental to the Sun. Moreover, the reason why they were vitiated with little glory and hindrance from enemies was because Jupiter was in its fall square Mars in its exile in the 6th, where it signifies enemies, both secret—through its opposition to the twelfth—and open because it rules the seventh.

And in addition it should be noted that the MC was then by direction in right trine to its ruler Saturn, whose RA I calculate at 31°24′. And without that correction there would be no direction to [a planet indicating] dignities.[2]

---

[1] Since the seventh house is empty, the planet in the opposite house (in this case, the Moon in the first) acts as if it were also in the empty house, thus assuming a double signification.

[2] The figure given is neither the RA of Saturn, nor the RA of its right trine. It may be a typographical error or it may be an arc of direction. If we take the given longitude of Saturn, viz. 20°20′ Gemini, its right trine, taken without latitude, would fall in 20°20′ Aquarius. The RA of that point is 322°44′; subtracting the given RAMC 289°47′, the arc of direction would be 32°57′, which, by the Naibod time measure, would correspond to about 5 months prior to the 34rd revolution. This is close enough to be considered as operative during the time of the 34rd revolution. Morin probably corrected the position of the right trine by the method set forth in Book 22, but I have not taken the time to make the calculation. If in fact the figure given as the "RA" is actually his corrected arc of direction, then his method has made the time of the direction more than two years before the 34th revolution, thus lessening its coincidence with the revolution.

Whoever wants to do so may compare our judgments with the judgments of Cardan that were cited above; and he will see: First, that in the judgments of the revolutions the significations of the geniture must always be considered. Second, How more reasonably and lucidly judgments proceed [when taken] solely from the determinations of the signs and planets according to our method in both the radix and the revolution, and how completely satisfactory they are in proving the phenomena, that is the effects of the stars, by reason. Third and finally, how superfluous, indeed how absurd, is the admission in this matter of those significators that Cardan calls "according to substance,"[1] from which he principally judges, and from which only error and confusion can arise in judgments, as can be demonstrated from [the statements of] Cardan himself at the end of Chapter 6 of the *Book of Revolutions*,[2] when the Moon is taken according to Ptolemy's opinion as the significator "according to substance" of the body, life, character, wife, mother, maidservants, daughters, and sisters. About all of whom he will be obliged to pronounce the same thing from the state of the Moon in the figure.

Furthermore, in proving a matter of such moment, a single revolution does not seem to be sufficient; therefore, we shall add others here.

First will be the 38th revolution of that magnanimous and unconquerable King of Sweden, Gustavus Adolphus, during which he was killed; and by his death he was also the cause of victory for his own army against the army of the emperor Ferdinand [II], which was commanded by Albert, Duke of Mecklenburg, Friedland, and Sagan, commonly called Walstein [Wallenstein][3]—the figure of whose revolution is such as to be worthy of note. See his [chart] in Book 17, Section 2, Chapter 2.

First, therefore, the ASC of this revolution set for Mainz, from Kepler's tables of [the geographical coordinates of] places, was the same as the radical [ASC]; and the Sun in the first with Venus and Mercury rulers of the tenth and seventh in trine to Jupiter ruler of the ASC and the Sun, which Sun was in partile trine to Mars in the ninth, that the Sun itself rules; moreover, the Part of Fortune in the tenth and sextile its ruler Venus, so that consequently this revolution would seem to be a very fortunate one, and, at first glance, absolutely free from any danger of either natural or violent death. And indeed in that year he did many outstanding things among foreigners, especially in opposition to the Count of Tilly,[4] Commander-in-Chief of the Imperial Army, whom he subdued and killed,[5] and likewise the Duke of Ba-

---

[1] What are more commonly called *general significators,* as the Sun for the father, the Moon for the mother, Venus for the wife, etc. Morin allowed them to have *analogy* with those persons, but he insisted that *accidental significators,* i.e. the rulers of the appropriate house cusps, were the true significators.

[2] Actually, at the end of Book V, where, in the famous passage that Morin had in mind. Cardan says: "And you should know that, as it has often been said, there are many things that are signified, but few significators, namely the seven planets, and the twelve houses, and a few fixed stars, as was said in the first book; on which account Ptolemy imposed a new fusion, by which he gave many significations to one signtficator; and he put the Moon as significator of the body, then of the mental characteristics, then of the life, and the wife, and the maidservants &. the daughters, and the sisters. How, therefore, will [the horoscope] be arranged for him, whose wife dies in childbirth, while he himself lives a long life, and his many daughters are unharmed, and his maids are fugitives, and his mother dies early, and he has a healthy body, and a bad and fickle mind..."

[3] Albrecht Wenzel Eusebius von Waldstein (1583-1634), Duke of Friedland, Sagan, and Mecklenburg. He was commonly called Wallenstein. He studied as a youth in Bologna, where he learned astrology and acquired a firm belief in it. In his later years he employed the Paduan astrologer Giovanni Battista Seni (1600-1656) as his personal astrologer. He also consulted John Kepler, who cast his horoscope (see *Notable Nativities* 920).

[4] John Tserclaes (1559-1632), Count of Tilly.

[5] Count Tilly was mortally wounded by Swedish artillery fire at Rain, Bavaria, on the River Lech on 5 April 1632; he was carried to Ingolstadt, where he died on 30 April 1632.

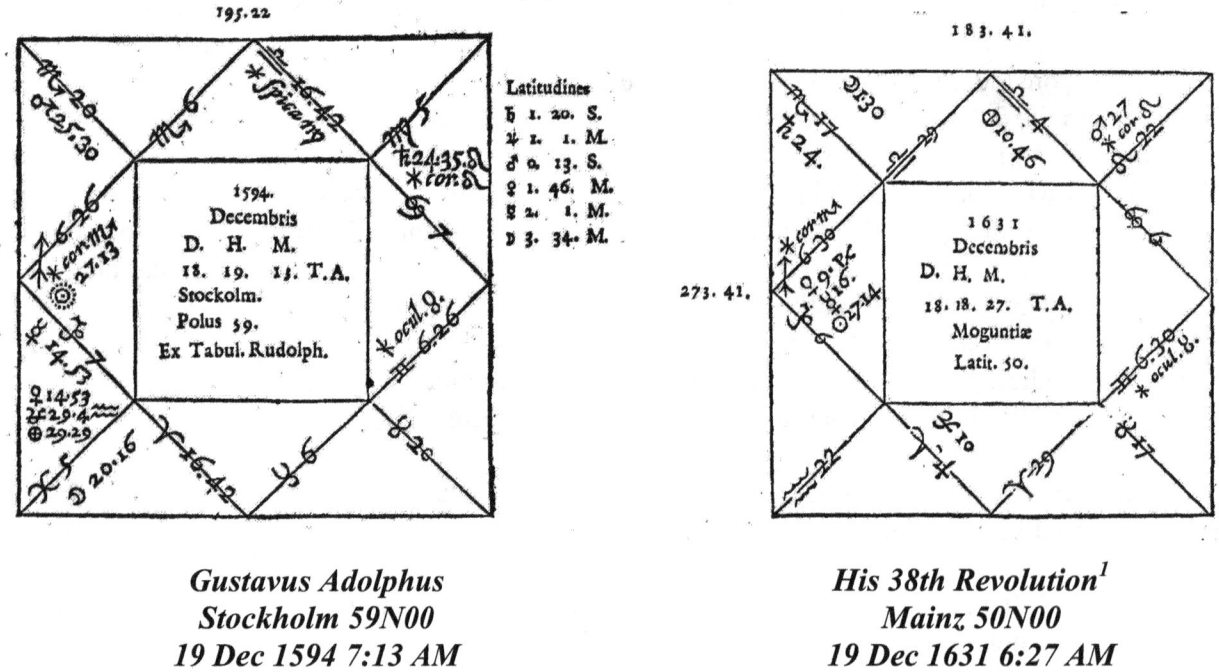

Gustavus Adolphus
Stockholm 59N00
19 Dec 1594 7:13 AM

His 38th Revolution[1]
Mainz 50N00
19 Dec 1631 6:27 AM

varia,[2] whose realm he subjugated. But finally, on 16 November 1632, in the morning, in battle against Wallenstein,[3] at the first encounter he was killed by a double blow of lead bullets,[4] because, going into battle, even though he had been warned, he did not want to wear armour—a fatal imprudence; for what could be more imprudent than for a king to expose himself naked to such a hail of bullets! But nevertheless, a prince very worthy of a Christian empire, if he had only been a Catholic.

But the signs of such a disaster were prominent in that revolution, since Jupiter ruler of the ASC in both the radix and the revolution is in opposition to the radical MC and square the radical Mercury ruler of the seventh, which in undertakings and actions, then in wars, portended something unfortunate. Moreover, Venus ruler of the MC of the radix was in the first [house] of the revolution with Cor Scorpionis,[5] a violent fixed star, and joined to Mercury ruler of the seventh [house] of the revolution, also presaging something unfavorable and violent in wars that he would undertake, and in his life. And in truth the Moon ruler of the eighth in both figures was in exile in [Scorpio] the domicile of Mars, a violent sign inclining to violent death.

---

[1] The Moon was actually at about 4 Scorpio 13 and the Part of Fortune at about 13 Libra 29.

[2] Maximilian I the Great (1573-1651), Elector and Duke of Bavaria.

[3] The famous battle of Lützen, in which the Swedes, roused to fury by the death of their king, who had been shot in the back when he led a cavalry charge earlier in the day, finally routed the Imperial forces under Wallenstein after a protracted engagement.

[4] Interestingly, Gottfried Heinrich (1594-1632), Count of Pappenheim, the Austrian Field Marshal *was* shot in the very

Nevertheless, all these things were too weak [to indicate] such a death, and another thing happened to concur that was truly atrocious. And this was the notable permutation of the places of Saturn and Mars in the geniture and in the revolution. If indeed in the geniture Saturn was in exile in Leo and in the eighth house with Cor Leonis,[1] it was afflicted by the square to Mars in Scorpio in the twelfth; and Saturn was partilely opposed to Jupiter ruler of the ASC, but Mars was square that same Jupiter. And these things strongly portended a violent death. But in the revolution Saturn is found in the place of the radical Mars, and Mars in the place of Saturn; therefore Mars in opposition and Saturn in square to the radical Jupiter ruler of the ASC—in both figures; whence a violent death was strongly portended in that year—in that year especially in which the direction of the MC was coming to the square of Jupiter and Saturn, and also to the body of Mars, all of which were, in the nativity, significators of violent death. And on the day of his murder, the transits of Saturn, Jupiter, Mars, and the Sun that were being made were also horrendous, as will be explained more fully in its own place. Moreover, the direction of the MC is about the result of actions, which very often (as it is here) is violent death.[2]

From this it is plain that this revolution did not have the [necessary] force from itself to signify death, and especially violent death, in that year (for nothing is discerned in this figure that is seen to be lethal in itself), but only with respect to the figure of the nativity.

Second will be the 57th revolution of Cardinal Richelieu, begun at Amiens in Picardy, of which the figure is like this:

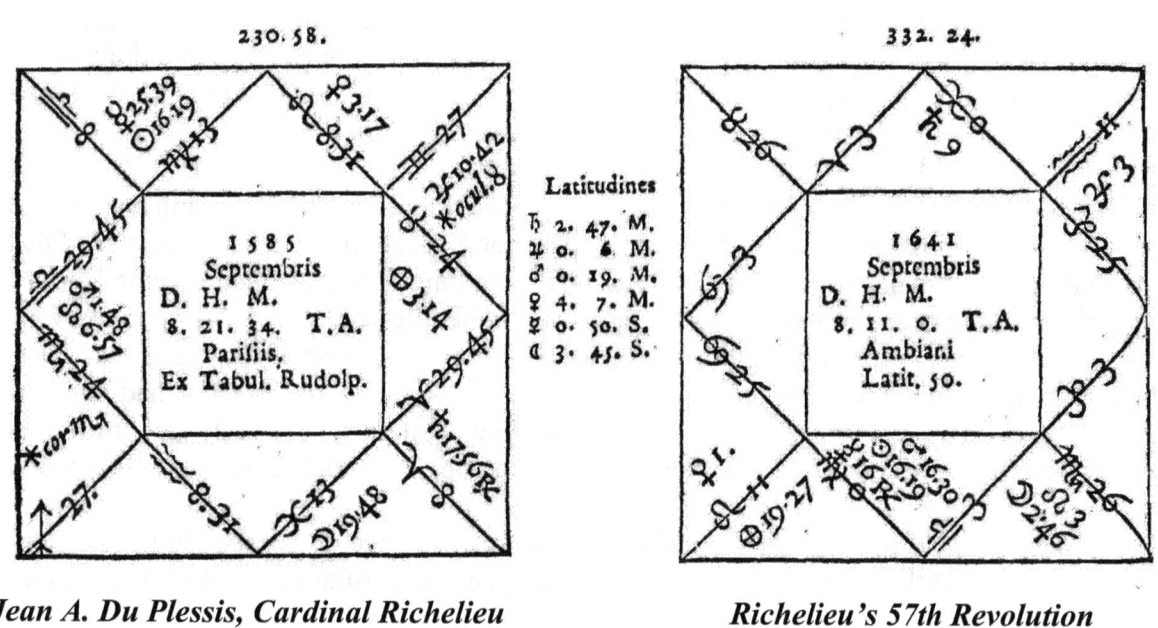

Jean A. Du Plessis, Cardinal Richelieu
Paris
9 Sept 1585 9:34 AM[3]

Richelieu's 57th Revolution
Amiens
8 Sept 1641 11:00 PM

---

[1] Regulus or α Leonis, which was at 24°43′Leo.

[2] Morin evidently meant to say that the result of actions *could be* (as here) a violent death.

[3] The RAMC should read 130°58′ rather than 230°58′, evidently a typographical error.

In this revolution the sign of the ninth [house] of the radix was ascending, and therefore it was signifying a long journey especially because the Moon ruler of the ASC was in the first of the radix and in the radical place of Mars. Add the fact that here Saturn ruler of the ninth is in the tenth; consequently, in this year he led King Louis XIII into the county of Rousillon; and that journey was fortunate for him for undertaking wars, having captured Perpignan by siege, on account of Saturn ruler of the seventh in the tenth in mutual reception by house with Jupiter trine the ASC, as well as the Moon ruler of the ASC; but on that journey he was twice in danger of his life. First, by illness; second, from a conspiracy designed to kill him, and whether in truth it was signified in that year namely, in which the direction of the ASC to the opposition of Jupiter in the eighth was completed, where it was afflicted by its sign [position], conjunct the Eye of Taurus,[1] a violent fixed star, and square the Sun ruler of the MC from that inimical sign that Jupiter was in; moreover, in this figure the Moon ruler of the ASC was afflicted several ways in the radical place of Mars, namely, in that same radical place of Mars, partilely square Jupiter in the eighth and then Venus ruler of the twelfth in [both] the radix and the revolution; Mars moreover ruler of the Moon and the first of the radix, the Sun ruler of Venus and the tenth of the radix, and Mercury ruler of the twelfth in the revolution and the eighth of the radix, were partilely conjoined in the fourth and afflicted by the opposition of Saturn ruler of the eighth, which in the radix was occupying the sixth in its fall and retrograde; Venus moreover ruler of the radical ASC was applying to Jupiter by an opposition which was the anaereta in both the revolution and the radix; and Saturn was signifying secret enemies in the radix, but in this revolution, open ones. Therefore, on account of these very bad and violent combinations, they were the causes affecting life, death, dignities, undertakings, and enemies, he was taken dangerously ill by a severe illness in which his right arm was mangled by surgeons, with Jupiter portending this, which planet in the radix was in Gemini with a violent fixed star, to which sign the arms are particularly subject in the microcosm; and he did not entirely recover from that illness, for he lingered on until his death which happened during the following revolution; but he did avoid a violent death from the conspirators by fleeing rapidly to Narbonne, where he took to bed, and he pushed his danger forward, both in delay by the conspirators and in flight from a condition of illness.

Before he departed from Paris, he wanted to know what I thought about his health and his life while he was on the road, but not in general ([this man] whom for 4 years I had not seen because of the remuneration that had been denied me for the method of finding longitude that I had invented, although by his own writing it had been promised to me); but, through the intercession of a magnate who was very faithful to him and [also] a friend of mine, namely the illustrious Count of Chavigny,[2] who as a third party requested my judgment on that matter, which I would have gladly declined if I had been able; but, since I was obligated by the favors [I had received] from that great man, and for the honor of astrology, I at last responded that the cardinal would become ill, with danger to his life, while on that journey.

He left Paris on the 30th of January [1642] at 2 P.M. when Cancer was ascending,[3] the sign on the ninth of the radix as in the figure of the revolution; and the Moon ruler of the ASC was in the eighth

---

[1] Aldebaran or α Tauri, which was at 4°40′ Gemini

[2] Probably, Léon Bouthillier, Count of Chavigny (1608-1652), French Secretary of State under Cardinal Richelieu. He is mentioned in Book 22, Section IV, Chapter 5 (p. 118 of my translation). He would appear to have been born at Paris 28 March 1608 at about 11:30 PM LMT (see G. Garollo, *Dizionario Biografico Universale;* also, AG 21, Sect. 2, Chapt. 3; and AG 22, Sect. 4, Chapt. 5)

[3] Here Morin has cast a horary chart set for a time certain. And he has compared it to the charts of the radix and the current revolution.

partilely joined to the Sun in Aquarius, and Saturn ruler of the New Moon was in the MC afflicted by a square of Mars from Sagittarius in the sixth house; and the place of the radical Jupiter, the anaereta, was on the cusp of the twelfth, which is [the house] of illnesses, and Jupiter itself was in Aquarius and in the ninth house. That hour in which he had departed was also very bad for illness and danger to his life, and I observed that, not without surprise that all these different causes were occurring at the same time.

Third will be the fifty-eighth revolution of that same Cardinal Richelieu, in which he finally died, who, having started wars throughout the whole of Europe, was the cause of death for so many millions of men from iron, flame, famine, pestilence, and other causes. And the figure of that revolution is like this:

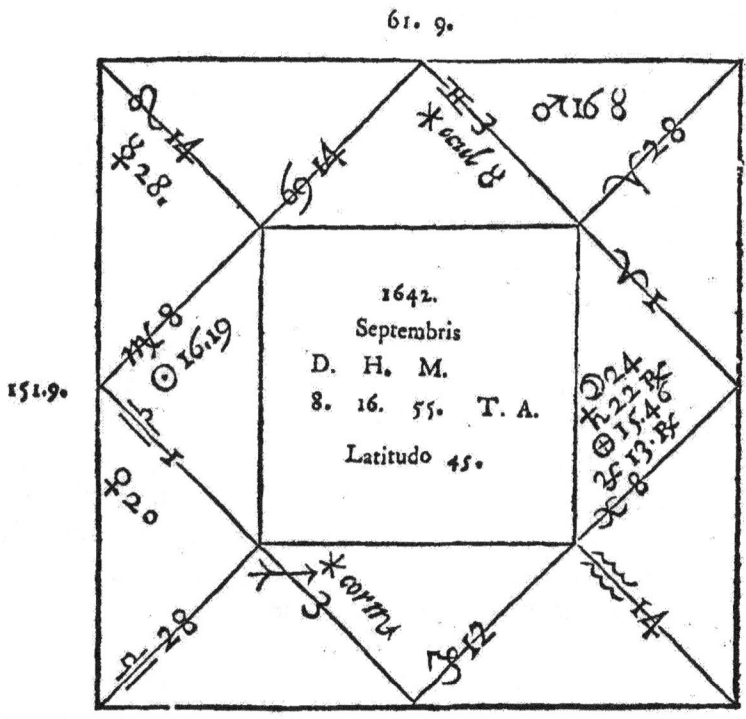

Richelieu's 58th Revolution
[Lyons]
9 Sept 1642 4:55 AM

This revolution began while, still ill, he had returned from the siege of Perpignan; and when four days had elapsed from the beginning of the revolution, he departed for Lyons; afterwards, without the king's knowledge and without his permission,[1] he gave the order to behead two important men, the royal favorite Henri d'Effiat,[2] who had conspired against the cardinal himself, and the Royal Counselor François Auguste de Thou [1604-1642] in the Privy Council, [who was] aware of the conspiracy; their

---

[1] Modern historians say that Louis had given the order to arrest Cinq-Mars and de Thou and try them for treason. The Cardinal evidently pressured the commission presiding over the trial to bring in a guilty verdict and sentence the prisoners to death. They were both beheaded at Lyons on 12 September 1642. The king may not have foreseen such a severe penalty, but he evidently shed no tears when he learned what punishment had been enacted.

[2] Heari Coiffier d'Effiat (1620-1642), Marquess of Cinq-Mars.

noteworthy nativities are shown elsewhere herein.[1]

Moreover, this revolution also signified a journey because Mars ruler of the first [house] of the radix and also in the first had come to the ninth of the revolution in partile trine to the Sun ruler of the radical MC, which was found in the first [house] of the revolution; and therefore the return was for illness [and it was] sufficiently fortunate, but truly notable and its mode one previously used by no mortal man. For in fact, in no inns up to the city of Paris, that is through about 200 leagues,[2] did he enter the door; but the wall had to have been destroyed and a bridge erected, by means of which the machine in which he lay, carried by 12 men across the bridge itself and through the broken wall, was introduced into the room prepared for it, since that machine was not able to ascend by way of the steps to the room prepared for it. What haughtiness and pride in traveling could Mars in the ninth, in partile trine to the Sun in the first, and sextile the Moon and Jupiter in the seventh, signify!

Moreover, Mercury, which was ruler of the eighth of the radix, was ruler of the year in the revolution, since it was ruler of the ASC, the Sun, and the MC, but it was in the twelfth house afflicted by a square to Mars ruler of the eighth, which was found conjunct the Head of Medusa,[3] which in fact portended a lethal illness in that year—especially since the Sun ruler of the twelfth and Mercury were in the first afflicted by the oppositions of the Moon, of Saturn ruler of the sixth, whose radical place is in the eighth, and then Jupiter, which was unfortunately placed in the eighth of the radix, and in particular it was the anaereta, to whose opposition the radical ASC had come in that year 1642. On account of these causes, and since this bad revolution succeeded the other bad one shown above, the malignant illness of the preceding year hung on with bad humors in his body, weakened by sleeplessness, treatments, and various sufferings. I had predicted to many friends that death [would result] from this revolution, which occurred on the 4th of December of that year 1642, and it was from illness. For the radical figure did not signify a violent death strongly, but only dangers of that kind of death, which he avoided many times. For no tyrant, with a terrible guard, with a carriage protected by iron plates, and with other such things, was more careful of himself and more on his guard against violent death, than Cardinal Richelieu, who was greatly afraid of that, both at home and away from home.

Fourth will be the forty-first revolution of the Most Noble Mr. Louis Tronson, a man distinguished for his learning, honesty, generosity, prudence, affability, and other virtues, whom the whole of France will always owe very much for his having liberated France from the tyranny of the Marquess of Ancre.[4] For he was involved in this most dangerous undertaking of King Louis XIII, by the Privy Council, with

---

[1] I have not found Cinq-Mars's nativity in the AG or elsewhere, but he was evidently born during the last week of March 1620. Henry de Boulainviller, Count of Saint-Saire, *Traité d'Astrotogie* (Garches, 1947), Chart 40, gives de Thou's birthdata as Paris 25 August 1604 at 2 AM.

[2] About 500 American miles or 800 kilometers.

[3] The fixed star Algol or β Persei was at 21°11′Taurus.

[4] Concino Concini (d. 1617), Marquess of Ancre, Marshal of France. He was a Florentine count who was a favorite, and some say a lover, of Marie de' Medici (1573-1642). who was married to the French King Henry IV (1551-1610) in 1600. Concini followed Marie to France and was systematically elevated in rank, becoming Marshal of France in 1614. Following the death of Henry IV, Marie became the Regent of France, since her son Louis XIII (1601-1643) was only 9 years old. For nearly four years 1613-1617 Concini was the power behind the throne and the real ruler of France. He was hated by most of the French noblity and by Louis himself, who resented being under the thumb of his mother's favorite. According to Maurice Lachatre, *Histoire des Papes* (Paris, c. 1875), vol. 3, p. 22, Louis also suspected that he was really the bastard son of Concini instead of the legitimate son of Henry IV, and this increased his hatred of Concini.

Lord Luynes[1] (who was afterwards Constable of France) and de Marsillac, and by his artifices and prudence the thing succeeded most happily during that revolution. After the murder of the Marquess of Ancre, everything having been set in order both inside and outside the royal household by the counsels of such men, the king himself retained Lord Tronson in his service and honored him in that same year with two outstanding dignities, namely membership in the Advisory Council and the Privy Council.

These things were signified in that same revolution. For its ASC was the MC of the radix, and the Moon along with the Sun, rulers of the 10th of the radix, were ruling the ASC of the revolution, and they were in trine aspect to each other; and the Sun was powerful from its exaltation in the MC[2] and in the place of the Part of Fortune, which was in the MC; moreover, the Moon, ruler of the ASC, was in her exaltation in the 10th, and her ruler Venus was joined to the Sun. And these things presignified the native's elevation by the king and his many honors and outstanding dignities; especially because the direction of the radical MC in that year was to the body of the Sun, ruler of the 10th,[3] and the Moon, Jupiter, and Venus in the 10th, and Mercury, ruler of the Sun, was in the revolution in the radical place of Jupiter and Venus with a trine aspect from Jupiter in Sagittarius; moreover, Venus had come again to the radical place of Mercury, which in the revolution is found in mutual reception with the Sun; and these [positions] were very outstanding and powerful.

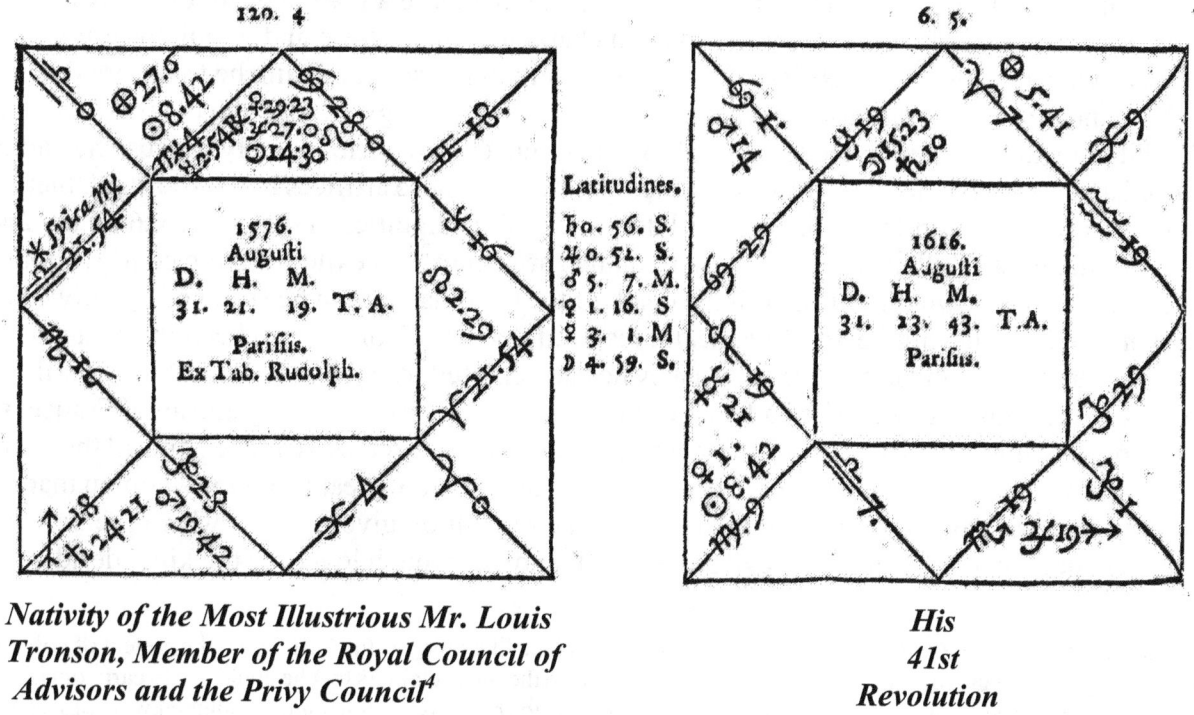

Nativity of the Most Illustrious Mr. Louis Tronson, Member of the Royal Council of Advisors and the Privy Council[4]

His 41st Revolution

---

[1] Charles d'Albert, Duke of Luynes (1578-1621), Constable of France. Acting under Louis's orders, he arranged the plot to murder Concini and was subsequently rewarded by being given all of Concini's lands and other assets and being granted the titles of duke and Constable of France.

[2] What Morin means is that the MC was in Aries, the sign of the Sun's exaltation; hence, the Sun "was powerful from its exaltation's being in the MC." See his statement at the end of this section.

[3] Since 28 Cancer was on the cusp of the 10th, and Leo was intercepted in the 10th, Morin feels justified in designating the Sun as ruler of the 10th rather than the Moon.

[4] The chart is correctly calculated for 21 Aug 1576 21:19 PM (= 22 Aug 1576 9:19 AM), not for 31 Aug 1576 as is shown in the center of the chart (probably a typesetter's error).

But Mars, ruler of the MC, in its fall in the 12th and square that same MC and [the Part of Fortune]; then the Moon, ruler of the ASC and Mars, afflicted by her conjunction to Saturn, ruler of the 8th in the 10th, were threatening imprisonment and the danger of death from undertakings and actions. Which certainly could have happened through the agency of that same Marquess of Ancre, in whom was the supreme power, if even a hint of the conspiracy had become known to him; but Mars was in sextile to the Moon, its ruler, and Saturn in trine to the Sun and Venus, its ruler; moreover, Mercury, ruler of the Sun, was in trine to Jupiter in Sagittarius in the 5th. These [positions], therefore, dissipated the noxious force of the malefics and made the native fortunate in his intelligence and his friends. Moreover, the Marquess of Ancre was slain on the 24th of April 1617.[1]

The fifth revolution will be the fifty-first of that same most noble Mr. Louis Tronson, member of the Advisory Council and the Privy Council of King Louis XIII, and most faithful Minister of the Royal Treasury, excelling all the courtiers on account of his notable honesty and other outsanding virtues and intelligence, and his official actions that were very frequent and dear [to the king]. [But], although the king had many times said to Cardinal Richelieu, who had very recently been elevated to the dignity of prime minister, that he trusted Mr. Tronson in all things above any others among the magnates and courtiers, and he had twice admitted him to the Privy Councils against the will of the Cardinal; the Cardinal said nice things about him then, [but] being unable to endure a man, indeed, of so great honesty and fidelity to the king, finally, when he had been charged with the false and iniquitous crime of lèse majesté, as well as with some false letters of trade and intelligence with Spain, he took care that it was brought to the king, who was easily deceived, [for] not only did he give too much credit to slanderers, but he did not want to listen to those accused (however falsely) by them, namely because he had been distracted and duped by the slanderers, or by their patrons. By these artifices of the Cardinal, therefore, Mr. Tronson was expelled from the court and despoiled of his dignities in the year 1626 on the 2nd of August, [while he was] ill at Nantes; and he remained at Nantes[2], an exile from the court without any compensation for his own dignities, until the death of the Cardinal, whom he survived by only 4 days.[3] Moreover, the king, having heard of his death, testified that Mr. Tronson had been the best and most faithful servant to him, and it is not recorded why he had departed from His Majesty. But that exile, with the losses of the dignities, which he had had for his good services from the king and all of France, were to Mr. Tronson himself and all of his family, a misfortune and the greatest damage. And all these things I learned from him personally, who was very friendly with me for 30 years, and for whom in that year I had predicted a fall from dignity from the figure of the revolution given below; which prediction that most excellent man, conscious of no evil for himself, and very much loved by the king, derided.

---

[1] According to Lachatre *(ibid.,* p. 22), the assassination took place like this: "Louis XIII, under the pretext of going hunting, had his regiment of guards mount their horses, since they were the only retainers that he could use to carry out his enterprise; the Captain of the Guards, l'Hopital-Vitry, betook himself to the Louvre with some gentlemen who carried pistols under their cloaks, and they stationed themselves on the drawbridge to wait for the Marshal of Ancre; he arrived with a numerous cortege as was his custom. The conspirators let everyone pass; then, when Concini was in the court, Vitry approached him, put his hand on his right arm to arrest him, and, drawing a pistol from his doublet, shot him in the chest; at the same time, another gentleman named Perray shot him a second time in his left side. The unfortunate Marshal fell dead from these shots. The conspirators made the air resound with cries of "Long Live the King!".... Louis XIII appeared then at one of the windows and said in a loud voice, "Many thanks to you, my friends; at this moment I am king." Thus was accomplished a murder that many people considered to be a parricide, having been accomplished by one that they regarded as the son of the Marshal."

[2] I have rearranged the order of the clauses of the Latin text and supplied a missing verb.

[3] Hence, Tronson died at Nantes on 8 December 1642. See also p. 95.

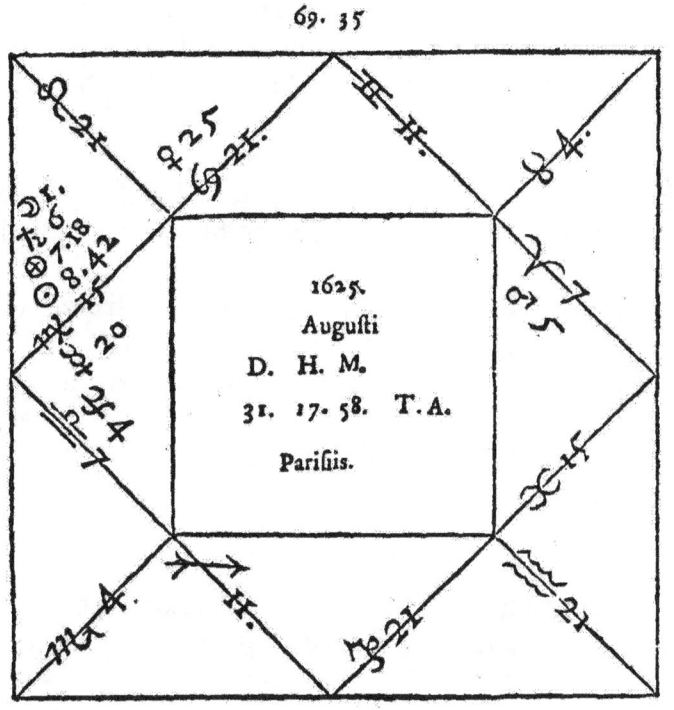

Louis Tronson's 51st Revolution
Paris
1 Sept 1625 5:58 AM

In this revolution, therefore, Mercury was the ruler of the year, indeed the ruler of the ASC, the MC, the Sun, and the Part of Fortune as well; and this planet was very strong in the 1st house; but in the radix it was in the 10th house, the ruler also of the Sun and the Part of Fortune; and the Sun was the ruler of the 10th, which is [the house] of actions and dignities; and therefore, because Mercury, the ruler of the radical ASC, was the ruler of the 9th of the revolution in the MC of the radix, a long journey was being signified in this revolution, and that he would handle many difficult negotiations for the king's benefit very happily, but especially between the king himself and Prince Condé,[1] who was absent from the court, and who in accordance with a conversation with Cardinal Richelieu wished to confide in no courtier besides Mr. Tronson, sent to him, on account of the tricks of Cardinal Richelieu himself. But the Sun and the Moon, rulers of the 10th of the radix, in the 12th of the revolution, afflicted by their conjunction to Saturn situated in that same 12th house, portended a huge evil of the nature of Saturn and the 12th house, certainly the loss of dignity, and an exile, also that he would be especially poor on account of the Part of Fortune's being with Saturn; and due to a secret enemy of great power who pretended to be his friend, on account of the Moon and the Sun, rulers of the 11th, in the 12th, which enemy was the Cardinal himself, by whose artifices he was expelled from court. Add [the fact] that Jupiter, which in the radix was the significator of honors in the 10th, was afflicted in the revolution by the very powerful opposition to Mars; moreover, the radical Saturn and Mars were hostile to honors, because Cancer, the fall of Mars, and Leo, the exile of Saturn, were in the 10th. For those reasons, he experienced those things at the end of this revolution, with another

---

[1] Henry II, Prince of Condé (1588-1646). By birth a Huguenot, he disavowed the Protestant cause and allied himself with the Catholic nobility.

one following[1] that was also very bad, in which the Sun was in the 10th house afflicted by the conjunction of Saturn and Mars. Moreover, a long and lingering illness by which he was distressed in that same year is evident from the Sun and the Moon conjunct Saturn in the 12th house,[2] which is the house of illnesses.

You will object. No signification of this exile and fall from dignity appears in the nativity, but quite the contrary; therefore, this revolution accomplished something not signified by the nativity.

I reply. Saturn, powerful from its exaltation in the 12th of the radix was inimical to honors because its exiles[3] were in the 10th house along with the fall of Mars in the MC, and Saturn and Mars in the 3rd portended some notable misfortune on a journey. And consequently, with the directions of Saturn and Mars in force for misfortunes in connection with dignities and journeys, that accident was sufficiently signified by the natal figure. Here in fact it is evident that the determinations of the planets by means of their exaltations, falls, exiles, and opposite houses are efficacious, as we asserted in Book 21, Section 2, Chapters 7 and 8.

The sixth will be the sixty-seventh revolution of this same Lord Tronson, in which he experienced the final fate of nature. But this was already preceded by the truly bad sixty-sixth revolution, in which

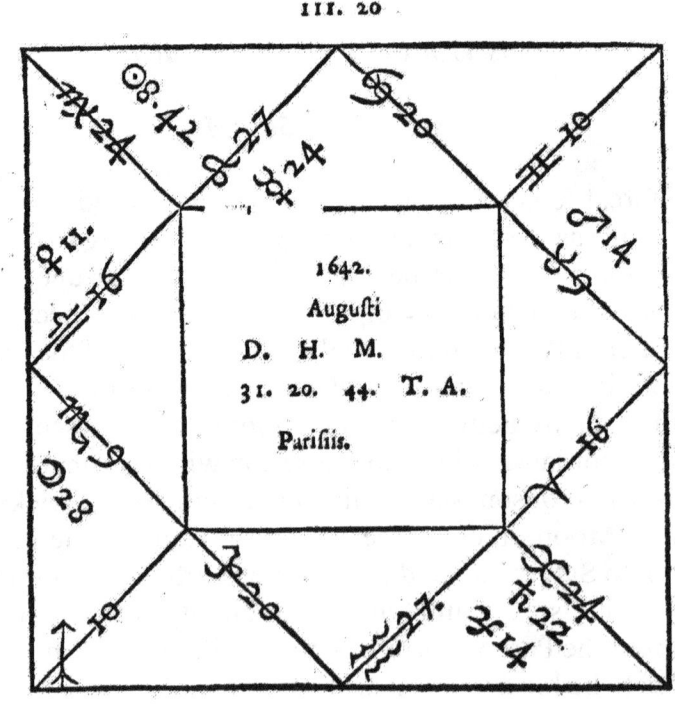

Louis Tronson's 67th Revolution
Paris
1 Sept 1642 8:44 AM

---

[1] The 1626 revolution.

[2] This statement refers to the 1625 revolution, which is shown in the figure.

[3] Both Cancer and Leo were on the 10th house, and both of them are the signs of exile of Saturn.

namely the Sun, ruler of the ASC, was afflicted by the conjunction of Mars and the opposition of Saturn in the 8th; moreover, Venus, the radical ruler of the ASC and the 8th, was in the 12th with the Moon in Cancer; and the ASC in that year came to the square of the Sun; therefore, it was necessary to be fearful of illness and death. And in fact he was ill with a fever for three weeks, a man otherwise rarely exposed to illnesses; but because Venus and the Moon were benefic in the 12th, free from bad rays of the malefics, he survived. But this bad revolution was succeeded by another bad one; it removed him from the living, as it happened with Cardinal Richelieu.

Therefore, in this revolution, Venus and Mars are still rulers of the 1st, and Venus ruler of the ASC and the 8th, as in the radix; and Venus is conjunct the ASC in the antiscion of Saturn, and Mars is in the 8th with the Head of Algol,[1] which is malicious and portends death by one's own fault; moreover, both of the luminaries are afflicted by oppositions of both of the malefics Saturn and Mars,[2] and Mercury ruler of the 8th of the radix and the 12th of the revolution is afflicted by the squares to the Moon and Mars, [both of them] badly afflicted, with the bad direction of the ASC to the square of the Sun still in effect.

Consequently, on the second day of October in the evening, after washing his lower legs with rather hot water, he experienced a rigor, with a double tertian fever, at which time the Moon was in the radical place of Mars; in addition, Mars and Venus were in partile opposition on the cusps of the 2nd and the 8th; and Mars was on the cusp of the 8th of the radix in 18 Taurus. With the passage of time, the double tertian degenerated into a double quartan, and that into dropsy, from which he passed to the fates—a man most worthy of Nestorean years,[3] and best and most faithful, husband of the noble Claudia de Sève, in appearance, intelligence, learning, piety, and all the aforesaid heroic virtues, and the two of them the very best parents of sixteen children, nine of whom, being well born, are still living, and both [of the parents] worthy of the Celestial Soul.

Seventh will be the eighty-fourth revolution of Constable Lesdiguières,[1] during which he died, and here is the figure of that revolution:

---

[1] Algol or β Persei was in 21°11′ Taurus.

[2] The Sun in 9 Virgo is opposite Saturn in 22 Pisces, and the Moon in 28 Scorpio is opposite Mars in 14 Taurus.

[3] In both the *Iliad* and the *Odyssey*, King Nestor of Pylos is characterized as a very elderly and wise man.

[4] The Latin text has 'Desdiguières'; I have changed it. Francois de Bonne (1543-1626), in his earlier years, was chief of the Huguenots in Dauphiné and commandant-general of the Protestant forces in their wars with the Catholics. He was created Marshal of France in 1609, Duke of Lesdiguières in 1611, and, having switched religions, Constable of France in 1622. He was in fact the last Constable of France (commander-in-chief of the armed forces), as the office was abolished by royal decree after his death.

Lesdiguières's 84th Revolution
[Valence] 45N
10 Apr 1626 11:24 AM

In this revolution, the Moon is the ruler of the 12th and of the ascending degree, but the Sun is the ruler of the rest of the 1st house; and the Moon was already the ruler of the 1st of the radix, and here Mars occupies its radical left square; but Saturn, the ruler of the 8th of the radix and of the revolution is here in opposition to the radical Moon, square Mars, and in the antiscion of the Sun, ruler of the 1st, which is joined to Venus and Mercury, rulers of the 12th of the radix; and the Sun applies by opposition to Jupiter, ruler of the 8th; consequently, this revolution was sickly and lethal to the old man, from which he died on 28 September of the year 1626. But if he had been younger, he would have escaped.

But for all that, lest someone say that this method appears conformable to the truth in one or another of any nativity, but is not true in each one, since it would be too long and tedious to confirm it with the revolutions of the previously mentioned persons, it seems good to establish it with a number of my own revolutions, in which something noteworthy happened to me; for the truths of astrology shine forth more in the more noteworthy accidents. And, having seen the succession of revolutions and accidents in the same nativity, it will be an occasion for admiration of rather than objection to the previously mentioned method.

First, therefore, will be my twenty-third revolution, which was very bad for me, and it produced two very noteworthy accidents for me: namely, on the 9th of July 1605, two very dangerous wounds because of a famous woman: one, a little below the heart, the other in the middle of the left thigh, both very deep, from which almost all my blood poured out, so that, while the first remedies were being applied, I was forced, not withstanding the opposition of the physician and the surgeon, to drink more than

6 ladles of wine[1] to prevent a sudden recurrence of *lipothemia*.[2] And, that I was not killed, I freely confess, was due solely to Divine Goodness. The second accident was my departure from my native place (after I had recovered from my wounds) for Provence, lest perchance some worse evil happen to me.

Moreover, the figure of the revolution is as is placed below; and the radical figure is given in Book 17, Section 2, Chapter 2.

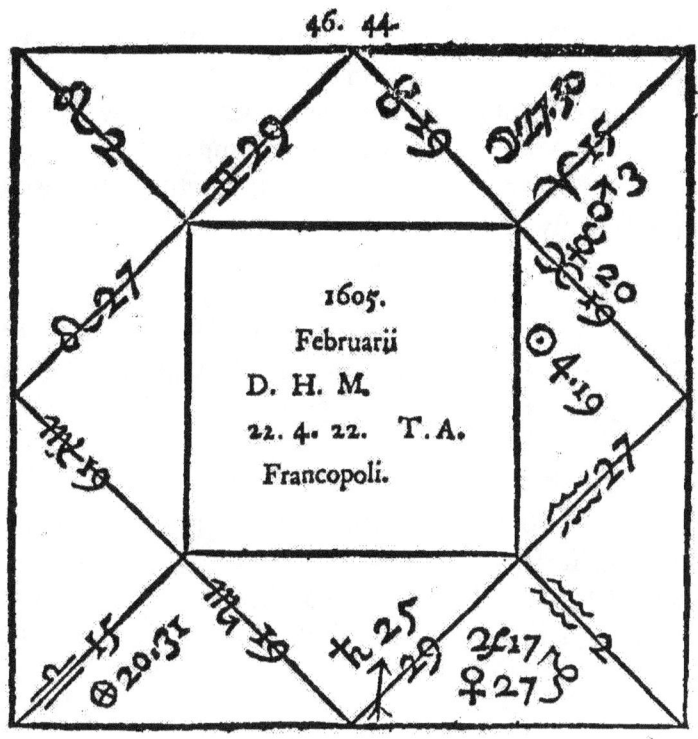

Morin's 23rd Revolution
Villefranche
22 Feb 1605 4:22 PM

Moreover, in judging this revolution, having had regard to the natal figure, it should be noted that because Venus, ruler of the radical 1st, is conjunct the Sun, ruler of the 5th, and Jupiter, ruler of the 8th is in the 12th house with Saturn, ruler of the MC, and it was in Pisces the exaltation of Venus, so many evils, misfortunes, and great dangers to life happened to me on account of women in my youth, that now I am stupified to recall them; and many more and perhaps worse things would have happened to me if the Divine Best and Greatest had not taken pity on me and had not liberated me from them; and astrology, around the 35th year of my nativity, in which I began to study that science, would have warned me from expeience of that unlucky and dangerous condition. Which granted, it is already plain at the outset that all the planets are situated in houses 5, 7, 8, and 9, to which the two accidents mentioned above belong.

Then, the Sun in the 12th of the radix signified hidden men, and they superior to me on account of the

---

[1] *Sex vini cyathos*, altogether, about half a pint.

[2] Fainting spell.

nature or the analogy of the Sun; and in the revolution, it, as the ruler of the 12th and of the ASC, [and posited] in the 7th, portended that such secret enemies would become open enemies, and that I would fall into their power; but Saturn, ruler of the 10th of the radix in the 12th, also signified hidden enemies superior to myself; but in the revolution, because it is the ruler of the 7th, it signifies open enemies that are going to harm me, especially because Mercury, ruler of the 1st,[1] is in the 8th, afflicted by the square of Saturn; and the place of the radical Mercury is on the cusp of the 7th of the revolution.

In addition, Venus, ruler of the 1st of the radix,[2] in the 5th of the revolution, presaged association with women, but with danger, because Venus was in square to the radical ASC [degree], conjunct Jupiter, ruler of the 7th and 8th of the revolution, which was also ruler of the 8th of the radix [and] conjunct Venus, with Cor Scorpionis, a very violent fixed star, occupying the 8th cusp of the radix.[3] And in addition, Saturn, ruler of the 7th cusp of the revolution, was conjunct the 5th cusp, to the square of which, Mercury, ruler of the 1st [and] badly afflicted in the 8th, was applying.

Therefore, wounds and a huge danger to life were portended by Mercury, ruler of the 1st in the 8th, whose radical place is on the cusp of the 7th afflicted by the conjunction to Mars, ruler of the radical ASC in the 8th, and square Saturn, ruler of the 5th and the 7th, Mars and Saturn also being square each other[4]; then, Venus, ruler of the 1st in the radix, in the 5th of the revolution, conjunct Jupiter, ruler of the 8th in both figures.

Finally, a long journey after the abovesaid [occurrences] is presaged by the Moon in the 9th of the revolution, partialy [posited] on the [degree] of the ASC of the radix in square to Venus, ruler of the 9th and the 10th, and trine Saturn, ruler of the 9th and 10th of the radix, which is found on the 9th cusp of the radix. Therefore, these effects square very well with the figure of the revolution, when it is referred back to the radical figure.

Second will be my thirtieth revolution, when I was a medical student at Aix-en-Provence in the year 1612 (for, with my studies intermittent during a ten-year period, these things by a warning from the most illustrious Chief Officer of the Avignon Senate, Guillaume Duvair [1555-1621], who was then my pupil in mathematics, in the 27th year of my age); therefore, in that year 1612, from an excessive drinking party with two Swiss, my fellow students in philosophy, and much bodily exercise in the noonday heat of the sun, during an eclipse that occurred on the 30th of May, I fell into a continuous fever on that very day that degenerated into a lasting and lengthy six months [illness], with *cachexia*,[5] *icterus*,[6] and dropsy, so that I was despaired of by the physicians, after having even employed [a form of] antimony prepared by them,[7] called *Algarot*, they finally advised me to go back to my native soil if I

---

[1] Since 27 Leo rises, Virgo occupies most of the 1st house; hence, Mercury is co-ruler of the ASC.

[2] In the radix, 28 Aries rises with the sign Taurus intercepted in the 1st; hence, Venus is co-ruler of the 1st house of the radix.

[3] Antares or α Scorpii was in 3°57′ Sagittarius.

[4] Saturn to 25 Sagittarius is barely within orbs of a square to Mars in 3 Aries. This is what would today be called a "heads and tails" aspect, since it is from the end of one sign to the beginning of another.

[5] A wasting disease.

[6] Jaundice.

[7] Antimony and its compounds were often used in medicine in Morin's day as a diaphoretic, febrifuge, and emetic. Since Morin was suffering from a chronic fever, the physicians used it as a febrifuge. Unfortunately, antimony compounds are poisonous in larger doses, so he may have been harmed more than he was helped.

was able. Which lengthy journey I undertook on foot with those Swiss who were very friendly to me, returning to my native place, and in the first few days having made only two leagues, by such exercise, change of air, and the generous use of white wine, very copious and wearying sweats broke out, especially at night, for more than the space of a month, which freed me from that illness, with the color of my hair having been changed to red with an Ethiopian curliness, which then little by little got back its natural color and state. Moreover, the figure [of the revolution] was such as is placed below.

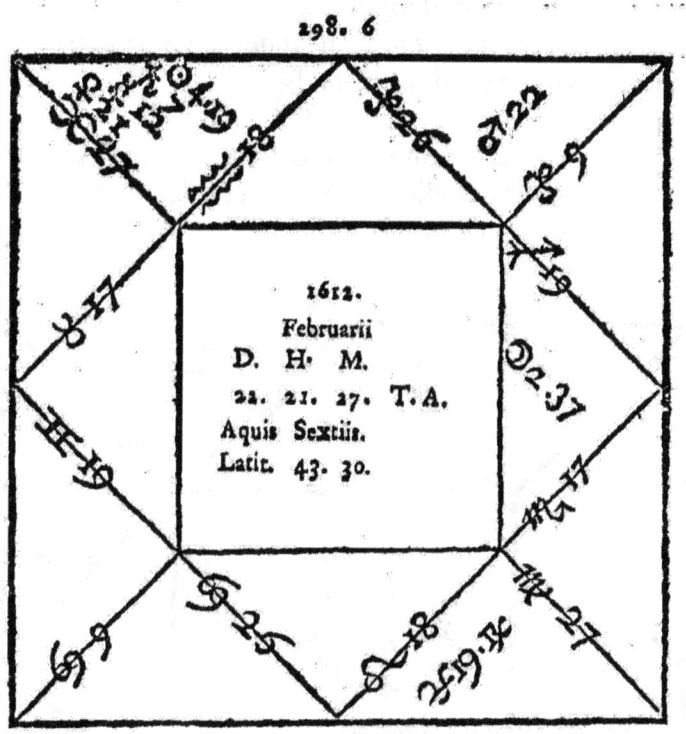

Morin's 30th Revolution
Aix-en-Provence
23 Feb 1612 9:27 AM

In which the position of the *caelum* is not much different from the radical position; and the Sun and the Moon, which were significators of illnesses in the radix, are here in square [aspect], and both are afflicted by Saturn, the chief significator of illnesses in the radix on account of its analogy [to illness] and its position in the 12th, for in fact [in the revolution] the Sun conjoins it and the Moon squares it, and it is the ruler of the 5th[1] along with Mercury, in the radix as well as in the revolution, which Mercury, ruler of the 1st, Saturn also afflicts by conjunction; moreover, Jupiter, ruler of the 12th and the 8th of the radix and of the revolution as well as of the Sun, Saturn, and Mercury, is in the 5th retrograde and square the ASC, but the Moon is in the 7th with Cor Scorpionis conjunct the 8th cusp of the radix. All of these, therefore, conspired [to cause] a great and dangerous illness.

A great illness happened on account of the Sun and the Moon being afflicted by Saturn; from social drinking and violent play in the heat of the Sun, on account of the Sun and Mercury, rulers of the 5th, which is the [house] of these pleasures, afflicted by Saturn, and then Jupiter, ruler of the 12th and the 8th [posited] in the 5th; a long [illness] on account of Saturn, dangerous on account of the Moon's being

---

[1] Because Libra is intercepted in the 5th, and Saturn is exalted in Libra.

with a violent fixed star and on the cusp of the 8th of the radix [while being] in the 7th of the revolution. And the journey was signified by Mars ruler of the ASC of the radix in the 9th of the revolution, exalted with a trine to the ASC, and Mars being opposite its radical [position and] on the cusp of the 9th; and the journey was salutary on account of Venus, ruler of the 1st of the radix[1] and the revolution, also exalted in sextile to Mars and to the ASC and free from the malefic Saturn. Therefore, these two planets, rulers of the 1st of the radix, and free from the unlucky rays of Saturn were rightly situated; and, with God willing, they preserved my life with the aid of my friends because Venus was ruler of the 1st in the 11th, even though the Sun, Saturn, and Mercury in the 11th, under the rulership of Jupiter in the 5th, signified illness from play and social drinking with those friends.

The third will be my thirty-first revolution which occurred while I was at Villefranche in the year 1613, in which I received the Doctor of Medicine degree at Avignon on the 9th of May; and the figure was such as follows:

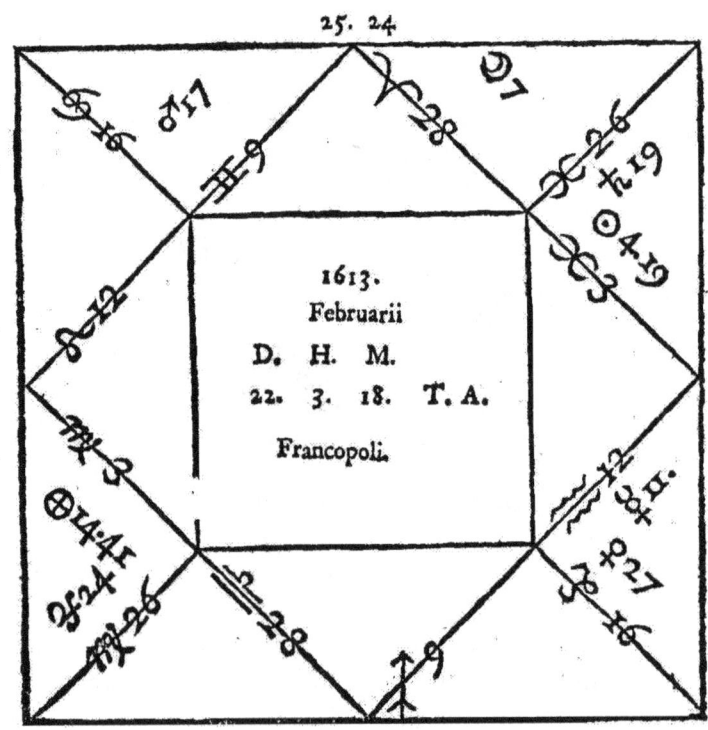

Morin's 31st Revolution
Villefranche
22 Feb 1613 3:18 PM

In which the Sun was the ruler of the ASC, with its exaltation in the MC, the radical ASC (which should be noted) square Venus, ruler of the Part of Fortune and the 1st in the radix, and here ruler of the 10th,[2] in the 10th house of the radix. And Mars, ruler of the MC was in partile square to the radical Moon, under the rulership of Mercury, and in trine to it, but square Saturn, ruler of the 10th of the radix, which in that year completed its own revolution, and in the 8th occupying the radical place of the Moon,

---

[1] Because Taurus is intercepted in the ASC of the radix.

[2] Because Taurus is intercepted in the MC.

with which it was conjoined in the radix in sextile to the MC; but the Moon is in the 9th determined to the sciences, in trine to the ASC, and sextile Mercury, which partially opposes the ASC from Aquarius, then in antiscion to Jupiter, which has a trine to Venus, ruler of the 10th, [and] is conjoined to it in the radix and is its ruler.[1] Then, therefore, there was a manifold and notable combination of the radical significators, both for the person and for his dignities; and in this figure, the radical ASC is in the MC, its ruler Mars in the domicile of and in trine to Mercury, which is well placed, the Sun powerful in the ASC and the MC, the Moon in the 9th applying next to Mercury, the ruler of Mars, which rules the MC, then Jupiter, which rules the Sun. All these things, I say, strongly presaged honors and dignity, and that of a Mercurial [nature], on account of Mars, ruler of the MC, in the domicile and trine of a well placed Mercury, and the Moon applying by sextile to Mercury; moreover, in addition, Venus, ruler of the 10th, was making a square to the MC and a trine to Jupiter, [and was] the ruler of the Sun; then Saturn, ruler of the radical MC, which had in that same year returned to its and the Moon's radical place, in sextile to the radical MC, and to Venus in the revolution, also ruled Mercury. Wherefore, I was made a Doctor of Medicine, which dignity is very much of the nature of Mars, Saturn, and Mercury.

But, because Mars was here afflicted by a square to Saturn, and Jupiter, ruler of the Sun, was also afflicted by an opposition to Saturn and a square to Mars, and the Sun itself was afflicted by a conjunction with Saturn and a square to Mars, that dignity was not a fortunate one for me, at least for financial gain, on account of Mars [in the revolution being] in the 2nd of the radix square Saturn; and therefore, after 12 years, [during which] I was the personal physician to two masters, who treated me, who deserved the best from them, most ungratefully, I abandoned the practice of medicine.

Fourth will be my thirty-third revolution, which occurred while I was at Paris in the year 1615, from whence I set out for Hungary for the sake of education and riches. And it was a fortunate journey for these things, but seven times during it I fell into danger of violent death, and four times in particular in the greatest danger to life; and in short, one time I was miraculously freed from a violent, indeed from an inevitable, death, on the first day of January 1616 at the first hour and 30 minutes after noon, having already begun a truly frightening fall into waters swirling to [the point of causing] bewilderment, along with the horse on which I was riding. Into which danger I had been thrown by a woman fortune-teller, because the day before, I and two young merchants had not wanted to take lodgings and spend the night at her place; and they also on that same day were thrown into other dangers, less to be sure, but inflicted upon them with evil [effect]; for one of them, during a very heavy hail storm, fell off of his horse into a river, and at night; and the other, carried away by his horse at full speed, was borne along very violently through thorn-bushes, ditches and hedges, with great danger to his life; while, when his companion had been extracted from the water, he wanted to mount his horse, and he ought to have gone back to the district, one German milestone distant, which we had passed according to the prophecy of the fortune-teller, who had said to them when they were leaving, that they would not go on the day that they thought they would, and that they would have some misfortune before they entered any other lodging. On the other hand, my danger was very much greater, but without any absolute evil; for I was truly freed [from it] in a miraculous manner; neither I, nor my horse, nor anyone mortal could have freed me or the horse from a fall that had already begun and from [subsequent] death; and this happened to me while I was returning from Hungary.

---

[1] That is, Jupiter is conjoined to Venus in the radix and its ruler. This entire sentence in the Latin is somewhat confused and ungrammatical.

Another time, moreover, while I was swimming in the Rhine just for fun, on the 7th of July 1615 at 10:30 or thereabouts, a catapult was thrown against me from a distance of three paces by a merchant of Cologne, who was guarding our little boat, who thought that robbers had crossed the Rhine to steal the boat, as often happened; and another fellow very nearly transfixed me with a sword; for, while swimming, I sought out our little boat in which we were going up to Mainz, and then I was going to catch hold of it. And in fact they were shouting at me in the German language, as they would at a robber, but I was ignorant of the language, and they were thinking that I had been slain by the shot from the catapult, or that I had been fatally wounded, and when I had heard the shouting and the language, that merchant ran far away, but, by the greatest goodness of God, I was not even injured. But there were other dangers on account of women, quarrels, duels, etc., and my mind always trembles whenever I remember all of these events, although by the greatest Clemency of God I was always uninjured, and I am terrified by the very magnitude of the past dangers that I have escaped from; for which, let there be everlasting honor and the giving of thanks to God from all the celestial host and from my own poor spirit. Amen. Moreover, the figure of that revolution was like this:

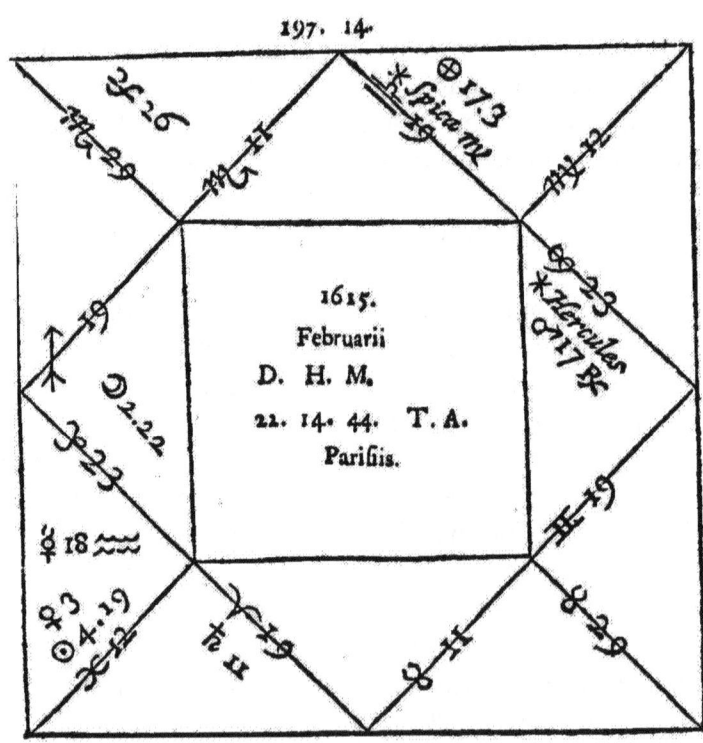

Morin's 33rd Revolution
Paris
22 Feb 1615 2:44 AM

From which, it should be noted that many and lengthy journeys were signified for me in the radix by Jupiter and Saturn, rulers of the 9th, with the Sun and the Moon in a cadent house and trine Mars, ruler of the ASC; and then dangers of a violent death from that same Jupiter, ruler of the 8th, with Saturn and the luminaries, then with Cor Scorpionis on the cusp of the 8th, and especially [death] in water on account of all the planets, except Mercury, being in water signs. Therefore, in this figure, Saturn, ruler of the 9th and the MC of the radix, in the 3rd of the revolution and its radical place on the cusp of the 3rd; then Mercury, ruler of the 9th of the revolution, applying to the square of Jupiter, ruler of the ASC of the revolution and the 9th of the radix, as well as the signs of the 9th and 10th of the radix in the 1st of the revolution, and the Moon in the 9th of the radix and the 1st of the revolution, [all] signify that long journey and that it would be for learning and riches, because that Mercury, ruler of the 9th was in the 2nd under the rulership of Saturn in his own sign Aquarius in the radix, for Mercury in the radix was ruler of the 2nd and 3rd in partile trine to the ASC and [also] in Aquarius.

Moreover, the journey was a lucky one and with honor among foreign magnates on account of the Mercury's being free from malefic aspects, in sextile to its ruler Saturn and trine the MC, in which Spica Virginis[1] shines, and Venus ruler of that MC in her exaltation and in her radical place with the Sun and in sextile to the Moon, also free from the malefics [and] in the 2nd house with Mercury and the Sun, whence I was sufficiently rewarded by the profession of medicine, especially because the Part of Fortune was in the MC with Spica and in trine to Mercury in the 2nd, and on account of my fame I was sent to the illustrious Cardinal of Forgách,[2] whom, as a patient, Johann Ruland, M.D., the son of Martin Ruland [1532-1602], was treating in the mountains of Hungary[3]; and I was honored with gifts by many magnates. Moreover, these things signified danger: First, that the ASC of the revolution was in square to the radical Moon in the 8th house; second, that Jupiter, ruler of the ASC, was under the rulership of Mars, both in water signs, and Mars itself, ruler of the ASC of the radix, was with Hercules,[4] a violent fixed star conjunct the cusp of the 8th house, and in its fall in square to Saturn also in its fall. Third, that the Moon, ruler of Mars and the 8th, was in its exile in the 1st, also afflicted by the square of Saturn and opposite Mars. fourth, that the MC of the revolution was afflicted by a square to the Moon[5] and Mars and an opposition to Saturn; and all of these were very bad.

Mars in the 7th conjunct the cusp of the 8th along with Hercules [and] in a water sign signified dangers of a violent death from quarrels, duels, and on the water; Saturn in its fall in a fire sign of Mars, occupying a water [sign] in the radix under the rulership of Jupiter, ruler of the 8th, by its own square to Mars, portended dangers in water, from fire and iron; Venus, ruler of the 5th and the 10th of the revolution, conjunct the Sun, ruler of the 8th in square to Jupiter, ruler of the 8th of the radix, dangers because of pleasure and women. From which it is sufficiently plain, how foolishly I followed the bad natal and revolutionary inclinations imprinted by the stars, certainly with great dangers, which I would perhaps more wisely have turned aside from, if I had then been skilled in astrology, for a corrupt nature is more efficaciously recalled from bad inclinations by the fear of temporal death than by the fear of eternal death, and especially during youth.

The fifth will be my thirty-fourth revolution, in which a great, malign, and lengthy illness befell me on the 16th day of April 1616, and the figure was like this:

---

[1] The Latin text has the symbol for Scorpio by mistake. Spica was in 18°28′ Libra at the time of the revolution.

[2] Ferencz Forgách (1566-1615), Archbishop (1605) and then (1607) Cardinal at Esztergom, Hungary.

[3] Morin doesn't say that he treated the Cardinal, but merely that he was sent for. Since the Cardinal died in that same year 1615, he may have passed away before Morin arrived; but in any case, the treatments that he received did not save his life.

[4] Beta Geminorum, more commonly called Pollux. It was in 17°54′ Cancer.

[5] Morin doesn't pay much attention to orbs. Here he puts the Moon in 3 Capricorn in square to the MC in 19 Libra, an orb of 16 degrees!

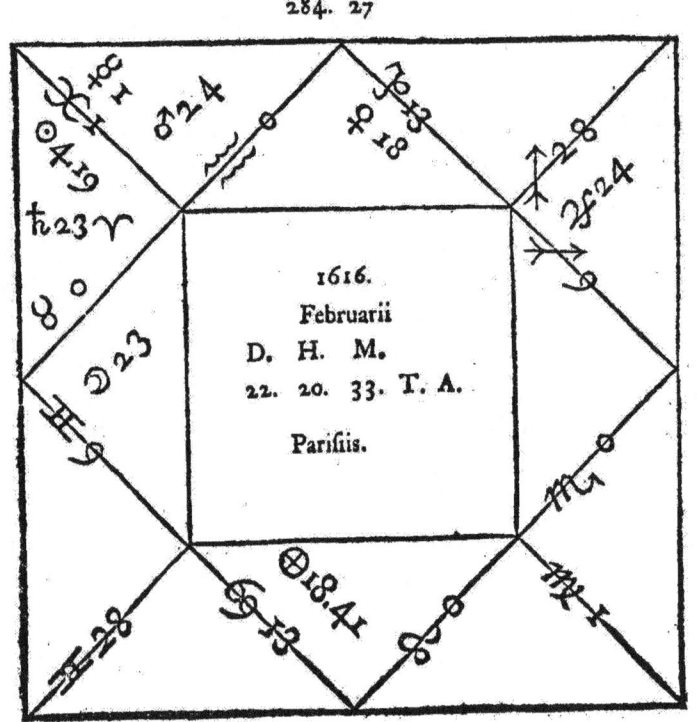

Morin's 33rd Revolution
Paris
23 Feb 1616 8:33 AM

How very similar this is to the natal figure, as far as the position of the *caelum*, as is the thirty-fourth of Cardan shown above; Venus, moreover, the ruler of the 1st of the radix and of the revolution, has migrated from the 12th of the radix to the MC of the revolution and the radix; and its ruler Saturn is in the 12th of the radix and the revolution conjunct the ASC of the radix; and Venus is applying to a square of Saturn in its fall; but the Moon has migrated from the 12th of the radix, where it it was conjoined to Saturn, to the 1st of the revolution, where it applies to a square of Mars in the 11th, which Mars also afflicts the Sun in the 12th, ruler of the 5th of the radix and the revolution.

Since, therefore, the ASC of the radix is then also directed to the square of Saturn, there was a great and powerful consensus of causes to bring about the kind of illness, from which I experienced outstanding misfortunes.

Sixth will be my thirty-ninth revolution:

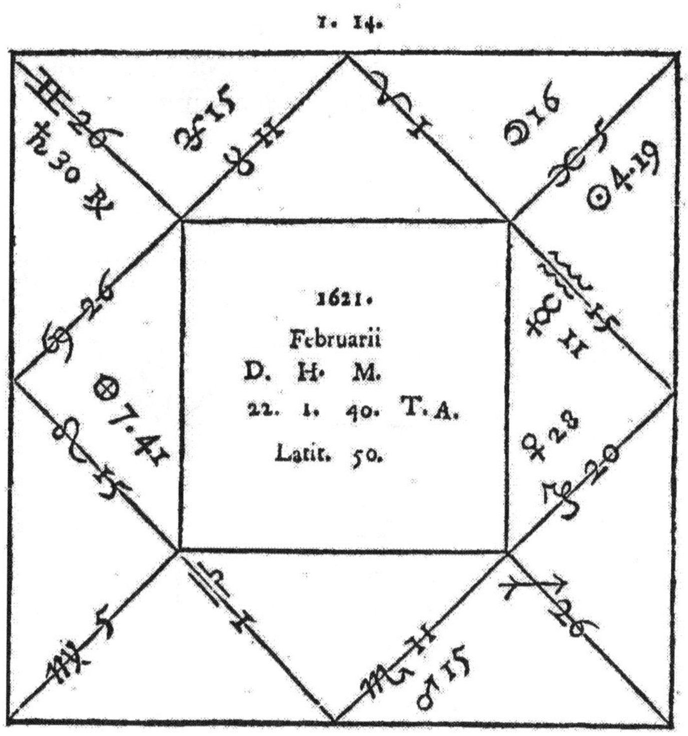

Morin's 39th Revolution
St. Evroult de Notre Dame 50N
22 Feb 1621 1:40 PM

which began at St. Evroult in Normandy[1] in the year 1621, in which in the month of October I betook myself by post horses to Montauban, which city King Louis XIII had besieged most unsuccessfully; and I was made regular physician to the Duke of Luxembourg,[2] a brother of the Constable de Luynes,[3] who had the greatest power [at that time]. That dignity was procured for me by the very noble Mr. Tronson, who was then close to the king and the very powerful de Luynes brothers, because he wanted to move me forward in the royal court, and therefore he brought this about for me with his own letters [of recommendation]. But that position was not a fortunate one for me; and I worked a field that was sterile and ungrateful. And the figure was as shown above.

The journey was caused by the Sun and the Moon, rulers of the first, in the 9th; the dignity by Mars, ruler of the ASC of the radix and the MC of the revolution, strong in trine to the Sun and the Moon; friends, [acting] with consideration and benevolence, on account of Jupiter, ruler of the Sun and the Moon, in the 11th and sextile them; but the misfortune was portended by the Part of Fortune afflicted by the squares of Jupiter and Mars, then the opposition of Mercury, whose ruler Saturn was in the 12th.

---

[1] The Latin *Sanctus Ebrulsus* is St. Evroult Notre Dame du Bois, Orne, France, a little town in 48N47 0E28, some 10 miles E of Gacé, Orne. Morin gives the latitude as 50 degrees, which would put it in the middle of the English Channel, but he may have guessed at the latitude and missed it a degree.

[2] Leon d'Albert de Luynes (d. 1630), who acquired the title of Duke of Luxembourg by marrying the heiress Charlotte-Margaret (d. 1680), Duchess of Luxembourg.

[3] Charles d'Albert, Duke of Luynes, mentioned above, a favorite of the king. He died in 1621.

The seventh will be my forty-seventh revolution, begun at Paris in the year 1629, in which, through the outstanding favor of the Most Serene Queen Marie de' Medici,[1] I was made Regius Professor of Mathematics. That [honor] was requested for me by the Most Eminent Cardinal Bérulle,[2] who, from his own kindness, thought me worthy.

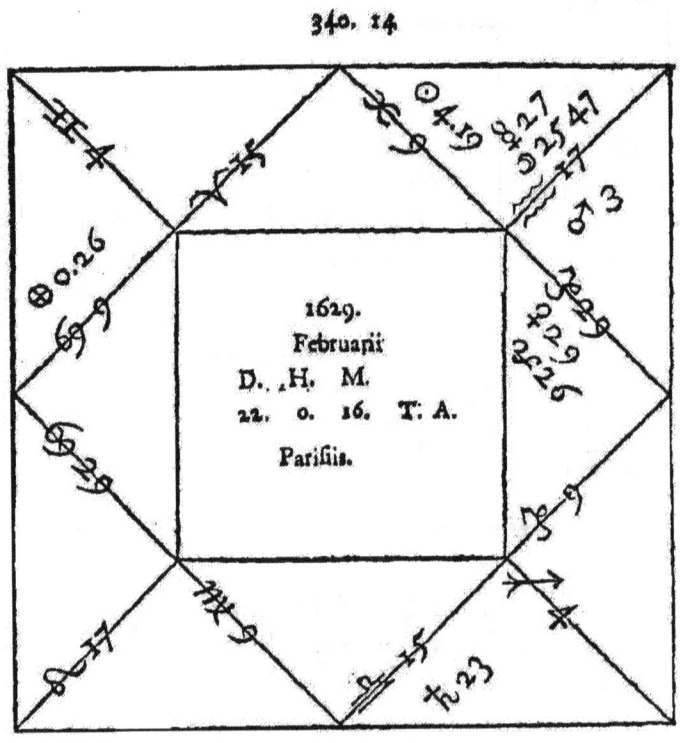

Morin's 47th Revolution
Paris
22 Feb 1629 0:16 PM

Indeed, foreseeing then from the direction of the MC of my nativity to my cluster[3] of planets, that there would be some brief dignity for me, but that it could not be hoped for from my master, the duke of Luxembourg, [even] after the outstanding services I had rendered him during a period of eight years, [and that] also with great dangers to my life; namely, because many times I had looked for some voluntary gratitude from him; I boldly decided to leave him, even though my friends were dissauding me; and a little while afterward that dignity presented itself to me. Moreover, the figure of the revolution is such as shown above.

In which there ascended the radical place of Mars, which was the ruler of my radical ASC. Moreover, the cluster of planets in my nativity, or its place, is in the MC of the revolution, to which the Sun itself is conjoined, unafflicted by the malefics. And these things presaged the honorable dignity very

---

[1] Marie de' Medici (1573-1642), widow of King Henry IV (1553-1610), and mother of Louis XIII (1601-1643) was Queen Regent of France.

[2] Pierre Bérulle (1575-1629), French Cardinal and Statesman.

[3] The Latin text has *cumulus* 'heap', 'mass', or 'cluster', sometimes called "stellium" today.

strongly in that year, along with fame and the celebrity of name, but they presented in return for the same effect other [occurrences] not more unworthy of being noted. For the direction of the MC of the radix in that year came partilely to Mercury in Aquarius, which was preceding the Sun before all the [other] planets; but in this figure Mercury had returned to its own radical degree according to the *Rudolphine Tables*, with the Moon, ruler of the ASC, in the 9th house, dedicated to the sciences, and both of them[1] applying to a trine of the exalted Saturn, their ruler, which was the ruler of the 10th of the radix; that, therefore, was outstanding, whence it is no wonder that, not withstanding certain oppositions raised by great men, the whole matter took place most fortunately by order of the Queen, especially because Venus, ruler of the 1st of the radix and the 11th of the revolution was conjunct Jupiter, ruler of the Sun and of the MC; and incidentally it ought to be noted here that in that year, as well as in the years 1613 and 1621, in which I acquired dignities, Venus, ruler of my Part of Fortune, was in Capricorn and square my radical ASC, or conjunct Jupiter, or in trine to Jupiter.

The eighth will be my fifty-second revolution, begun at Paris in the year 1634, [which was] certainly outstanding, both in the position of the planets and also in what transpired. For the beginning of this revolution [fell] of course on the 30th of March. In the larger court of the Royal Arsenal, before 8 Commissioners assigned to [query] me by Cardinal Richelieu, the Prime Minister of France, and more than 300 men who were Magnates of the Court, [members] of the Privy Council of the King, or the regular Councils, Presiding Officers, Advisers, Nobles, Religious Persons, Mathematicians, and others, I gave a perfect demonstration of the Science of Longitudes[2] that I had invented, a matter both scholarly and scientific, for the discovery of which a great prize had been established and promised by the kings of Europe, which is said to have never been done for any other purpose. And in that so celebrated discussion that lasted around six hours, I very fortunately overcame the envy of the mathematical commissioners (whom I was thinking were friends of mine) and the plots against my honor, so that they were compelled to approve my demonstrations, by the judgment given out publicly before so illustrious a gathering.

But, 10 days having passed, the Mathematical Commissioners Pascal, Mydorge, Beaugrand, Boulenger, and Hérigone,[3] met again by the order of Cardinal Richelieu, so that from [4] articles of that doctrine, selected for them by that same Cardinal, [and] already previously discussed and judged, they might once again render judgment on that doctrine. And when alone, I having neither been called nor heard [in defense], they thoughtlessly and impudently rendered a different [judgment] from their prior one [and one that was] plainly contrary to the mathematics involved, and presented it to the Cardinal, by whose order they immediately handed it over to the printers, so that it might be known to everyone what they (God willing) had acknowledged in its warning to the Cardinal himself, added to that opinion of his own. And so it resulted that I was defrauded of the prize that had been offered by those commissioners and by Cardinal Richelieu. I appealed that second judgment to the more famous astronomers of Eu-

---

[1] The Latin text has the symbol for the Sun, inserted by mistake.

[2] This was a badly needed method of finding the geographic longitude of ships at sea. Morin's method consisted of observing lunar distances from stars or planets, from which, by calculation from an ephemeris, the time on the standard meridian of the ephemeris could be determined. Then, by comparison with the locally determined time of the ship at sea, its distance from the ephemeris meridian could be determined. This method had been advocated by Regiomontanus (1436-1476), but Morin had evidently revised and perfected it.

[3] The fame of these learned men has not endured. I was unable to find their names in the usual reference sources.

rope, to whom I wrote and transmitted my book,[1] all of whom, by their own replies to me,[2] approved the first judgment, and they unanimously condemned the second for falsity and injustice; and yet, during the life of the Cardinal, this was absolutely useless for me, according as all this is set forth in our *Astronomy Restored*[3]; and Saturn in my nativity, ruler of the 11th in the 12th, signified false and envious friends and in fact secret enemies, by reason of the determination and analogy well-known to me.

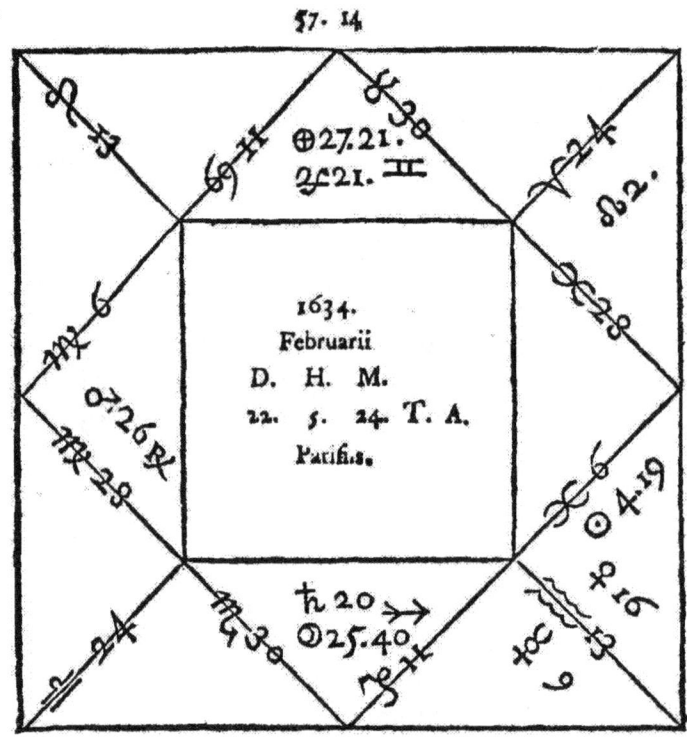

Morin's 52nd Revolution
Paris 22 Feb 1634 5:24 PM

Moreover, in this figure of the revolution, there occurs at the first glance a celestial spectacle not more unworthy of note than the one in the natal figure. For in fact both luminaries and the 3 superior planets, Saturn, Jupiter, and Mars, are in mutual opposition and square to themselves and to the Part of Fortune,[4] [and] they are also in the 4 angles of the figures, while in the radix they were conjoined in the cadent 12th house. For, what other sort of thing was portended for me than something great, public enemies, celebrated quarrels, huge oppositions, and hindrances to good fortune, just as all these things happened to me in that same year? as you can see] in the figure above.

---

[1] *Longitudinum terrestrium nec non coelestium nova et hactenus optata scientia...* the New and Hitherto Longed for Science of Terrestrial as well as Celestial Longitudes] (Paris: J. Libert, 1634 4to 164 pp.)

[2] Morin published their replies in the book, *Lettres escrites au Sr Morin par les plus célébres astronomes de France, approuvant son invention des longitudes...* [Letters written to Mr. Morin by the Most Celebrated Astronomers of France, Approving his Invention of Longitudes] (Paris: The Author, 1635.8vo55 pp.].

[3] *Astronomia jam a fundamentis integre et exacte restituta...* [Astronomy, Now from its Fundamentals Completely and Accurately Restored] (Paris: The Author, 1640. 4to 361 pp. Diagrs.)

[4] Here again Morin disregards orbs, as he considers the Sun in 5 Pisces to be opposite Mars in 26 Virgo.

In fact it can be seen that the opposition of the 5 radical planets, Venus, Sun, Jupiter, Saturn, and the Moon, that I had in the 12th of the radix, was ascending, and their [radical] places were in the 7th of the revolution. And that presaged the great and open oppositions to me by secret enemies. Moreover, the Sun, ruler of the 12th, on the cusp of the 7th, when it had already been in the 12th of the radix, signified that a secret enemy magnate would become an open one in that year, and it was the Cardinal himself, [who acted] with public injustice towards me. But Jupiter, ruler of the Sun and the Moon, elevated over all the planets in a domicile of Mercury and well disposed, presaged ingenuity and prudence of intelligence in undertakings and actions with good luck, especially because Venus and Mercury, rulers of the 10th, were conjoined in trine to Jupiter. And so my actions proceeded very fortunately, as far as those things that resulted from them, as is plain in [my book] *Astronomy Restored*. And yet, the square of Mars and the oppositions of Saturn and the Moon to Jupiter and the Part of Fortune stirred up publicly against me disputes, detractions, slanders, and the most atrocious and false invectives by envious, good-for-nothing, and disreputable persons, and they signified that my action would be rendered unfortunate by injustice and fraud. Moreover, the withholding of the lucrative prize and the fraud [perpetrated] by both hidden and open enemies was signified by Mars, retrograde on the cusp of the 7th, and square the Part of Fortune and Saturn, ruler of Venus and Mercury, rulers of the 10th and the 2nd, especially because in the nativity Mars, ruler of the 12th and the 7th, was my significator of hidden and open enemies as well as disputes, and Saturn of hidden enemies. Therefore, this revolution agrees remarkably well with the events of that year.

The ninth will be my 60th[1] revolution, in which on the 2nd of November I contracted a long and drawn-out fever with a stupendous evacuation, and then with a swelling and pain in the spleen, that finally released urine in a flood, so long and copiously that, with the flesh [itself] then [as it seemed] turning to liquid, I really feared death from the *marasmus*.[2]

And the figure was like this:

---

[1] The Latin text says *sexcenta* 'six hundredth' by mistake.

[2] A withering or wasting away of the body.

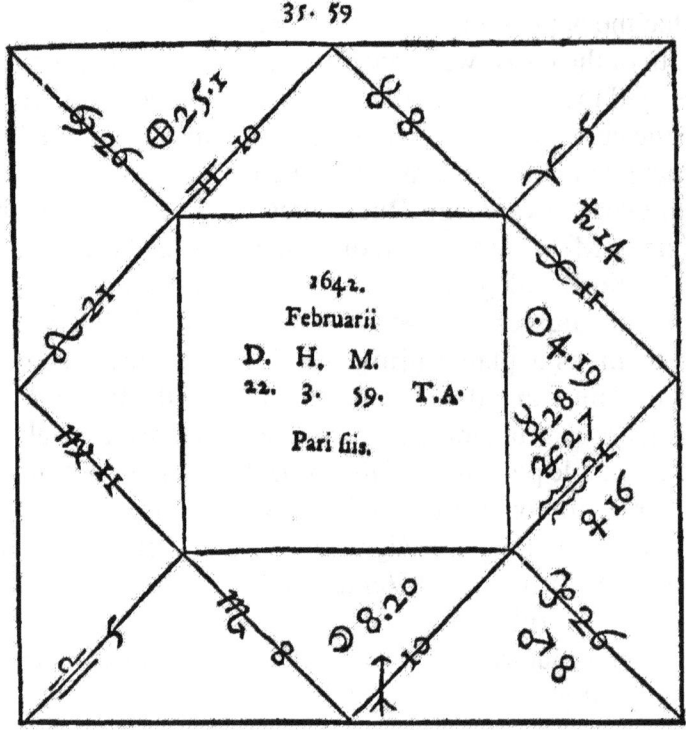

Morin's 60th Revolution
Paris
22 Feb 1659 3:59 PM

In which [the positions of] both luminaries should be noted, which were significators of illnesses in the nativity, because they were in the 12th; but in the revolution, the Moon, ruler of the cusp of the 12th, is on the 8th cusp of the radix, which is [a significator] of death. Moreover, the sun, ruler of the ASC, is conjoined to the 8th cusp of the revolution, and Saturn, which has returned to its radical place, is in the 8th, very badly afflicted by its own conjunction to the Sun and its square to the Moon; moreover, Jupiter, ruler of the 8th, is opposed to the ASC; and Mars, ruler of the radical ASC, is found in partile opposition to its own natal place. All of which, but especially Saturn in the 8th afflicting the Sun and the Moon, rulers of the 12th and the 1st, signified a long, difficult, and dangerous illness, but [also] its clearing up, on account of Jupiter and Venus being opposed to the ASC of the revolution, in sextile to the radical ASC, and the mutual reception by domicile of Jupiter with Saturn in a water sign, which in that year came by direction to a sinister square of the Moon. And it should be noted that, in this revolution as in that of the year 1612, the Moon is found conjunct the 8th cusp of the radix, in square to Saturn, which is conjoined to the Sun; and there were two great illnesses that were long and dangerous. The tenth will be my sixty-second revolution, begun at Paris in the year 1644, whose figure is like this:

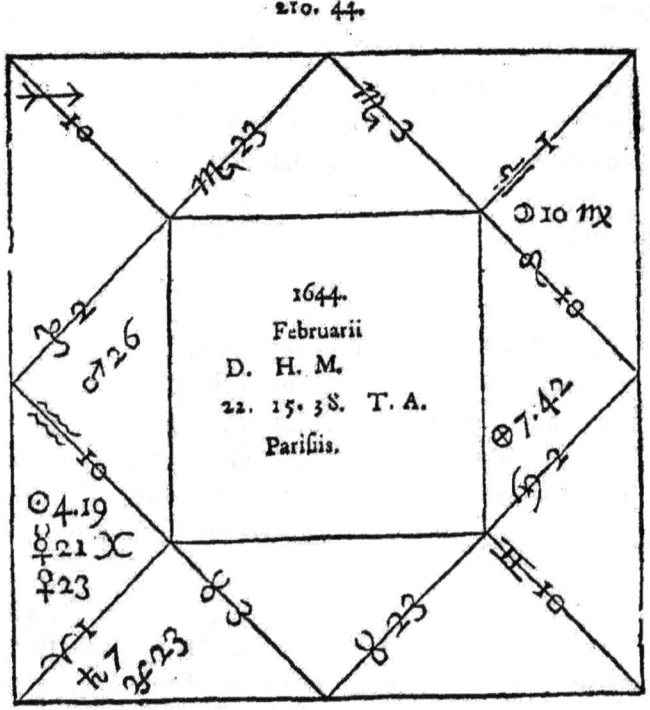

Morin's 62nd Revolution
Paris
23 Feb 1644 3:38 AM

In which Mars, ruler of the radical ASC is found in the 1st, exalted, and in mutual reception by domicile with Saturn, in sextile to Venus and square Jupiter. And it is the ruler of the MC, where the trine of the radical cluster of my planets is found, which [trine] occupied the 7th of the radix, which has to do with quarrels; and the radical place of Mars is in the 7th of the revolution; and the Part of Fortune is on that same place. Furthermore, in this revolution Mars was very strong for conferring bravery and audacity for difficult [tasks] and for engaging in quarrels in the hope of good results.

Having inspected this revolution, [and] with Cardinal Richelieu dead, from whom while yet alive I could never obtain the promised remuneration for the *Secret of Longitudes* that I had invented, I decided to request that from the Royal Council, although all my friends and some magnates were dissuading me, because in that Council the spirit of Cardinal Richelieu, and the comrades and satellites of his fortune yet remained powerful, and for that reason I would not accomplish anything with them opposing.

Nevertheless, I composed the text of my request with as much skill as I could employ, so that the injustice perpetrated against me by Cardinal Richelieu, when he encouraged my Commissioners to render a second judgment against me, one absolutely contrary to the first and true judgment. And that could not be decided without [giving] shame to France. Then, in the month of September, I sent that [document] containing 43 pages to the printers, and after that I began to distribute it as much as I could with propriety; and after so many expenses already made in vain, amounting to 100 livres,[1] I was reluc-

---

[1] About $6,000 in today's money.

tant to set this forth vigorously in the matter. But those who examined that statement, even if they had formerly been very favorably inclined to Cardinal Richelieu, would have been able to think that there was anything in it worthy of censure or rejection, but everyone acknowledged the justice of my petition. Still, I decided not to present the case to the Royal Council in that year, but only to set it in motion, to prepare minds and bring together my friends, which also luckily succeeded on account of Mars and Jupiter, rulers of the 11th, of which Mars was exalted in the 1st and Jupiter was applying to the radical ASC. Consequently, I began to hope in God and the stars that I would accomplish something in the following year.

In addition, I was maligned without cause in that same year by Ismael Boulliau [1605-1694] in his *Astronomia Philolaica*[1] in connection with the equation of time. And the Moon was presaging that, being the ruler of the 7th in the 8th, and in a sign of Mercury opposed to the Sun and inimical to the ASC[2]; then Saturn ruler of the ASC in its fall in quincunx to the Moon, and square the radical place of Mars in the 7th. But Mars, ruler of the MC, exalted in the 1st and sextile the exalted Venus, was signifying a victory for me, not only strongly but also with good effect I issued a rejoinder at the end of my *Astronomy Restored*.

Then, the Sun, Mercury, and Venus in the 2nd, in trine to the MC and the Part of Fortune, then Jupiter, ruler of the 2nd,[3] and powerful in the place of the Part of Fortune,[4] applying to the radical ASC, caused me [to obtain] a sufficient amount of gain from astrology in that year, and I received a thousand livres[5] for judging the nativity of a certain most Serene and Magnanimous Prince, whose very famous name I have omitted here. And yet, I have never sought to gain money from astrology, but rather I fled from [doing so], and as often as I could, without offending friends or magnates, I refused the work, namely so that I might devote all my time to establishing the theory of astrology.

The eleventh will be my sixty-third revolution, begun at Paris in the year 1645, of which the figure is like this:

---

[1] A set of astronomical tables based upon Kepler's *Rudolphine Tables;* they were published at Paris in 1645 and were thus in competition with Morin's own version.

[2] I suppose he says it is "inimical to the ASC" because it is in the 8th house; it is not inimical by aspect, since it is trine the ASC.

[3] It is co-ruler of the 2nd because Pisces is intercepted in the 2nd.

[4] The Part of Fortune is in Cancer, and Jupiter would be powerful in Cancer, the sign of its exaltation.

[5] About $62,000 in today's money.

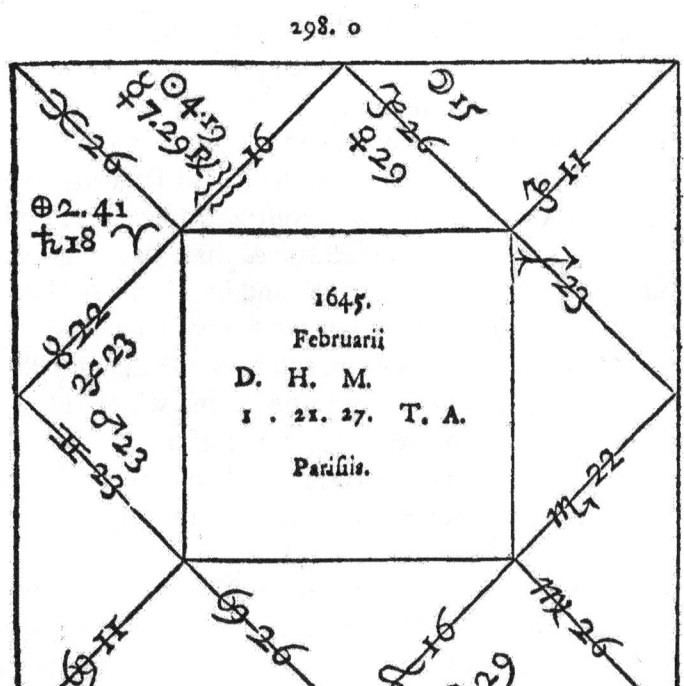

Morin's 63rd Revolution
Paris
22 Feb 1645 9:27 AM

In this revolution, Venus is found again at the end of Capricorn, namely square the radical ASC, as in the years 1613 and 1629, and in trine to Jupiter, as in that same year 1613; and therefore, at first glance, some good was prophesied, as happened in those years. But much more in this year, namely because she was the ruler of the ASC in the MC, while in the radix whe was the ruler of the 1st[1] and of the Part of Fortune.; moreover, Jupiter, ruler of the Sun, is in the 1st of the radix and in the ASC of the revolution and trine Venus, its ruler. For from these things, great good fortune in undertakings and actions is signified, also in connection with dignities and increase in riches. Moreover, the Sun, ruler of the 5th of the radix and the revolution, in the 12th with Mercury in sextile[2] to the Moon and Jupiter, signify friends of a solar nature, certainly princes and ministers of the kingdom, then too, Mercurial types and learned men, and their favor, because of Jupiter, ruler of the Sun, in the ASC and trine Venus and the Moon. Then, Jupiter and Mars, rulers of the 7th of the radix and the revolution, one of them in the ASC, and the other on the cusp of the 2nd, signify lawsuits because of rich men, but not unfortunate ones, because Jupiter and Mars are not afflicted by Saturn, and Mars is in its own radical antiscion.

Therefore, prophesying well from this revolution, I put forth special care and work at the beginning of that year, so that the case of my remuneration for the year 1644, fortunately begun, would be referred to the Royal Council, and one way or the other it would be terminated, so that as quickly as it could be done, I might be freed from the cares, disgusts, and expenses of that business. Therefore, having seen

---

[1] Venus was co-ruler of Morin's ASC because Taurus was intercepted in the 1st house.

[2] Here again, Morin pays no attention to orbs: Mercury is 7 degrees from an exact sextile to the Moon and 15 degrees from an exact sextile to Jupiter.

those Most Serene gentlemen, the Duke of Orleans,[1] Prince Condé,[2] the King's Ministers, the Chancellor, and other Magnates, all of whom had with good will promised their own help to me in a matter as just as this, it finally happened that, on the 8th of April, when the case had been set forth in the Royal Privy Council, I was granted an annual pension of 2,000 livres[3] above the first vacant ecclesiastical benefice, along with 1,000 livres to be paid to me from the Royal Treasury. And this indeed was not really enough for the remuneration for the *Secret of Longitudes* I had invented (for which a very large prize had been offered) and also for the *Astronomy Restored* that I had established[4]; but at least this was done with the very free consent of all [those involved], and in this matter I experienced a very prompt and fortunate success; and I received that honorific prize not withstanding the envy of the supervising commissioners and other secret enemies. But Saturn, ruler of the 9th, the 10th, and the Moon, being in its fall in the 12th with the Part of Fortune and square the Moon, which ruled the 2nd, [and] with Mercury in its detriment, cadent, combust, and retrograde, signified the pettiness of the remuneration. Moreover, I was given the hope that my pension would shortly be assigned to some benefice before this fortunate revolution was finished. And that also happened fortunately.

From the things said above, therefore, my eleventh revolution was rather good; and it is plain that the annual revolutions of the Sun are especially effective the more closely they correspond to the natal figure. But since these are only about things of the past, I am pleased to add here my sixty-seventh revolution, which will begin in the year 1649, and whose figure is as follows:

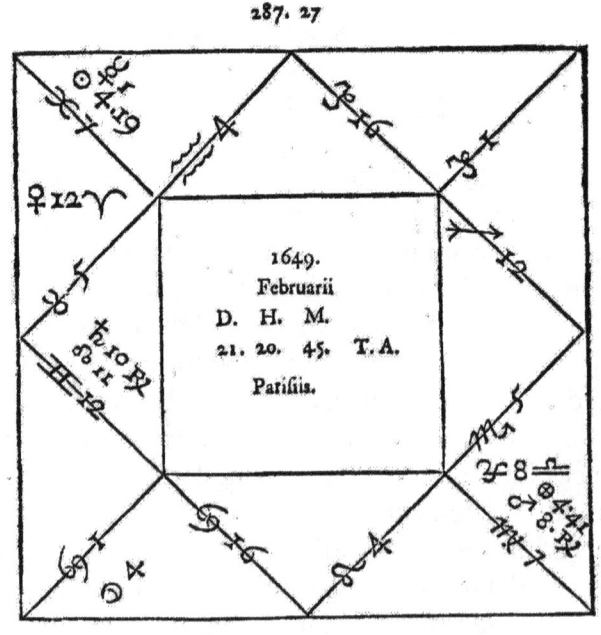

Morin's 67th Revolution
Paris
22 Feb 1649 8:45 AM

---

[1] Jean Baptiste Gaston, Duke of Orleans (1608-1660), younger brother of King Louis XIII.

[2] Henry II, Prince of Conde (1588-1646).

[3] About $125,000 in today's money.

[4] These are references to his previously published books on finding longitudes and to his astronomical tables based on Kepler's theories and tables.

In the year 1649 on the 25th of May at 10:15 [P.M.] at Paris,[1] the Moon will undergo a total eclipse in the 5th degree of Sagittarius, square the radical Sun and Jupiter, which in my nativity signify illnesses and death. and immediately after this eclipse, Mars applies to Saturn, also a significator of illnesses in the radix, which is then found in partile square to the radical Moon, which was also a significator of illnesses in the nativity; and therefore, this eclipse threatens me powerfully with death, especially because it was on the cusp of the 8th of the radix, where the very violent fixed star Cor Scorpionis[2] is found, and in the place of the revolution that is afflicted by the opposition of Saturn and the square of Mars.

At the beginning of this revolution the Sun is directed to the square of Saturn in the ecliptic; and Jupiter, the ruler of the Sun and of the 8th and 12th [houses] of the radix and the revolution, is directed with the Moon to the same square with latitude; and Saturn in the revolution is found in the place of the direction, afflicted by the square from Mars in the 6th. Moreover, the Moon is in the radical place of Mars, and therefore these are also very bad and lethal directions.

Finally, the figure of the revolution shown above is also very bad. For the Sun is afflicted by the square of Saturn and the opposition of Mars, of which the latter is in the 6th and the former is in opposition to the cusp of the 8th; and Venus, ruler of the ASC is badly placed in the 12th house and in opposition to Jupiter, ruler of the 12th and 8th of the radix and the revolution, which is found in the domicile of Venus and the exaltation of Saturn, and also in square to the Moon, which is in the radical place of Mars in the 3rd, with which malice of figure the situation of the *caelum* is similar to that of the radix, but here it is still worse.

All these things agree most powerfully [in pointing] to my death; and, after having escaped the danger of a violent death on so many occasions, this figure still threatens something violent. By iron, by poison, by fire, by water, let the will of God be done, Amen! For I am mistaken if I will evade so strong an alliance [of evil indications], however as an Astrologer and Physician I shall have tried to overcome such a storm of evil influxes. Nevertheless, I shall beware as much as I can of illnesses and violent accidents, especially from blood relations, or servants because of Mars and jupiter in the 6th and Venus, ruler of the 6th, afflicted in the 12th with an opposition to Jupiter and a square to the Moon and the 3rd [house]. But, for how many and how great evils this revolution will have produced, see in the my abbreviated version of the *Rudolphine Tables*, pp. 108 & 109.[3]

Since the rest of the examples above are only those of natural or secular things; and, unworthy as I am, I had chanced to make the acquaintance of the Most Reverend Father Charles de Condren,[4] formerly the General of the Congregation of the Oratory of Jesus, a man skilled in all the sciences, pious, innocent in his morals and very well known for his sanctity, who knew astrology, and for the defense of which he wrote, and many times he approved this labor of mine, to absolve it as he gave praise to God,

---

[1] Unless 10:15 PM is a misprint in the text. Morin has calculated the time of this eclipse incorrectly. From modern figures we can calculate that mid-eclipse occurred at Paris on 26 May 1649 at 3:01 AM LAT. Th. von Oppolzer [*Canon of Eclipses* (New York: Dover Publs., 1962)] gives the half duration of the partial phase as 112 minutes and of the total phase as 51 minutes. So it began at Paris at 1:09 AM, and the total phase began at 2:10 AM LAT. Morin's version of the *Rudolphine Tables* would put the time of mid-eclipse about 5 minutes earlier.

[2] Antares or α Scorpii, which was at 3°57′ Sagittarius at Morin's birth in 1583.

[3] Fortunately, despite all these evil indications, Morin lived another 7 1/2 years,

[4] Charles de Condren (1588-1641), French theologian and politician.

so that it should be plain to all, not just to us, that it embodies a natural propensity to divine things or to religion, which is said by astrologers to pertain to the 9th house of the figure; but in many voluntary things too we also are aroused by the stars to religion, piety, and other virtues at a particular time, no less so than to ambition, rapine, murder, fornication, impiety, and other vices, according as good things or evil things were [present] in the celestial constitution of each person. Still, I shall set forth some solar revolutions of that Blessed Father, born to outstanding religion and piety, relating to his ecclesiastical life, so that the mouths of those may be shut up who will have it that there are no parts of nature in religious or divine things, as if God had established with those things that are contrary and inimical to Himself, and had not rather wished for all of nature, and especially the stars (the corporeal Governors of the World, subordinates of God Himself) to stir up man and move him toward his own understanding, love, and care. Therefore, thoughts from nature of piety and Divine worship are inherent in even a Pagan man, by means of which, if Divine Grace does not intervene, nature then is not destroyed, but rather it is perfected. And so that the Devil notices the bad influences of the stars on a man, by which he may more effectively throw him down into sinful acts and dangers of a violent death by means of his own suggestions, just as the nativities of men bear witness, in which such things always occur under unlucky inspirations; why on the contrary will God not notice at which time the *Caelum* pours in agreeably and fortunately, to motivate man by its own particular and supernatural concourse through its anticipation, and then through that which they commonly call efficacious, but more rightly sanctifying grace; and thus nature will comply with grace, and grace will perfect nature, and it will devote itself to that one, when it shall have been pleasing to God?

First, therefore, will be his twenty-first revolution, begun in the year 1608, in which the man decided to lead the religious life of God, having rejected the world and its vanities, so that he might serve God in a more holy and free manner. And that revolution was this, along with the genethliacal figure.

Rev. Father Charles de Condren
General Superintendent of the Oratorical
Congregation of Jesus Christ   *Revolution*

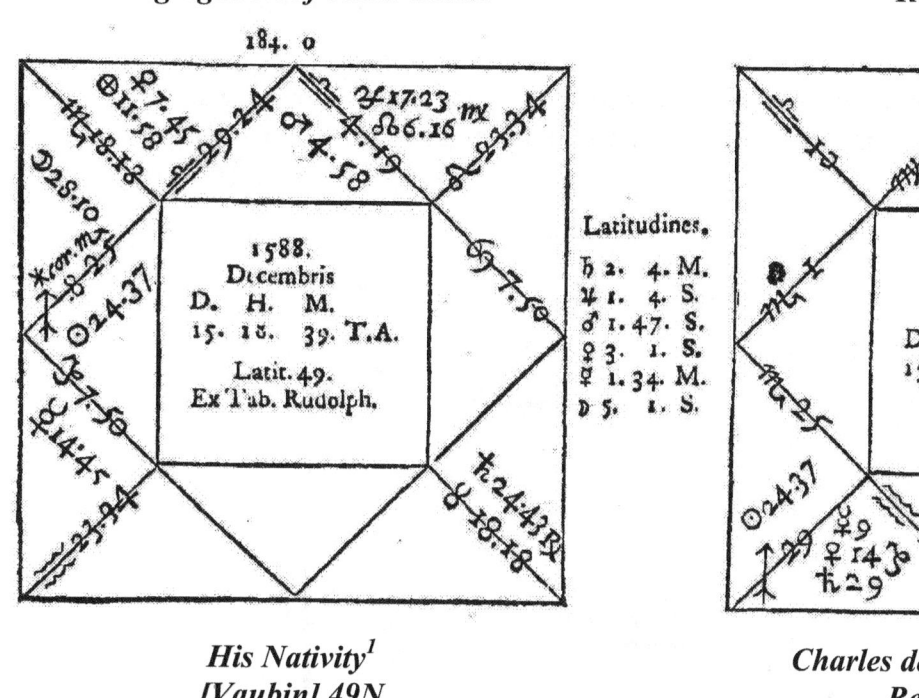

His Nativity[1]
[Vaubin] 49N
16 Dec 6:39 AM

Charles de Condren's 21st
Revolution[2]
[Vaubin] 49N
16 Dec 1608 3:15 AM

In this revolution, four planets are found in the 3rd house, which is a house of religion, like the 9th to which it is opposed; namely, the Sun, ruler of the MC, conjunct the cusp of the 3rd, which was in the 1st of the radix, ruler of the 9th; Mercury, ruler of the 9th of the radix[3]; Venus, ruler of the radical MC, which is found with Mercury in the radical place of Mercury, and Venus's radical place is in the 1st of the revolution; and then Saturn, ruler of the 3rd of the radix, having [the sign of its] exaltation in the MC of the radix; moreover, Mercury is the ruler of the cusp of the 9th of the revolution; and Mercury and Venus are in trine to Jupiter, ruler of the Sun and the cusp of the 3rd, [and] which in the radix was the ruler of the ASC in the 9th house. Finally, Mars, which was in the 10th of the radix, and now is ruler of the ASC, is in its own radical antiscion, in sextile to Mercury, Venus, and Saturn, and also in trine to the 9th[4]; and the Moon, ruler of the 9th[5] is in trine to the Sun. Powerfully, therefore, are the significators of inclinations, profession, and religion combined among themselves, both in the radix, and in this revolution; and Venus and Mercury are joined to Saturn under his rulership, who by essential analogy presides over those who are devoted to hermits, monks, religious persons, and the contemplative life; and conse-

---

[1] The position of Mars is incorrect; it should be 9.58 Libra, evidently a typographical error.

[2] The position of the Moon was accidentally omitted and is not shown in the chart. Judging from the position of the Part of Fortune, Morin had calculated the Moon to be in 14 Aries.

[3] Mercury, which was actually in 14 Capricorn, is joint ruler of the 9th because Virgo is intercepted in that house.

[4] He means that Mars in Pisces is trine to the sign Cancer, which is intercepted in the 9th house. Note that Morin considers an aspect to the sign in an empty house to be valid.

[5] The Moon is co-ruler of the 9th because the sign Cancer is intercepted in that house.

59

quently, they were the natural and powerful cause of why in that year the man devoted himself to God and decided to enter the religious profession. Moreover, Mars, ruler of the 4th of the radix, was square in the revolution to the Sun, ruler of the 1st, signified great opposition and hindrance from his father, which also took place then.

Second will be the 25th revolution of that same Rev. Father, which began in the year 1612, in which he was initiated into the orders of sub-deacon and deacon, the figure of which was thus:

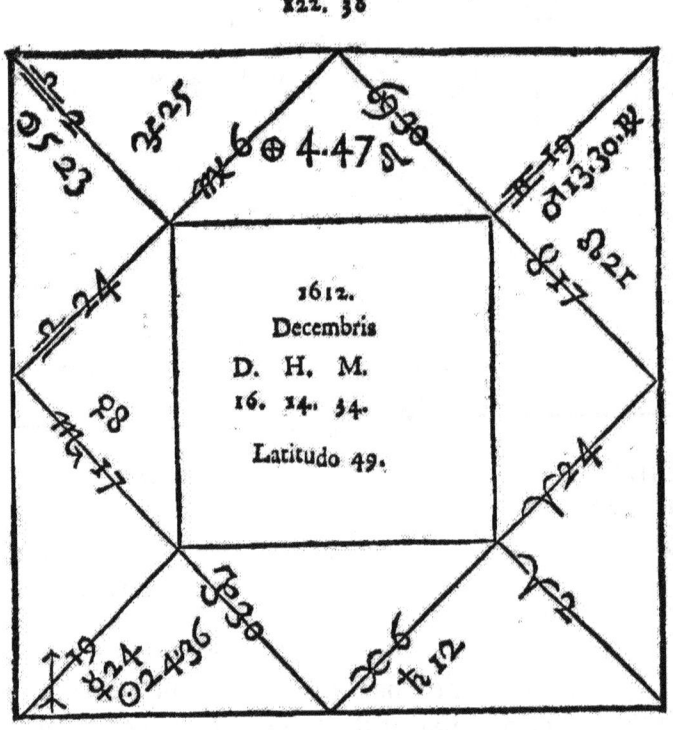

Charles de Condren's 25th Revolution
[Vaubin] 49 N
17 Dec 1612 2:34 AM

In which there is again a powerful combination of significators of his person and of his inclinations, with the significators of dignity or profession and also of religion. For the Sun and Mercury, rulers of the 9th in the radix, are found again in the 3rd house [and] also partilely joined together in a partile square to Jupiter, their ruler, which has returned to its radical place in the 9th of the radix; and Jupiter and Mercury are in mutual reception by domicile. Moreover, in the radix the Sun, ruler of the 9th, was in the 1st. But in the revolution it is the ruler of the 10th in the 3rd; in addition, the Moon, ruler of the 9th of the revolution is in the MC of the radix; and its ruler, Venus, has returned partilely to its radical place in the 1st of the revolution. These [indications] therefore greatly agreed with ecclesiastical dignities—not to be sure with splendid dignities but with power in subordinate matters, because the luminaries are in cadent houses, and Mercury, ruler of the 9th, and the Sun, ruler of the 10th, are afflicted by a square to Saturn and an opposition to Mars, while Jupiter is square Mars and opposite Saturn, but only common to religious persons on account of Saturn's being square to the Sun and Mercury and on account of Saturn's opposition to Jupiter, especially [since it is also] peregrine and square Mars.

Third will be the 26th revolution of that same Rev. Father, in which he was raised to the dignity of priest; and the figure was like this:

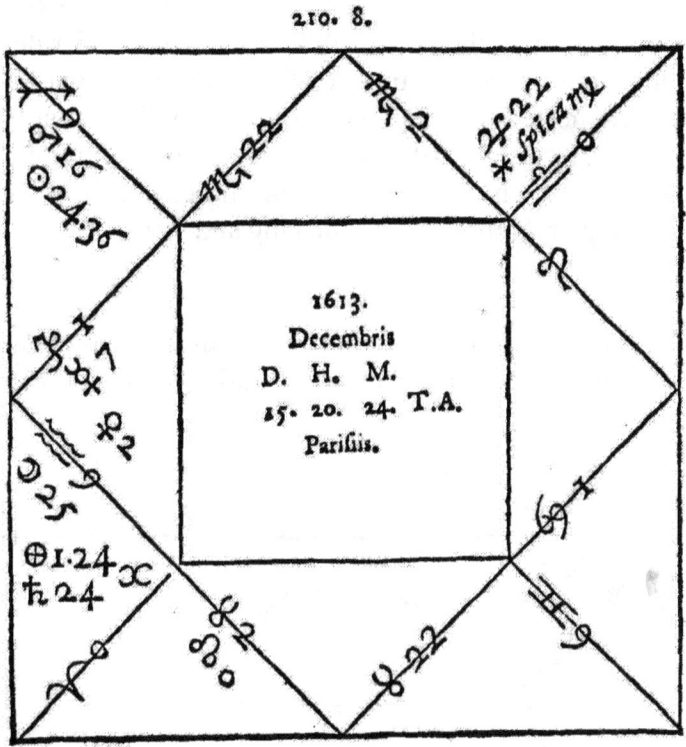

Charles de Condren's 26th Revolution
[Vaubin] 49 N
17 Dec 1612 2:34 AM

In which Mercury,[1] ruler of the 9th of the radix, and Venus, ruler of the MC of the radix and the 9th of the revolution, are found in the 1st and in domiciles of Saturn in opposition to the radical Jupiter[2]; moreover, Jupiter is the ruler of the radical ASC and Sun; then in this revolution the ruler is Saturn; also, Mars, which rules the MC, is found in the 9th with Spica,[3] under the rulership of Venus in the 1st, applying by trine to the Moon, which is also posited in a domicile of Saturn[4]; and the Sun and Mars are in sextile to Jupiter and the Moon. These [indications], therefore, greatly agreed with inclinations towards religion with ecclesiastical dignity, but without power over subordinates, and only to some sort of ordinary religious post, on account of Saturn's ruling Mercury, Venus, and the Moon, [and] in square to the Sun and Mars, ruler of the MC.

And the truth of the matter was that at that time and always thereafter his mind was only turned towards a religious life, without any further ambition for power over subordinates, to which he was

---

[1] Mercury was in 3 Cap 11, not in 7 Cap.

[2] Neither Mercury in 7 Capricorn nor Venus in 2 Aquarius is opposite the radical Jupiter in 18 Virgo. Either Morin made a mistake here or some words of his text were omitted when the book was set in type.

[3] Spica was in 18 Libra 27, but Jupiter was in conjunction with it, not Mars.

[4] First, the Moon applies to a planet, not a planet to the Moon; and second, it is Jupiter that is trine the Moon, not Mars. Morin evidently saw the Jupiter symbol and inadvertently thought it was the Mars symbol.

averse, preferring rather to be a subject, rather than to be in charge; and he had this [trait] from Saturn and Mars in his nativity, of which the latter was in exile[1] in the 10th, ruling the Moon in the 12th., and the former was retrograde in the 6th, the ruler of Mercury, which ruled the 9th,[2] applying by trine to Jupiter, [and Saturn was] in opposition to the Moon, although the Sun was ruler of the 9th, and it was in the 1st, and Jupiter in the 9th and fortified by a trine to Mercury its ruler, was the ruler of the Sun and the ASC. [All these] correctly prophesied that he would someday hold a great dignity in the church, and that he would hold it reluctantly, in fact that of General Prefect of the Congregation of Oratory of Jesus, to which he had dedicated himself, which [rank] he many times tried in vain to give up; and, having been offered [the post of] Bishop or Archbishop by the king and by Cardinal Richelieu, he always strenuously refused it.

The fourth will be the 29th revolution of that same Rev. Father, in which he joined and devoted himself to the Congregation of Oratory of Jesus, so that he could serve God more faithfully and fruitfully; and the figure was like this:

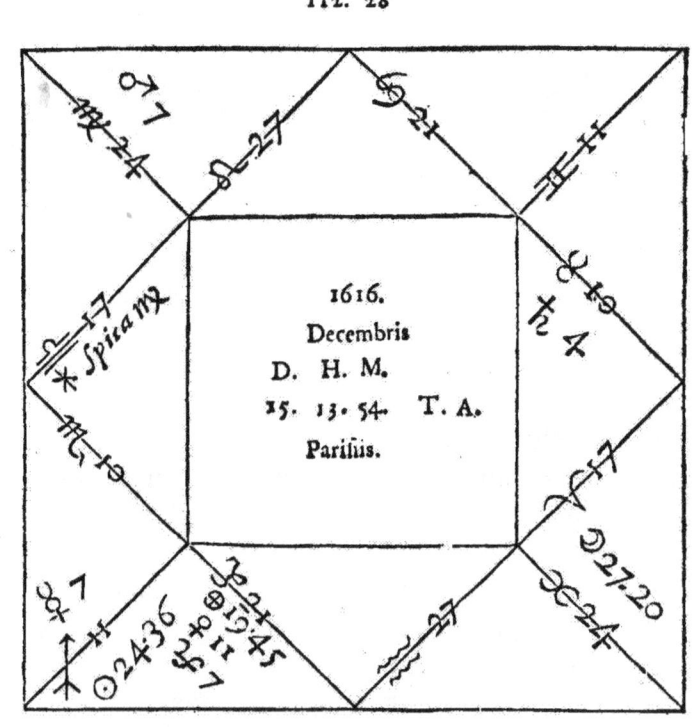

Charles de Condren's 29th Revolution
Paris
16 Dec 1616 1:54 AM

In which the Sun and the Moon rule the 10th, and the Moon is in the 3rd of the radix and the Sun in the 3rd of the revolution, mutually square. The Sun, moreover, was in the 1st of the radix, the significator of the native and of his inclinations, and then also of religion because it was the ruler of the 9th of the radix. Then in the 3rd of the revolution, which is [the house] of religion by reason of its oppo-

---

[1] That is, in its detriment.

[2] Mercury was co-ruler of the 9th.

62

sition to the 9th, four planets are found, viz. Mercury, ruler of the 9th of the radix, which has come to the ASC of the radix [and] is conjunct the cusp of the 3rd of the revolution; the Sun, of which we have spoken; Jupiter, ruler of the ASC of the radix, which was in the 9th of the radix; and Venus, ruler of the MC of the radix and of the ASC of the revolution, with which is found Spica; and Jupiter and Venus are on the radical place of Mercury, ruler of the 9th of the radix and the revolution, with the Part of Fortune in the [same] house and trine Saturn, and also trine Mars, which is found in the radical place of Jupiter, and its partile trine in the revolution.

Here again, therefore, the significators of inclinations, of profession, and of religion are powerfully combined. But the famous fixed star Spica, the one most beneficent for the moral nature, in the ASC, and Venus, ruler of the ASC, with Jupiter and the Sun in the 3rd, influenced an extrordinary piety and cultivation of religion in that year, and they inclined tha native to a religious life that would greatly profess piety, in which the abovesaid Congregation by unanimous consent surpasses the rest, which the Blessed Father himself chose; and Venus trine Saturn with mutual reception by domicile and conjunct Jupiter supported piety and humility.

Fifth will be the forty-first revolution of the Blessed Father, in which, after the death of the Most Eminent Cardinal Bérulle,[1] General of the Congregation of Oratory of Jesus, while the Father himself was away in Lorraine, he was elected to be the successor of the Cardinal as General [of the order], notwithstanding the artifices by which an attempt was made to divert that election from him. And the figure was like this:

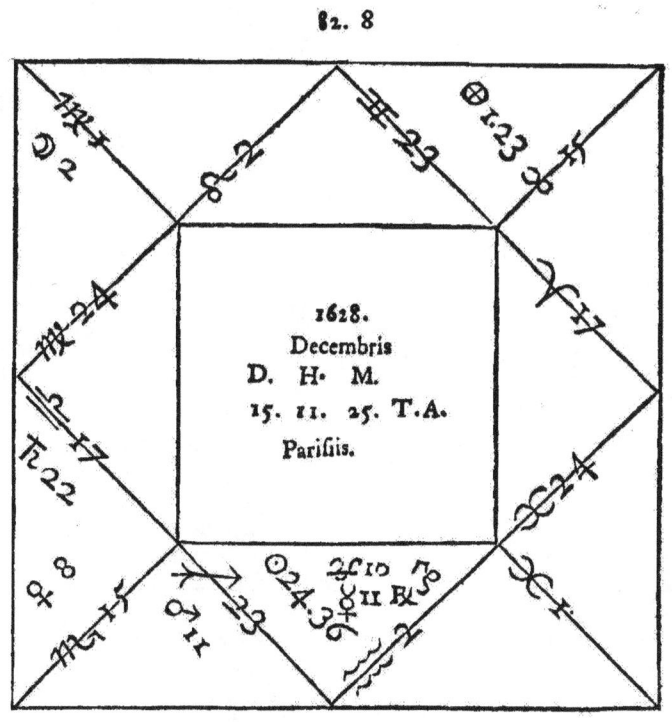

Charles de Condren's 41st Revolution
Paris
15 Dec 1628 11:25 PM

---
[1] Cardinal Pierre de Bérulle (1575-1629), who had founded the Congregation of Oratory of Jesus in 1611.

In which the ASC is partile square the Sun and also square the radical place of Jupiter, which was in the 9th; and Jupiter, ruler of the Sun and the radix ASC, as well as Mercury, ruler of the 9th of the radix, are conjoined in the 4th, almost partilely on the radical place of Mercury; and Mercury is ruler of the ASC and of the 9th and 10th of the revolution; and their ruler, Saturn, is in his own exaltation with Spica in trine to the MC, where it is allotted the triplicity [rulership].[1] Moreover, the Sun, ruler of the 9th of the radix, is on the cusp of the 4th [of the revolution], applying to the Moon,[2] ruler of the 10th, [and] in sextile to Saturn; and the Moon herself is applying by trine to Jupiter and to Mercury, which rules the Moon. Therefore, since the Sun, Jupiter, and Mercury are in the 4th, which, by reason of its opposition to the 10th, signifies dignities, and the Part of Fortune is in the 9th, a notable dignity was presaged especially by these, but also by the others already mentioned; and this would be an ecclesiastic one, because the Sun and Mercury were rulers of the 9th and Jupiter was in the 9th of the radix. Add to these the fact that Venus, ruler of the MC of the radix and the 9th of the revolution, has returned in this year to its own radical place in sextile to the Moon, then to Jupiter and Venus; therefore, in this conformable revolution, even though absent and reluctant, he was elected Superior General of his own order.

The sixth will be the 53rd revolution of that same Blessed Father, in which from a continued fever he suffered the extreme fate; and the figure was like this:

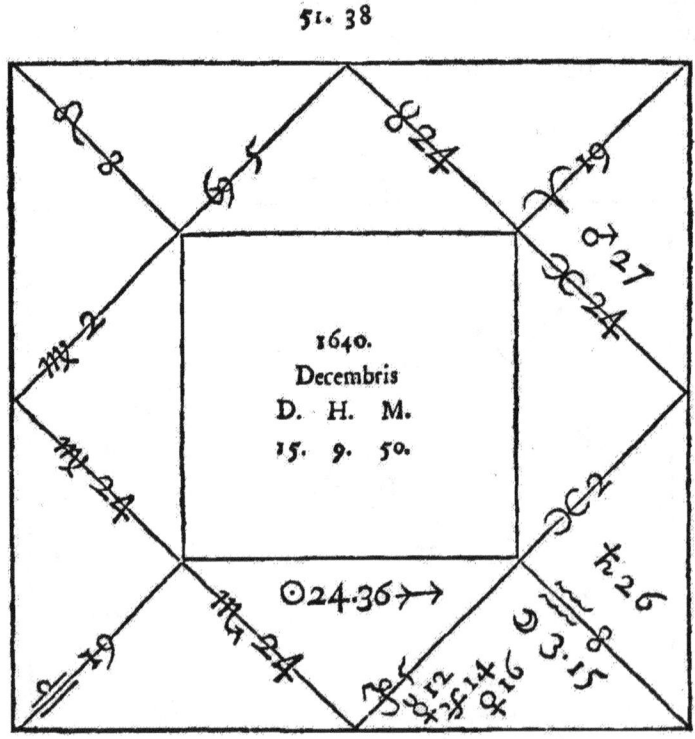

Charles de Condren's 53rd Revolution
Paris
15 Dec 1640 9:50 PM

---

[1] Saturn is the day ruler of the air triplicity, which includes the MC sign Gemini.

[2] This is wrong! The Sun cannot apply to the Moon. In this chart, The Moon in 2 Virgo is *separating* from a trine to the Sun in 25 Sagittarius.

In which Jupiter, ruler of the ASC of the radix and the Sun in the [radical] 1st house, is the ruler of the 8th of the revolution, and its ruler Saturn is in the 6th, which it occupied in the radix, opposed to the Moon in the 12th, and Saturn is in its own [domicile] and square the radical Moon; moreover, Mercury, ruler of the ASC of the revolution, applies to Jupiter, ruler of the 8th in its fall; but the Sun, ruler of the 8th in the radix [and] in the 1st, is in the revolution the ruler of the 12th in the 4th, afflicted by the square of Mars, ruler of the 12th of the radix and the 8th of the revolution,[1] in which it is situated. But the Moon, ruler of the 8th in the 10th of the radix, is found in its own radical antiscion in the revolution, opposite the cusp of the 12th, under the rulership of Saturn, when in the radix it was under the rulership of Mars. Therefore, all things in this revolution united in [indicating] an illness with danger to his life. Consequently, since the Sun in the 1st of the radix was the apheta, and in this year it was directed to the square of the Moon, ruler of the 8th in its fall in the 12th, and Saturn in the revolution was in the place of the direction and in the 6th house, on the 30th of December 1640 he fell into a fever, and on the 6th of January 1641 he fell asleep in the Lord, a man truly holy, who thereafter became my pious intercessor with God in Heaven, Amen.

But let these things [that we have shown] so far suffice to demonstrate astrologically from their effects that the revolutions of the Sun always act in conformity with the significations of the radical figure, not indeed [producing] anything of note contrary to or surpassing [it]. And this [is true] not only in natural, mortal, and secular matters, but also in spiritual and ecclesiastical ones, for which, as was demonstrated above, the *caelum* was aptly and effectively disposed, in the radix as well as in the revolution.

You will object: If the revolution can [do] nothing contrary to or surpassing the decrees of the nativity, then this brings in [the concept of] fatal necessity, and there will be no truth in Aphorism 5 of the *Centiloquy*: *One who is aware [of them] can avert many effects of the stars*, namely the evil effects signified by the nativity, from which St. Thomas deduced that *A wise man will rule his stars*. But if he can avert these, why could he not attain the good things denied by the nativity with a fortunate revolution favoring [them]? Therefore, a revolution can [act] to surpass or contradict the nativity.

I reply: A revolution cannot by itself accomplish anything contrary to or surpassing the radical influx for the reasons often mentioned, and because its influx is weaker than the radical influx, and therefore it yields to it; but it can [do so], through an accident, if a strong determination of will (which is superior to natural fate) is added to the influx of the revolution, at least in those things which are within its power, but the effect will not occur without great opposition, and it will not be complete, but [will remain] imperfect, or unworthy, or unfortunate because of the resisting radical influx. As, for example, if the nativity denies marriage to the native, and a revolution promises [it], the native will have in mind to marry a whore or a girl of low degree, much inferior to himself [in rank], but [certainly] not equal or superior to himself, either in wealth or family status. Therefore, in these and similar matters, the radical figure introduces a fatal necessity, not of course inevitably immutable,[2] as is Divine Providence, but capable of being changed by human will, [but] with difficulty and imperfection, as has been said. And so, Aphorism 5 of the *Centiloquy* can be true and that which is deduced from it in objection. See Chapter 24 of Book 22, where we have discussed God's Providence, fate, fortune, and misfortune, and this doctrine is elucidated at greater length.

---

[1] Mars is co-ruler of the 8th.

[2] As a devout Catholic, Morin was obliged to accept the doctrine that man can change his fate if he chooses to do so, for otherwise a man would be born either saved or damned without any possiblity of redemption. But as an astrologer, he was evidently not so sure.

Chapter VIII.

Whether the Annual Status of the Native can be Sufficiently Known from the Revolution of the Sun Alone if the Revolutions of the Other Planets are Omitted.

It is the custom of astrologers to judge the annual state of the native solely from a revolution of the Sun, having omitted the revolutions of the other planets. In fact no small difficulty ensues for us to elucidate this matter. Namely, whether the revolution of another planet is necessary to understand the native's state more perfectly.

Many think that the Sun is the source of all celestial virtues, from which the virtues deriving from all the rest [of the planets] derive their powers to act. But the Moon is the dispenser of these virtues, not only of those of the Sun, but also those of the other stars. With which opinion Cardan agrees in his *Book of Revolutions*, saying:

> "That he who has both luminaries impedited will never obtain anything outstanding, for he will have everything vitiated as it were, even with the [other] planets disposed in the best manner." And, in his *Book of the Mutations of the Air*, "It is not possible for any effect to be produced in this world either in the mutations of times or in the course of life of men and in their fortune, unless the Sun and the Moon in that same hour and minute of the hour are in some principal place signifying that effect or unless they are connected to the significator of that same thing by a perfect opposition or square."

Whence it will not be difficult to persuade the aforesaid [astrologers] that the Sun's revolution for its own annual effects and those of the other planets.

But in fact the abovesaid opinion about the virtue of the Sun and the Moon is contrary to reason and experience. For the individual planets differ among themselves in their kind and therefore in their formal virtue [as we explained] in Book 9, section 3, Chapter 2, and they are particular sources of influential virtues diverse in their kind, the Sun to be sure of the solar kind, the Moon of the lunar kind, Saturn of the saturnian kind, etc., and they are, therefore, the 7 principal celestial governors of this lower world. Consequently, the virtue of Saturn is not produced by the Sun, [whic is] also contrary to the nature of the Sun; and the Sun will not excite the force of Saturn by its own virtue, since the planets do not act influentially in a mutual manner among themselves, but each planet acts with its own virtue on these lower-world things and in its own individual manner. Moreover, in their mutual concourse to effect something through their determination, they help or impede each other in turn, as is said elsewhere; whence, it cannot anymore be said that the sun excites the force of Jupiter than that Jupiter excites the force of the Sun; but, so much greater is the force of the Sun's virtue than that of the others, that as often as the Sun concurs with another planet in rulership or in an aspect or a conjunction, they produce greater effects than if that planet was concurring with another planet; whence the opinion has arisen that the Sun is the source of all celestial virtues, and it excites the forces of the other planets to act. And the same thing can be said about the Moon, which, because it is the dispensor of the virtues of the planets, they are spontaneous. It is therefore seen that the revolution of the Sun alone does not suffice for understanding fully the native's annual state. And that is confirmed [by what was said] in Chapter 3, where we have also declared from the mind of Cardan that the revolutions of the other planets are also efficacious and useful.

Moreover, there is a notable difference between the revolutions of the Sun, at least those of Saturn, Jupiter, Mars, Venus, and Mercury, for these are only satellites of the Sun and are bound to it and to its motion., and the Sun itself carries them with it wherever it goes, being always constituted in their midst, the center of their orbits as it were. By which system Nature certainly teaches that the Sun is like the King of those planets, and a cause superior to them, indeed a universal one; but they are subordinated to the Sun as less universal causes, serving the Sun with their proper contributions by means of their own universal effects; consequently, their forces and status belongs in a way to the status of the Sun, like the status of the satellites of Jupiter and Saturn. For this reason, the revolution of the Sun was also the more universal; and since in this, not only the status of the Sun itself is seen, but also the status of its satellites, both their inherent status and their status with respect to the Sun, the force and signification of that status extends itself [to cover] all kinds of accidents [that befall] the native, viz. the accidents of life, riches, brothers, parents, etc., that can occur in the year of that revolution. But the revolutions of Saturn, Jupiter, Mars, Venus, and Mercury have signification only to those accidents that by their own proper or particular determination, by bodily position or by rulership they signified in the figure of the nativity. And take note of this!

But this can be confirmed in this way, because if in a revolution of the Sun anyone of its satellites shall have returned to its own radical place, that one is by the common consensus of astrologers thought to be in that year most efficacious in moving forward those things that it presaged in the nativity, as is quite evident in the revolutions of Saturn, which, because they are more rare and because it is the highest of all the planets, they also produce more notable effects, in accordance with the radical determination of Saturn itself, and hence that very revolution of the Sun is strengthened, namely because it is rendered more conformable to the genethliacal constitution; and likewise many revolutions of the planets act in the same way. From which it follows, that even though a revolution of the Sun is universal with regard to all the native's accidents, as was explained above, nevertheless, when his satellites return to their own radical places, it is useful to erect the figure of their revolution if it can be done, and to contemplate that figure, so that a more certain judgment can be made from it about those things that they inherently signify by their own particular determination.

But that [also] pertains to the Moon, since it, just as the Sun, is a primary planet in no way bound to the Sun itself, but just as the Sun itself is arranged [to revolve] around the earth,[1] and of the greatest strength after the Sun [in acting] upon these inferior things, to which it is the nearest of all the planets. So certainly, just as the annual revolutions of the Sun have a noticeable effect on the annual accidents of every sort that must be foreseen for the native, so it is entirely compatible with reason that the monthly revolutions of the Moon [in which it returns] to its radical place exert no mean influence on the monthly accidents of the native. For the Sun and the Moon, according to Genesis, Chapter 1, are made in days, and months, and years[2]; and the

---

[1] Morin had adopted Tycho Brahe's model of the solar system, in which the Sun revolved about the earth, but all the other planets (Mercury, Venus, Mars, etc.) revolved about the Sun. This model was satisfactory for computing the position of the Sun and the planets and had the virtue of avoiding conflict with the Catholic Church, which still maintained that the earth was the center of the universe.

[2] Not quite an accurate quotation. In the Latin Bible, Genesis i. 14 says *Fiant luminaria in firmamento caeli, et dividant diem ac noctem, et sint in signa, et tempera, et dies, et annos, ut luceant in firmamento caeli, et illuminent terram.* 'Let there be luminaries in the firmament of heaven, and let them divide the day and the night, and let them be for signs, and times, and days, and years, so that they may shine in the firmament of heaven, and light up the earth'. Months are not mentioned.

Sun (as is plain in nature) is the moderator of the years, and the Moon of the months; and so it seems to me that the construction of a revolutionary figure is necessary. For this is much more natural than Cardan's method, who, in his *Book of Revolutions*, chapter 2, wants to have a figure of the revolution of the Moon erected every month [when] it returns to the place that it occupied at the time of the revolution of the Sun. For if the revolutions of the planets should be noted and their figures] erected, these should also be erected [for their return] to their own radical places, as is done in the case of the Sun itself; for the Sun is first in the rank of the planets because it is the rule of the rest of them in the manner of acting through their influences; and the voice itself of the revolution clearly indicates the return of a planet to some fixed place, which is its radical place, but not some changeable place such as the planet's place at [the time of] the revolution of the Sun.[1] And this is confirmed by the fact that the place of the radical planet is determined to the native radically for that very planet and no other; and during the whole life of the native, the strength of that planet in that place will be principally active, and through that place in the places of it aspects. So that, therefore, in a revolution of the Sun, this does not determine any other place for the native than the radical place; and so, neither the Moon nor the other planets in their own revolutions should determine any place for the native other than the radical place, which they also determine *de novo* by their own revolutions, and the force of the radical determination impressed upon the native at birth, they excite *de novo* to produce they things that they signified radically, according to their own state, both celestial and terrestrial, in the revolution.

Since, therefore, the Sun rules the years, as a cause that is more superior and more universal, and the Moon rules the months, as a an inferior and lesser universal cause, nor is that the function of the other planets, as is established in nature; therefore, it is necessary that that rule be followed for their revolutions, viz. the annual revolutions of the Sun and the monthly revolutions of the Moon.

Furthermore, the annual revolution of the Sun is two-fold. First, is the revolution or return of the Sun to the beginning of Aries, because that was its first radical place with respect to the whole world. And if this is only seen in the caelum, it is [still] the universal cause of the whole sublunary world. But if it is referred to any [particular] place on earth by a figure erected [for that location], it is [thereby] made a cause for that particular place, but one that is nevertheless still universal with respect to the living creatures in that very place, either in that city or in that region, to which individuals that universal constitution pertains equally per se. But second is the revolution of the Sun to that point of the zodiac that it occupied at the beginning of the nativity or the origin of any particular thing, such as a man. and this is only a particular cause with respect to that thing, for those things that happen to him annually, but in no way pertaining to the rest of the individuals that are in that same place or in that same city. See Book 23, chapter 3.

Similarly, the monthly revolution of the Moon is two-fold. First is the true conjunction of the Sun and the Moon, and it is called "the synodic revolution," which is universal for the whole terrestrial globe, or for any region, or any particular city, as was said above about the Sun. but second is the revolution or return of the Moon to that point of the zodiac that it occupied at the time of origin, or of the birth of any particular thing, such as a man; and it is called "the periodic revolution," which is only a particular cause with respect to that man, in no way pertaining to the rest of the individuals of that place

---

1 Cardan, *De Revolutione Annorum, Mensium, et Dierum, ad dies Criticos, et ad electiones Liber,* Chapter 1 (not 2), *Post haec singulo mense tempus praecise notabis, quo Luna ad eundem punctum pervenit, in quo in revolutione anni fuit, et hora illa figuram eriges...* 'After this, you will take note of the precise time in each month when the Moon comes to the same point where it was in the revolution of the year, and you will erect a figure for that hour...'

or city. And in fact it is in conformity with reason that because the Sun and the Moon are prime universal causes, the former namely for the year and the latter for the month, the second [type of cause] moreover of the Sun and for a particular man for the year, therefore the second [type of cause] of the Moon is also for a particular man for a month. And two-fold is that revolution, or two-fold that month, namely synodic and periodic, which are especially conspicuous in nature—indeed, the synodic and universal one in the tides of the sea, and the periodic and particular one in acute illnesses.

And it should not be objected that the Moon has its own particular signification in a nativity, to which it is determined, and that therefore its revolution cannot be made for anything signified in the nativity; for the same thing could also be objected for the Sun, and that is false as is established by experience. For the revolution of the Sun shows the status of the year, either its good fortune or its bad fortune, for whatever was signified by the natal figure, even more so for those things that it signified from its own determination in the radical figure; consequently, the same thing should be judged to apply to the Moon. Moreover, that function only applies to the Sun and the Moon as primary planets, and not to the others, which are only secondary and less universal. But that the revolution of the Moon to its own radical place is very efficacious will be plain from the examples that will be put below; from which the error of Cardan, who judged the place of the Moon in the revolution of the Sun to be of greater force for the whole year than its radical place. And it will also be noted that th revolution of the Moon do not act above or contrary to the figure of the nativity, but rather in conformity with it, as was proved in the case of the Sun in the seventh chapter.

Chapter IX.

How the Figure of the Revolution of the Moon should be Erected.

First of all, an accurate radical place of the Moon is required, which the astronomical tables do not yet supply to us, and will not supply until they have been constructed according to the principles of astronomy that we have restored; and it is shameful that in this old age of the world there is still found among the more celebrated astronomers a difference of around one degree in the motion of the Moon, as is plain from the *Ephemerides* of Argol; which difference causes a great error in the erection of a figure of the revolution of the Moon, namely because one degree is nearly the Moon's motion in two hours, in which time there is a great change in the figure of the *caelum*. Still, because it is probable that all that [much] difference but only a part of it, either in excess or deficit, is in the true place of the Moon, [taking into consideration] that error, it will always be useful to erect that figure of the revolution of the Moon; and therefore it will be even more useful the smaller the error in the lunar tables.[1]

---

[1] Morin evidently believed that the positions of the Moon given by his tables, which were derived from those of Kepler, were close to the truth. Unfortunately, while they were somewhat closer than those of Argol, they were still not very close. They had an error that could reach a maximum of 30 minutes of arc or a little more. And, unlike the case of the Sun, the error in the natal position was independent of the error in the revolutionary position. Consequently, in a worst case, the combined error could be as great as one degree. And, as Morin says, that could cause an error of two hours in the time of the lunar revolution. It was the middle of the 18th century before lunar tables and published ephemerides began to appear that were capable of producing lunar positions with an error of no more than 1 minute of arc in the longitudes.

Secondly, for the year, month, and day on which the lunar revolution to be erected falls, it should be sought from the ephemerides or tables from which the radical place of the Moon was taken at what hour and moment the Moon will return to its own radical place in the ecliptic, without any consideration of its radical latitude, to which it does not return, but taking note of its latitude at the moment of the revolution for the purpose of directing the Moon itself monthly. And thus the mean time of the revolution of the Moon to its own radical will be had, which must be doubly corrected, and then the figure must be erected, as it is done in Chapter 5 by the first method for erecting a revolution of the Sun. For, just as the figure for the revolution of the Sun must be erected at the place where the native is at the beginning of the revolution, so it must be judged proper for revolutions of the Moon. For the same reason is proper to both, even though the native, during the entire time of the revolution of the Sun, may be traveling from the East to the West. For, from the individual revolutions of the Sun as well as those of the Moon, he receives a new impression that lasts during the entire revolution. And, just as the revolution of the Sun actuates potential causes of the radix, so the revolution of the Moon actuates potential causes of the radix and the revolution of the Sun. And similarly, just as the revolution of the Sun accomodates or refers itself to the figure of the radix in whatever place on Earth the native is situated [at the moment], so the revolution of the Moon accomodates itself to the figures of the radix and the revolution of the Sun in whatever place on Earth the native may be at the moment of the revolution of the Moon.

Chapter X.

In Which the Force of the Revolutions of the Moon is Shown Through Their Effects in Several Genitures

In order that the truth of the doctrine that we have set forth here about the periodic revolutions of the Moon may be made plain, it also seems to be necessary to demonstrate and prove it with some examples, leaving any one [who wishes to do so] free to examine it with more; since indeed I have experienced scarcely any notable effect to happen in the life of a man that was not closely preceded by a concurring revolution of the Moon.

First, therefore, will be the revolution of the Moon to its own radical place in the nativity of Gustavus Adolphus, King of Sweden, which closely preceded and signified his death [in battle], the figure of which on the following page is worthy of note.

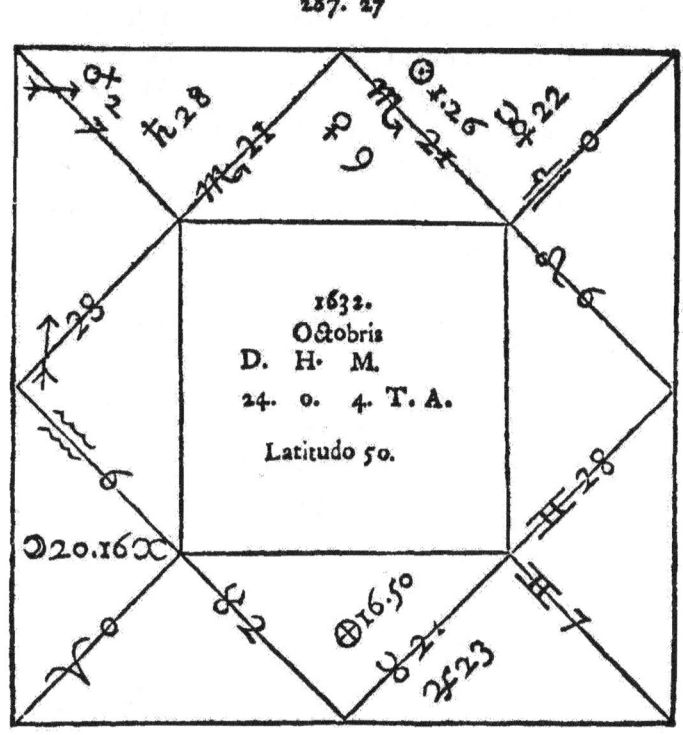

Gustavus Adolphus Lunar Revolution
Nürnberg 50 N
24 Oct 1632 0:04 PM[1]

In this revolution, begun at Nürnberg, the Moon rules the 7th, which is [the house] of wars and battles, and it is opposite the 8th. Moreover, Jupiter, ruler of both the Moon and the ASC of both the radix and the revolution, is in its own radical square, opposed to Saturn, ruler of the 1st, which is found in square to the radical Jupiter and the radical place of Mars, which places were already afflicted in the radix and the revolution by their own square and opposition, and it is conjoined to Mars itself, which is with the Heart of Scorpio[2] in the ASC of the radix. Moreover, the Sun, ruler of the 8th both of the radix and this revolution, is in the domicile of that same Mars in the MC with Venus, ruler of Jupiter and Mercury, but in her exile; moreover, the Sun was in the first of the radix and its annual revolution, and here its radical place is in the ASC; therefore, here it is the significator of the person himself, his moral nature, actions, and death.

All these things clearly signified a battle, because of the radical place of the Sun in the ASC and the Sun itself in the MC [of the revolution], and its ruler, Mars, with the radical ASC, but an unlucky and lethal one, because Jupiter, ruler of the Moon and the ASC, a afflicted by the opposition of Saturn in the

---

[1] Here we have an example of the errors that were possible in calculating lunar returns from the *Rudolphine Tables*. In the first place, the natal longitude of the Moon was 20 Psc 26 not 20 Psc 16, as Morin calculated. Second, the true time of the lunar return on 24 Oct 1632 was about 11:30 AM LAT at Nürnberg, not 0:04 PM, a difference of 34 minutes—partly due to the error in the natal longitude and partly to the error in the calculated longitude of the return. The true RAMC of the lunar return was about 201°31′ rather than about 210°00′ (the figure 287°27′ above the chart is completely wrong—either a miscopying of Morin's or a typesetters blunder; and the MC should read 2 Scorpio, not 21 Scorpio). As good luck would have it, the error in the time does not alter the chart sufficiently to have affected Morin's judgment in this instance.

[2] This is the star Antares or α Scorpii; its longitude was 4 Sag 38.

radix and in this revolution; and because Saturn, the radical anaereta was already in a very bad place, apply to Mars in the radical ASC with the Heart of Scorpio; moreover, the Sun, ruler of the 8th in the MC under the rulership of Mars, and the Moon, ruler of the 7th, which is [the house] of battles, in the 2nd. And it is worthy of note that here the Sun comes partilely to the place of the Moon in the annual revolution, in which the Moon was ruler of the 8th house; Jupiter comes to the opposition of Saturn, and Saturn to the square of Mars in that same revolution. He was killed [in battle] on the 16th of November 1632 at about the ninth hour of the morning.

Second will be the revolution of the Moon in which Cardinal Richelieu died on the 4th of December 1642; and the figure was like this:

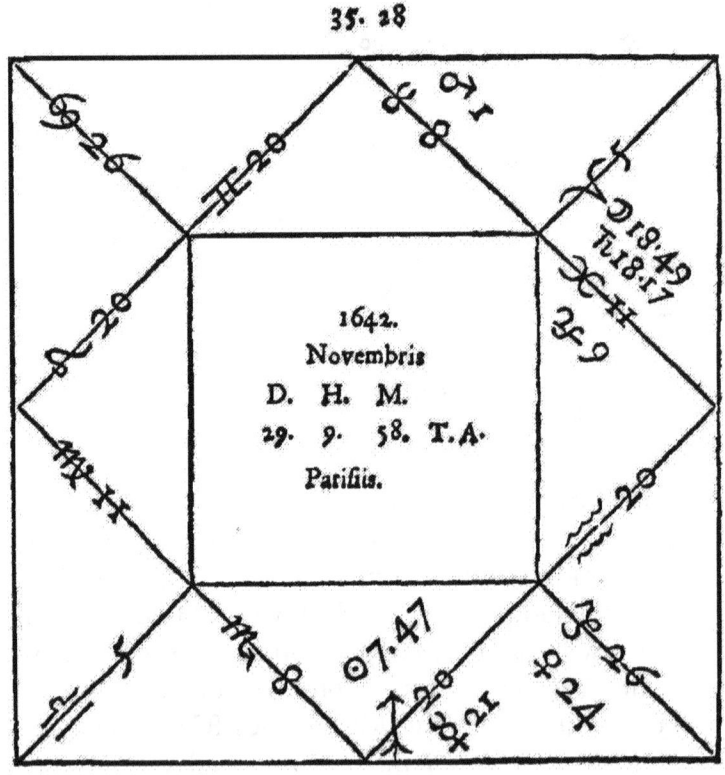

Cardinal Richelieu Lunar Revolution
Paris
29 Nov 1642 9:58 PM[1]

---

[1] Here we have an even larger error than that in the preceding lunar revolution. The true natal longitude of Richelieu's Moon was 19 Psc 49, which is quite close to Morin's figure 19 Psc 48; but his lunar revolution chart puts the Moon at 18 Psc 49, while the true longitude at the time given was 19 Psc 09. There are in fact two errors here: (1) Morin inadvertently calculated the chart of the revolution for a lunar longitude of 18 Psc 49 rather than 19 Psc 48, and he also miscalculated the time by about 10 minutes; and (2) the actual return of the Moon to the true natal longitude occurred at 11:07 PM LAT rather than the 9:58 PM that he calculated. His error was thus 1:09, which rotates the lunar revolution chart 17 degrees, so that the MC was actually about 25 Taurus (rather than 8 Taurus), and the ASC was about 3 Virgo (instead of 20 Leo). Mercury (whose true longitude was about 27 Sagittarius rather than 21 Sagittarius) was therefore in the 4th house rather than in the 5th, and Jupiter was in the 7th rather than close to the cusp of the 8th; the other planetary house positions remain about the same; but the signs on the cusps of the 1st, 5th, 6th, 7th, 11th, and 12th houses are all changed, so that the cuspal rulers of these houses are also changed.

In which the Moon was in the 5th of the radix and as the ruler of the ASC of the annual revolution of the Sun again in the 5th, and [the Moon], ruler of the 12th is now in the 8th partilely conjunct Saturn, which was in its fall in the 6th of the radix and was the ruler of the 8th of the annual revolution; moreover, in this revolution, it is again the ruler of the 5th, and Venus is in that house, ruler of Mars and the MC. Jupiter, moreover, both in the radix and in this revolution, is ruler of the 5th, in the 8th, and applying to Saturn and the place of the Moon. In addition, the Sun, ruler of the ASC and the 12th of this figure, who was the ruler of the 12th in the 1st of the annual revolution, is found in his own square, afflicted by a violent fixed star,[1] square Jupiter, ruler of the 8th, and then Saturn and the Moon in the 8th. And finally, Mercury, ruler of the 8th of the radix and the 1st of this revolution, is found in the 5th in exile and afflicted by a square from those [planets]; moreover, it was the ruler of the ASC in the 12th of the annual revolution; and Jupiter, the radical anaereta has now come to its own radical square on the cusp of the 5th of the radix and the 8th of this figure.

Therefore, so great and so manifold a combination of significators occurs, viz. of the 1st, the 12th, the 5th, and the 8th, that the lethal illness already signified by the annual revolution happened during this monthly one, from the former of which he languished for a long time without being cured, which arose (as it were) from the things signified by the 5th, to which rumor Venus, ruler of the ASC, and Mercury, ruler of the 8th of the radix, are [both] found here in the 5th, with Mercury badly afflicted, attest in no small measure; and his illness was of this sort—a sudden fever that struck on the very day of the revolution of the Moon because of its partile conjunction with Saturn in the domicile of Jupiter and the exaltation of Venus.

The third will be the revolution of the Moon, in which the most noble Mr. Tronson was exiled from the royal court with the loss of his dignities through the evil artifices of Cardinal Richelieu, who was pretending to be his friend; and the figure was like that shown on the next page.

In which Venus, ruler of the ASC, and the Moon, ruler of the MC of the radix and of this revolution are afflicted by the conjunction of Mars; and Venus is besieged by malefics in the 11th, of which Mars rules the 7th and Saturn is in the 12th, whose ruler, Mercury, was in the 10th but opposite the radical Mars, [and] partilely square the Part of Fortune. The Cardinal wanted him to be imprisoned for crimes with which he was falsely charged, but the king was unwilling; and Jupiter in the radical ASC and in the 1st of this revolution with the Part of Fortune freed Mr. Tronson from the more serious evil and saved his life when he was very sick; moreover, the bad luck happened on the 2nd of august 1626.

The fourth will be the revolution of the Moon preceding the death of that same very noble Mr. Tronson; its figure is on the next page.

In which the Moon is in the 12th house afflicted by a square to Mars in exile and ruler of the 8th; also, the Sun is in the 4th and is also square the Moon, ruler of the 12th. Moreover, Mercury, ruler of the ASC, in which is found the radical place of that same Mercury, is in exile in the 4th afflicted by a square to Saturn and to Jupiter, ruler of the 8th, who is found in the 7th, with Saturn conjunct the 8th cusp; these things threatened death from illness; and therefore he died on the 8th of December 1642 at around 9 in the morning.

The fifth will be the revolution of the Moon preceding the death of the unconquerable Constable

---

[1] Antares or α Scorpii, which was at 4 Sag 47.

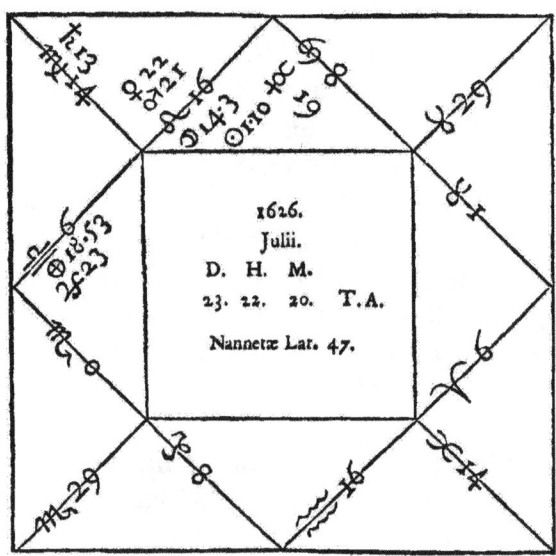

Mr. Louis Tronson Lunar Revolution
Nantes
24 Jul 1626 10:20 AM[1]

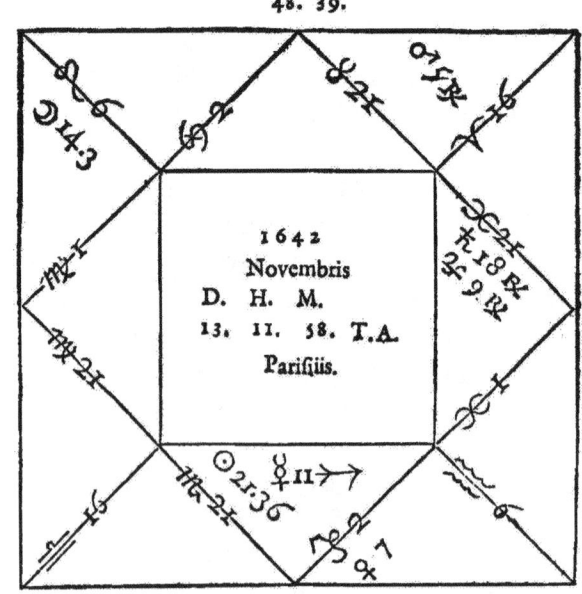

Mr. Louis Tronson Lunar Revolution[2]
Paris
13 Nov 1642 11:58 PM

---

[1] Here Morin was more fortunate. Recalculation shows that the true time of the lunar return was about 10:12 AM LAT or only 8 minutes earlier than the time that Morin deduced. This small difference would not affect his analysis.

[2] Here, Morin has made a large error of 2:03. The Moon was at about 15 Leo 04 at the time shown above. But recalculation shows that the true time when the Moon returned to its natal place of 14 Leo 03 was at about 9:55 PM LAT, at which time the MC was about 19 Aries, the ASC 8 Leo, and the 8th house cusp 28 Aquarius. A good bit of his analysis of the chart is therefore invalid.

Lesdiguières, shown below:

Constable Lesdiguières Lunar Revolution
Grenoble
6 Sept 1626 10:02 AM[1]

In which there ascends the opposition of the radical Mercury, ruler of the 12th of the radix; and Mars, ruler of the ASC, is with Saturn, ruler of the 8th of the radix and of the annual revolution; and Saturn and Mars with the Sun are opposed to the Moon, which was ruler of the 1st of the radix and was therefore the principal significator of the [native's] life; and consequently, both luminaries are very badly placed here, since in particular Saturn, the Sun, and Mars are in square to the Mars of the annual revolution. Moreover, Jupiter, ruler of the Moon, is in the 12th with Venus, ruler of the cusp of the 8th and Mercury, ruler of the Sun and the 8th,[2] is in the place that the Moon occupied in the revolution of the Sun.. Therefore, all of these things inclined to illness and death; and consequently, on the 28th of September 1626 he died, a man most fortunate in war and in military dignities. Moreover, he began to be ill on the 11th of August; and a revoloution of the Moon that had preceded that, in which the Sun was in the 17th degree of Leo, which is square the radical places of both Mars and Saturn, which are conjoined in this revolution.

The sixth will be the revolution of the Moon in the year 1605 very closely preceding the day of that year on which very dangerous wounds were inflicted upon me, of which this was the terrifying figure:

---

[1] This time is close. Recalculation of the natal chart and the lunar revolution puts the true time of the revolution at about 10:13 AM LAT with MC 16 Leo, ASC 7 Scorpio, and the Moon in 17 Psc 22.

[2] Mercury is ruler of the 8th because its sign Gemini is intercepted in that house.

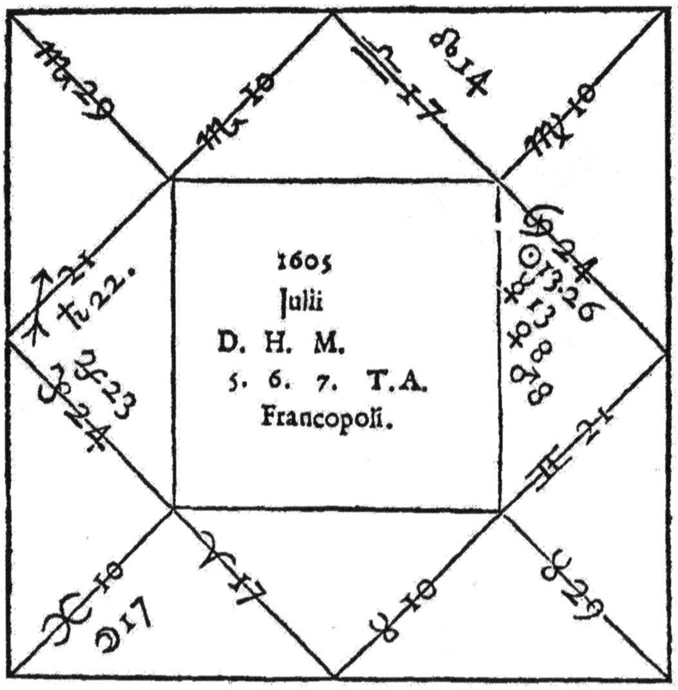

Morin Lunar Revolution
Villefranche
***5 Jul 1605 6:07 PM*[1]**

In which the sign of the 8th [house] of the radix ascends, and Saturn is in the ASC; moreover, Jupiter, ruler of the ASC, is opposed to the 8th cusp, with the Sun, Mercury, Venus, and Mars situated in the 7th house, which is [the house] of open enemies; and Jupiter itself is in its fall; and in fact the Moon is the ruler of Mars, Venus, Mercury, and the Sun, as well as being ruler of the 8th, along with the Sun,[2] and the Moon is square the ASC and Saturn, to which it was conjoined in the 12th in the radix. These [positions], moreover, portended wounds with a notable danger to my life, first from a secret enemy and then from an open one; and it was on account of a woman because the sign of the 1st [house] of the radix was in the 5th [of the revolution], and Venus, its ruler, was in partile conjunction with Mars in the 7th on the radical place of Mars; and indeed Venus was in the 5th and Mars in the 8th of the revolution of the Sun. But because Jupiter, ruler of the ASC, was not afflicted by the malefics, and further because the Moon, ruler of the 8th, was in sextile to Jupiter and in trine to Venus, some hope for life arose, even though the Moon was afflicted by a square to Saturn, and the Sun was conjunct Mars; and so, with God taking pity on me, my life was preserved, but almost miraculously. And that misfortune happened to me on 9 July 1605 at around 8:20 P.M.

The seventh will be the revolution of the Moon closely preceding the 30th of May 1612, on which day I fell into a very dangerous illness, as was mentioned in [my discussion of] the revolution of the Sun for that year; and the figure was like this:

---

[1] Recalculation shows that the true time would have been about 5:46 PM LAT with 17 Sagittarius rising.

[2] Because Leo is intercepted in the 8th house.

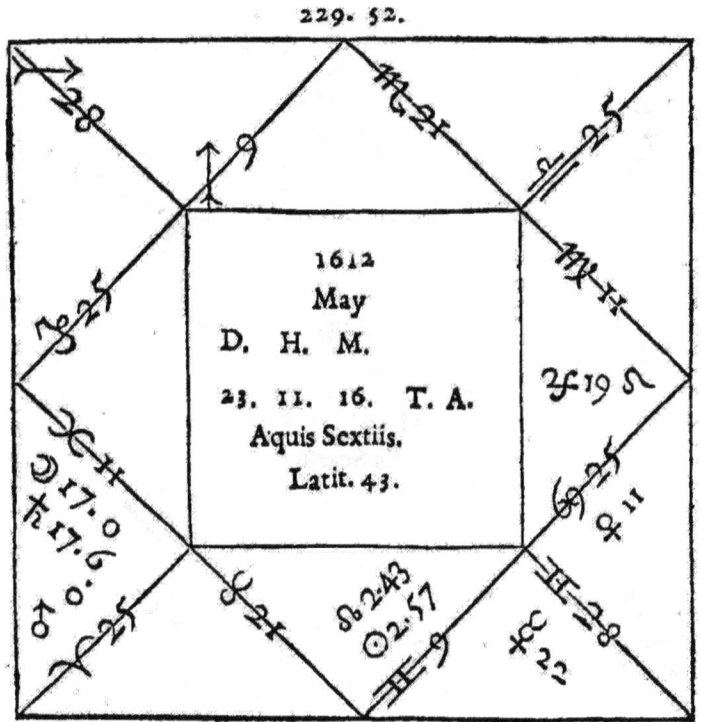

Morin Lunar Revolution
Aix-en-Provence 43 N
23 May 1612 11:16 PM[1]

In which the square of the radical ASC ascended, and Saturn, ruler of the 12th and the 1st, was partilely conjoined to the Moon; in the revolution of the Sun, she was square to him; and Saturn and the Moon, together with Mars, are opposed to the 8th and square Mercury, ruler of the 8th, which certainly portended and illness with danger to life. Moreover, Jupiter, ruler of Saturn and the Moon, has returned partilely to its own place in the revolution of the Sun, where it signified an illness from play and social drinking,[2] and it confirms that same thing in this figure, where it applies to Mercury, ruler of the 8th situated in the 5th, which is the house of pleasures, [and] in square to Saturn, ruler of the ASC and the 12th; with the Sun, ruler of Jupiter, situated partilely in opposition to the place that the Moon occupied in the revolution of the Sun, and that [place was] with a violent fixed star[3]; therefore, this revolution of the Moon agreed with the revolution of the Sun with regard to the abovesaid illness.

The eighth will be the revolution of the Moon closely preceding the 9th of May 1613, when I attained the degree of Doctor of Medicine; and the figure was like this:

---

[1] Recalculation shows that the true time would have been about 10:58 PM LAT with 21 Capricorn rising.

[2] Reading *compotatione* 'social drinking' rather than *computatione* 'computation'.

[3] Antares or α Scorpii, which was in 4 Sag 21.

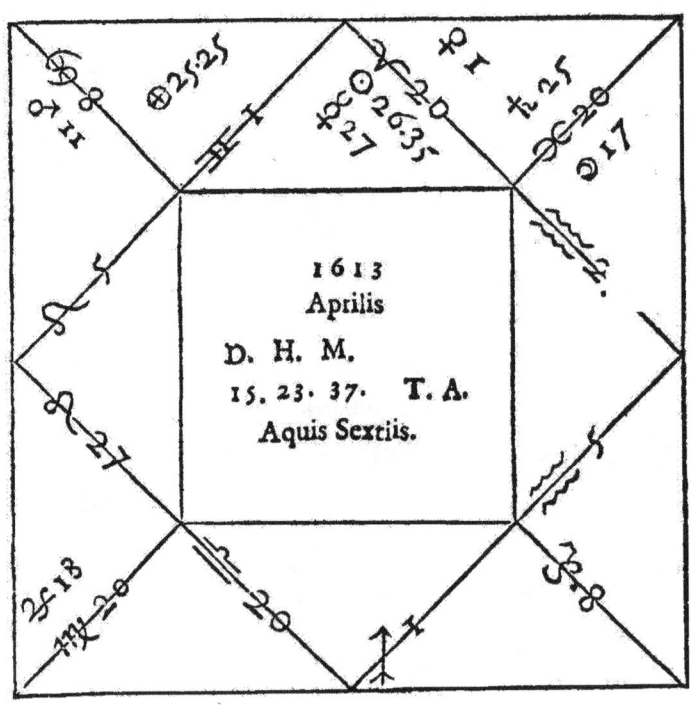

Morin Lunar Revolution
Aix-en-Provence
16 Apr 1613 11:37 AM[1]

In which the *caelum* is disposed as it was in the revolution of the Sun, and the Sun, ruler of the ASC, is exalted in the 10th, with Mercury, ruler of the Part of Fortune and of Jupiter, ruler of the Moon; moreover, the Sun and Mercury are found on the radical ASC and on the MC of the annual revolution; and this presaged a dignity very strongly, because in particular, Saturn and Mars, that were powerful in the MC of the radix, have returned to their radical places in this revolution; and Mars, ruler of the ASC of the radix and the MC of both revolutions, was in trine to the Moon, its own ruler, which is in the 9th, which has to do with the sciences, with Saturn, ruler of the MC of the radix, and it was applying to an opposition of Jupiter, its own ruler. Therefore, during this monthly revolution I received the degree of Doctor of Medicine, from the nature of Saturn, Mars, and Mercury, because of Mars ruler of the MC and the Sun, because of Saturn in the 9th conjunct the Moon, ruler of Mars; and because of Mercury, ruler of the Part of Fortune in the 10th, [it was] also with much honor. But Jupiter, ruler of the Moon, in his exile and opposed to the Moon and Saturn, and both Jupiter and Saturn square the Part of Fortune, signified that the doctorate would not be useful nor that profession stable, especially because the MC was in a mobile sign, and its ruler, Mars is also in a mobile sign in the 12th house.

The ninth will be the revolution of the Moon preceding the notable danger that befell me while I was swimming in the Rhine on the 7th of July 1615 at around 10:30 PM; and the figure was very worthy of note, as [is shown] below.

---

[1] Recalculation shows that the true time would have been about 11:15 PM LAT with 1 Leo rising.

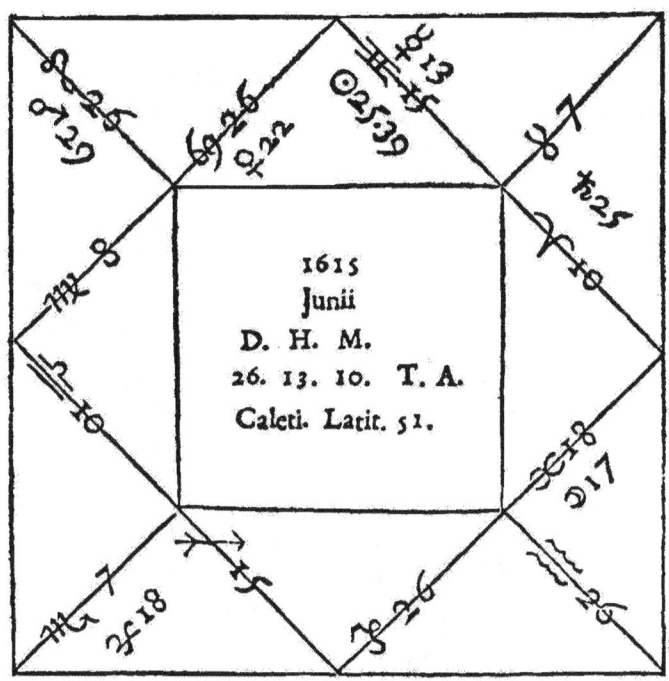

Morin Lunar Revolution
Rhine River [near Köln] 51 N
17 Jun 1615 11:10 AM[1]

Namely, in which the Moon is on the cusp of the 7th, opposed to the ASC; and the Sun and the MC and Mercury, their ruler [posited] in the MC, in square to the ASC and the Moon, with the Sun claiming the rights of the exaltation for itself in the 8th[2]; moreover, this portended a danger to life, since in fact the Moon in the 7th customarily occasions either a violent death or the danger of it; and so a missile was hurled at me from [a distance of] not more than three paces, [and] a sword was brandished, while I was amusing myself by swimming in the Rhine, as I mentioned in [my discussion of] the revolution of the Sun. And a great danger in the midst of pleasure was signified by Saturn, ruler of the 5th in the 8th, and Mars in a fire sign; further, by Mars itself, ruler of Saturn and the 8th, which [planet] is found in the 5th of the radix and the 12th of the revolution, the two of them portending the danger of a violent death by iron or by a hot globule of lead. And going into the water was signified, because the Moon, and Venus, ruler of the 9th of this revolution, and Jupiter, ruler of the 9th of the radix [posited] in the 3rd of this figure, were [all] in water signs. but because they were in trine aspect, and in addition Jupiter and Venus were in sextile to the ASC, whose ruler, Mercury, was strong and free from the malefics, Mars and Saturn, just like both of the luminaries[3]; consequently, with God's most merciful consent, I was saved

---

[1] The date & time shown in Latin in the center of the chart are wrong; it should read 16 Jun 1615 at 23:10 T.A. (= 17 Jun 1615 11:10 AM LAT); also, the ASC is wrong—it should be 18 Virgo instead of 8 Virgo; and the RAMC is wrong—it should read 73°42′ instead of 37°42′ (probably a typesetter's error); but the chart is actually set for 11:14 AM, not 11:10 AM, Recalculation shows that the true time would have been about 10:58 AM, when the ASC was about 15 Virgo. Mercury was in 10 Gemini 14, rather than in 13 Gemini; and Venus in 23 Can 54, rather than 22 Can.

[2] Since Aries is on the cusp of the 8th, Morin assigns the Sun as co-ruler of that house.

3 But the Sun is sextile Mars, although the aspect is not completed before Mars leaves the sign it is in.

while in such great danger, and also uninjured; and here appear the causes of my safety, which are not found in the revolution of the Sun.

The tenth will be the revolution of the Moon, during which I experienced the horrifying danger of falling from my horse from a high place into swirling waters, on the 1st day of January at around 1:30 PM[1]; and the figure was like this:

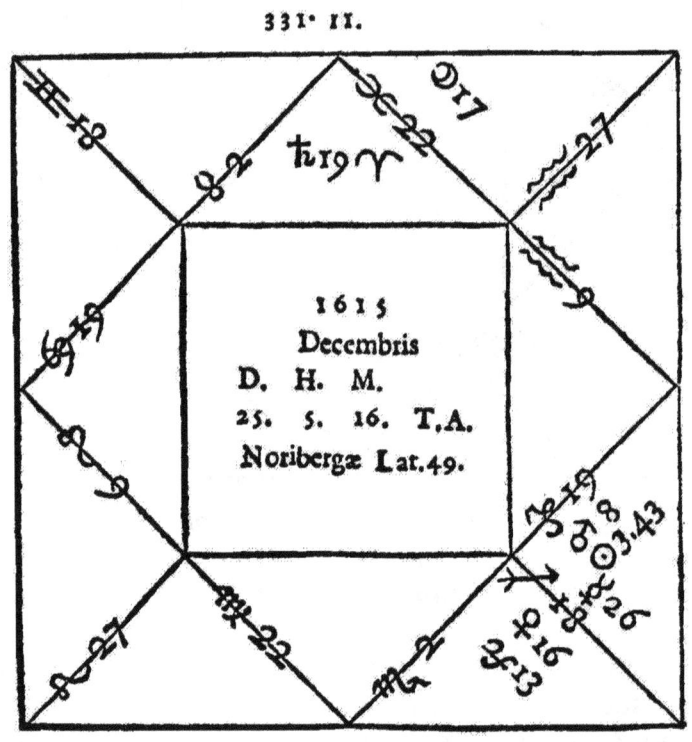

Morin Lunar Revolution
Nürnberg 49 N
25 Dec 1615 5:16 PM[2]

In which the sign of the 8th [house] of the revolution of the Sun is ascending, in which [revolution] the sign of the 8th [house] of the radix was ascending; and the ASC is the place of Mars in that same revolution, which is close to the violent fixed star called Hercules.[3] Moreover, the Moon, ruler of the ASC is in the 9th, said to be [the house] of long journeys, and it is square Jupiter, Venus, and Mercury, which are in the 8th of the radix and in the 6th of this figure around the ASC of the revolution of the Sun. These positions, therefore, gave warning of the danger of death during a journey; but Saturn, ruler of the 6th, 7th, 8th, and 9th, was in the 10th partilely square the ASC, in its fall in the domicile of Mars; consequently, it was signifying a fall from a height; and its ruler, Mars, was in the 6th on [the place of] the opposition to its own radical [place], conjunct the Sun and square Saturn, ruler of the 8th, portending danger from animals and especially from horses because of the nature of Mars itself and because of Sat-

---

[1] I assume that 1:30 PM is what is meant by *hora prima cum 30 circiter minutis*.

[2] The RAMC 331°11′ is wrong; it should be close to 353°. But recalculation shows that the true time of this revolution was about 7:04 PM LAT, with RAMC 20°, MC 22 Aries, ASC 10 Leo, 8th cusp 0 Virgo.

[3] Now more commonly called Pollux or β Geminorum; it was at 17 Cancer 55.

urn's being in the domicile of Mars. consequently, in that lunar month, returning from Hungary, by the fall of a running horse that was carrying me, I incurred the danger of a lethal fall from a height into a dreadful torrent between great rocks foaming with waves and whirlpools. From which surely either God the Best and Greatest or a Guardian Angel freed me, as I have said in [my discussion of] the revolution of the Sun. For against the abovesaid dangers the Moon in trine to the ASC could not have [prevailed] against the abovesaid [positions], since the ASC was the place of Mars and the cusp of the 8th in the revolution of the Sun; therefore, the effects of Saturn and Mars agreed with [that of] the Moon, and by no natural cause could it have freed me from [a lethal continuation] of the fall, once it had begun.

The eleventh will be the revolution of the Moon, in which by the notable favor of the Most Serene Queen Marie de' Medici[1] I obtained on the 3rd of August 1629 an appointment by King Louis XIII [to the post of] Regius Professor of Mathematics; and the matter was undertaken on the 30th of June. The figure [shown on the next page] was such as is very worthy of note.

The sign of the 10th [house] of the radix is ascending, and Saturn, ruler of the ASC, is in his own exaltation with Spica, near the cusp of the 9th, dedicated to the sciences; moreover, the Sun and Venus, partilely conjunct in the 7th with the Moon as their ruler, were in trine to the MC, whose ruler and that of the radical ASC is Mars, conjoined to the radical Part of Fortune, [and] in trine to the Part of Fortune in this figure, which Mercury rules in the sign of the Sun, and in the 7th house with the Sun ; and Mars in partile sextile to the Moon and then to the Sun and Venus, its ruler; and the Moon in partile sextile to the ASC, which also has a partile trine to Mars, which lays claim to it through its exaltation.

Moreover, all these things were strongly presaging an honor and a royal dignity, along with the notable favor of friends, who were the Reverend Father de Condren, who persuaded me to apply for that dignity although I was unwilling and reluctant [to do so], and on my behalf he spoke about that matter to Cardinal Bérulle, by whom I was esteemed, and who had influence with the Queen. He spoke to the Queen on my behalf, to whom I had already become known because of [my practice of] astrology; and the Queen sought that dignity for me from the King, although in the private office of that Queen, she explained to him that she had already sought that same dignity for another learned man.

Moreover, this favor was signified by Jupiter in the 1st house, ruler of the 11th and the Moon; and the Moon herself in partile sextile to the ASC [and] ruler of the Sun. Wherefore, with the Queen Mother in favor and indeed making an effort, the matter was so quickly and favorably accomplished, that I myself marvelled at it; especially, because the King, who was at that time almost 150 leagues from Paris, and with Cardinal de La Rochefoucauld,[2] by whom the Regius Professors were accepted, repeatedly opposed the Queen's action; which the Sun in the 7th brought about and Saturn conjunct the cusp of th 9th in partile square to the ASC and the Sun.

---

[1] Marie de' Medici (1573-1642). Her help came just in time, for she was banished from the court late in 1630.

[2] Cardinal François de La Rochefoucauld (1558-1645) the Grand Almoner of France.

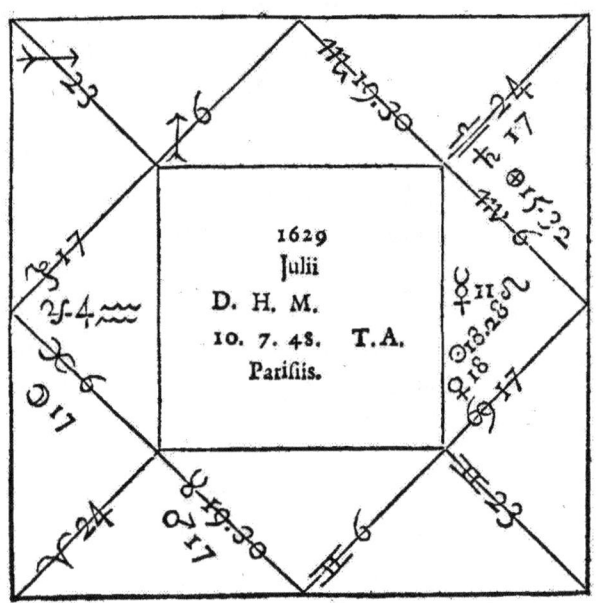

Morin Lunar Revolution
Paris
10 Jul 1629 7:48 PM[1]

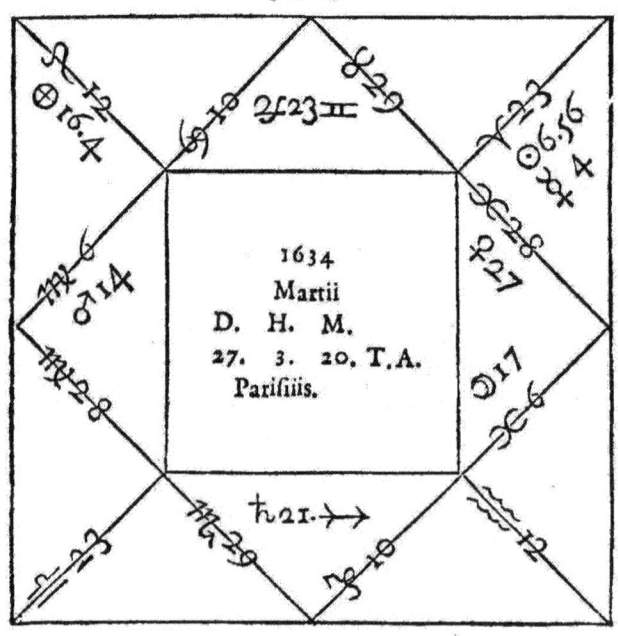

Morin Lunar Revolution
Paris
27 Mar 1634 3:20 PM[1]

---

[1] Recalculation shows that the true time of the revolution was about 8:00 PM LAT, with MC 22 Scorpio and ASC 21 Capricorn.

[1] Recalculation shows that the true time of the revolution was about 3:33 PM LAT, with MC 1 Gemini and ASC 7 Virgo.

Twelfth will be the revolution of the Moon, during which I publicly demonstrated the Science of Longitudes, in the presence of 8 Commissioners and more than 300 men, both magnates and learned men, with great honor and praise; but afterwards, a notable injustice was perpetrated against me by Cardinal Richelieu and my Commissioners; and the figure was such [as is shown above], very worthy of note.

In which, the caelum is in fact disposed in the same manner as in the revolution of the Sun; and the ASC is opposite the cluster of the radical planets, which is found in the 7th house, [which is] assigned to lawsuits and disputes; in it is found the Moon afflicted by an opposition to Mars in the 1st; and Jupiter, ruler of the Moon, is in the 10th afflicted by an opposition to Saturn in the 4th; and these 4 planets not only corrupt each other by their oppositions but also by mutual squares from the 4 angles of the figure, which was indeed portending great enemies, celebrated disputes, and huge oppositions, in general as in the revolution of the Sun; especially because Saturn was applying by square to Venus, ruler of the MC.[1] Moreover, Venus was in her own exaltation; and Mercury, ruler of the 10th and the 1st, was conjunct the Sun, which was signifying fame and praise, and Mercury was in mutual reception by domicile with Mars in the 1st, which was presaging shrewdness and ingenuity of intelligence as well as animosity; but the Part of Fortune[2] was in the 12th under the rulership of the Sun in the 8th of this figure and in the 12th of the revolution, which was portending a Magnate as a secret enemy and damage to success. And these individual things happened during the course of this monthly revolution.

The thirteenth will be the revolution of the Moon preceding by only 3 hours the [onset of] the long and difficult illness by which I was seized on the 2nd of November 1642. The figure is such as is shown on the next page.

---

[1] But in fact Venus was *separating* from the square to Saturn.

[2] Reading the symbol for the Part of Fortune rather than the symbol for the sign Cancer.

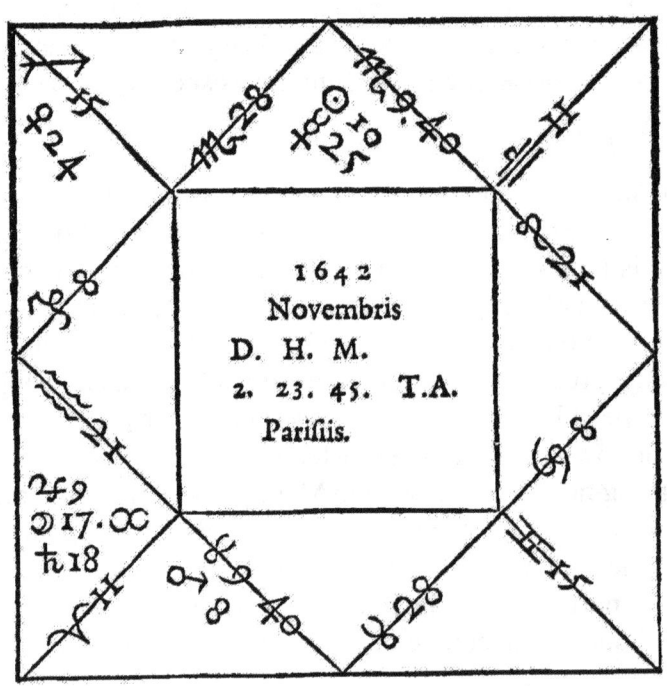

Morin Lunar Revolution
Paris
2 Nov 1642 11:58 AM[1]

In which there first ascends the opposition to the radical Mars, and that [planet] rules the Sun, the ruler of the 8th, [and is] in the MC, which [in turn] is afflicted by an opposition ray from Taurus, where Mars is in exile; and the Moon is besieged by Jupiter, ruler of the 8th of the radix, and Saturn, to which it applies partilely, which I have already very often observed to be very bad in a revolution of the Moon, especially when Saturn is the significator of death or of illnesses in the radix. Moreover, Jupiter, the Moon, and Saturn are conjoined in the 2nd; this is opposite the 8th house, which aggravates the evil of the configuration in that regard. Therefore, it is not surprising that an illness that an illness began closely with such a configuration; and it was long because of Saturn, and indeed difficult, because no planet was able to temper the evil of this configuration, since all of them, either in the radix, or in this figure, or in both, were significators of either illnesses or death, or of both.

The fourteenth will be the revolution of the Moon, during which a prize was given to me in the Royal Council for my *Secret of Longitudes*; and the figure was as shown on the next page.

---

[1] The date and time in the box are not quite conect. The chart is actually set for 1 November 1642 at 23:58, which is equivalent to 2 November 1642 11:58 AM LAT. Recalculation shows that the true time of the revolution was about 0:26 PM LAT, at which time the RAMC was 224°17′ with MC 16 Scorpio 46 and ASC 14 Capricorn 27.

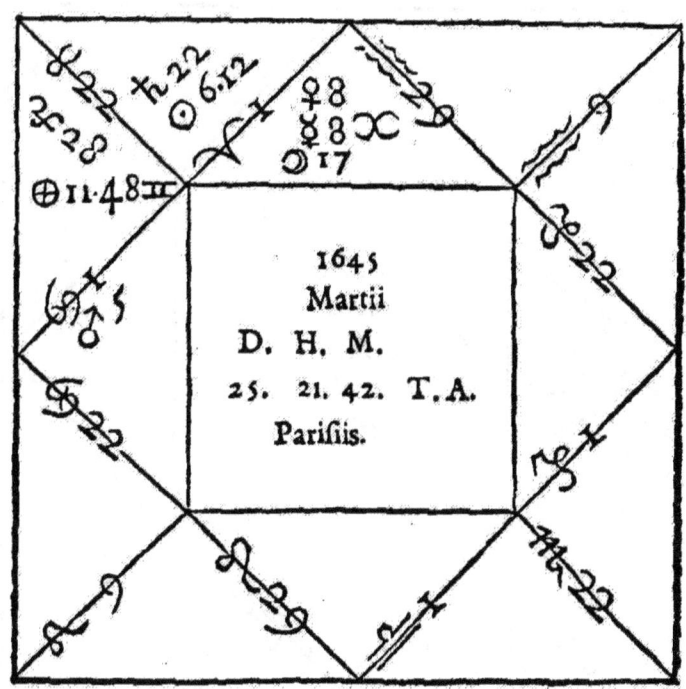

Morin Lunar Revolution
Paris
26 Mar 1645 9:42 AM[1]

In which there ascends the trine of the radical cluster of planets, whose place is in the 10th house, where Venus, Mercury, and the Moon, ruler of the ASC, are found. And in the MC is the radical place of Mercury, ruler of the Part of Fortune, which were presaging fame, good fortune, and wealth in undertakings and actions, and that through the favor of the Queen, Princes, and Minister of the Kingdom because of the Moon, ruler of the ASC, in the 10th with the exalted Venus, partilely conjunct Mercury, ruler of the Part of Fortune; and then because of the Sun exalted in the 11th, whose ruler, Mars, is in the 1st. And therefore, on the following 8th of April, my case, a petition for the prize for my having discovered the science of [finding] longitudes and the restitution of astronomy, was heard in the Queen's Council in the presence of Princes and Ministers of the Kingdom, and, with the consent of all, I was awarded a prize, but a small one, which Jupiter, ruler of the Moon and the 10th [house], in the 12th with the Part of Fortune, seemed to portend, and also the Part of Fortune itself in square to Venus, Mercury, and the Moon.

The fifteenth will be the revolution preceding the demise of the Blessed Father Charles de Condren, the figure of which is very worthy of note.

---

[1] Recalculation shows that the true time was about 9:37 AM LAT, with MC 28 Aquarius and ASC 0 Cancer.

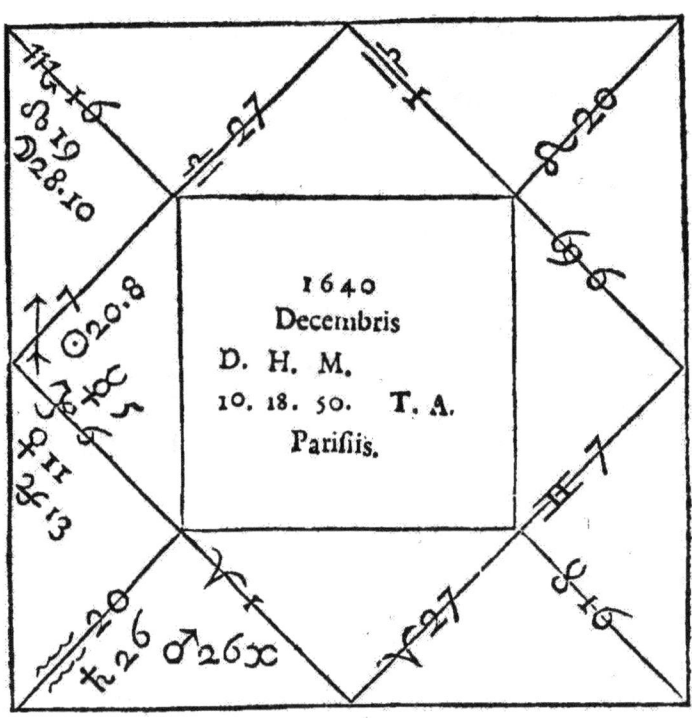

Charles de Condren Lunar Revolution
Paris
11 December 1640 6:50 AM[1]

In which the *caelum* was disposed just as it was in the radix; and the Sun and the Moon, rulers of the 8th of the radix and of this revolution, were in the 1st and 12th as they were in the radix, but both of them afflicted—the Moon in fact was square a strong Saturn, to which she was opposed in the radix, and the Sun was square Mars. These things, then, were portending a lethal illness so very strongly, that it could scarcely be [indicated] more powerfully, since in [both] the radix and in this revolution the Moon was the significator of illnesses and death and the Sun of life and death; and Jupiter, ruler of the ASC, [even] with Venus could not help because it was in its fall and opposed to the 8th, nor was the ASC fortified by any fortunate rays. Consequently, he died on the 6th of January 1641 at about 6 A.M.

---

[1] This chart is completely wrong! At the time stated, the Moon was in 25 Scorpio 06, not in 28 Scorpio 19, where it should have been. Possibly, Morin mistakenly made his calculations for a lunar position of 25 Scorpio 10 rather than 28 Scorpio 10. Recalculation shows that the true time of the lunar revolution was about 11:53 AM LAT or 5 hours and 3 minutes later than the time shown above. Here we have an example of the danger of reading a chart after the fact. The true lunar return is shown on the next page with some brief comments by the translator. The reader should compare the two charts and the comments made about them.

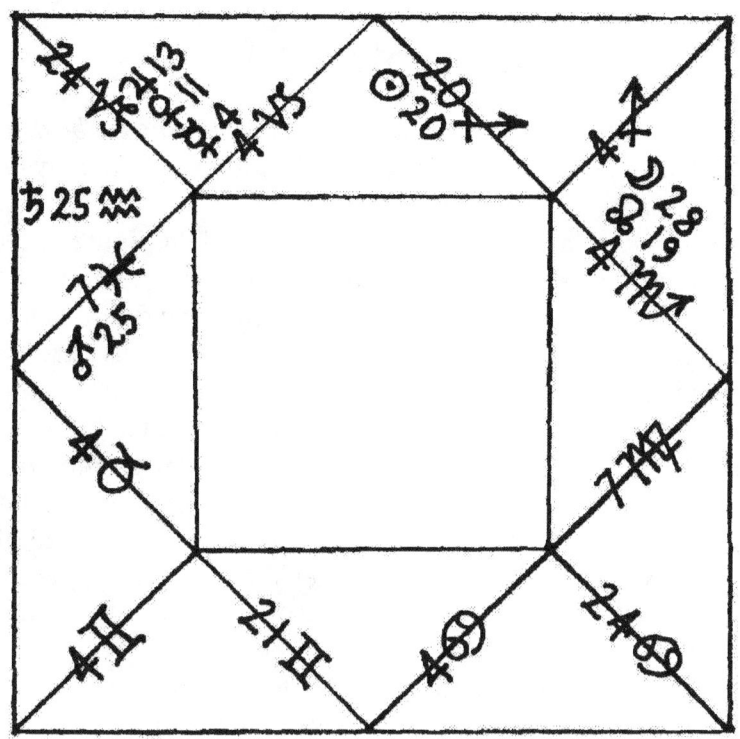

Charles de Condren Recalculated Lunar Revolution
Paris
11 December 1640 11:53 AM

Translator's Comment

Some of the ominous signs that Morin noted in his chart are also present in this one; in particular, the squares of the malefics to the lights. The Moon, co-ruler of the 6th house is in the 8th in its fall and square Saturn in the 12th. Mars, ruler of the Moon and the 8th, is in the 1st and square the Sun on the cusp of the MC. The Sun is co-ruler of the 6th, so both of the co-rulers of that house are afflicted by squares to the two malefics. According to Morin, the 12th house is the house of illness rather than the 6th, but in this chart the 6th is empty, and Saturn opposes it from the 12th. Jupiter is ruler of the ASC, and it is in the 11th in conjunction with Venus, but Jupiter is in its fall in Capricorn, so, as Morin says, it cannot help much, although, contrary to what Morin said of the other chart, here the ASC does receive fortunate rays, namely a sextile from Venus and the weak Jupiter. Still, I think this chart is also an ominous one, and even the position of the Sun on the cusp of the MC may merely have been indicative of the fact that Father de Condren's demise was that of a notable person, and his funeral was attended by many important persons.

No doubt Morin would have noted some other dangerous features of this recalculated chart, but these are the principal ones that come to my mind.

Chapter XI.

Whether the Genethliacal Revolutions of the Sun and the Moon should be distributed into Quarters, and whether their Figures should be Inspected for Accidents Signified by those Revolutions.

Cardan, *Book on Revolutions*, Chapter 2, after having erected the figure of the annual revolution of the Sun, then wants the figure of the revolution of the Moon to be erected for the individual months when it returns to the same place in the ecliptic that it occupied in the figure of the solar revolution. Furthermore, he also wants figures to be erected for the quadrants of the individual months, when the Moon by her own proper motion has come to the places that are square and opposite her place [in the revolution]. And so, notice should be taken of both the former and the latter figures—the former, so that a judgment can be made of the [whole] month and the first quadrant of the month, and the latter, so that a judgment can be made about the rest of the quadrants. But since, however, we have rejected these revolutions of the Moon, but those revolutions that are made to the **radical** place of the Moon have been proved [to be effective], it might be questioned whether they too should be divided into quarters or weeks like those [of Cardan's]?

But I say that if the revolutions of the Moon should be divided into quadrantal figures, then the same thing ought even more to be done with the genethliacal revolutions of the Sun. And indeed in the case of the mundane revolutions of the Sun, Ptolemy says, *Quadripartite*, Book 2, Chapter 9, "That that principle ought to be accepted in any conversion of the Sun, from its return into the place from which it departed, as that thing teaches with its own effect, then also by its name," which is worthy of note for revolutions of the Moon and the other planets, both in mundane and in genethliacal [charts]. But because a circle exhibits no beginning per se; and even as a pagan was ignorant of the creation of the world and the position of the Sun at the beginning of the creation in an uncertain point of the zodiac, from which it [then] began to move; therefore, thinking about that same zodiac and the 4 points of principal virtue, which are of course the beginning points of Aries, Cancer, Libra, and Capricorn, which are the radical place of the Sun at the beginning of the world and its squares and opposition; and not knowing which of these first received the Sun, he assumed these 4 beginnings, at which he directs figures to be erected for the quarters of the mundane revolution of the Sun; which it certainly seems he would not be going to do, if he had known the first location of the Sun in the zodiac, from which it began to move. For using [all] four beginnings, he [obviously] did not know [which was] the first, i.e. the radical one, from which one the others receive their force; and he could not confute their subordination and judge about them the wrong way around, at least in their influential effects. Therefore, similarly, it does not seem that the genethliacal revolutions of the Sun ought to be divided into quarters; and consequently, in similar fashion too, the revolutions of the Moon should not be subdivided.

Nevertheless, it is proved by experience that a great force is inherent in the figures of the quarters, not only of the mundane revolution of the Sun, but also of the synodic revolutions of the Moon; therefore, those revolutions should be subdivided into quarters; and consequently, in similar fashion, the genethliacal revolutions ought to be subdivided for the reason just stated, because the prior things should be models and rules for the later things.

To this [argument] it can be replied first that in both universal and particular revolutions of the Sun and the Moon that force of the quarters should most certainly be attributed to the transits of the Sun and the Moon through places [in the zodiac that are] square and opposed to their own radical places. For these aspects are noteworthy in the circle of celestial virtue through their determination. But because the Sun and the Moon, when they are in their own radical places, determine other points of that same circle by their own aspects of quincunx, trine, sextile, and semi-sextile, they do not seem proper for erecting figures subdividing a revolution, but more by their aspects that are malefic by nature, the square and opposition, rather than by the benefic trine and sextile; especially since Cardan, *Book on Revolutions*, chapter 13, declares that the custom of the Egyptians was to erect figures for individual months for the return of the Sun to the same degree and minute of each sign of that sign in which the Sun was [posited] in the geniture. Indeed, the custom of the Egyptians in this regard certainly smacks of the old cabala of astrology from its first parents, by which every planet by its own place in the *caelum* determines 12 places of the *caelum* and no more to its own nature, according to the force and type of their own aspects, as we have said in Book 16, Section 1, chapter 4.[1]

Second, it can be replied that synodic revolutions of the Moon are not peculiar to the native, and they are not tied to any radical genethliacal beginning, but they are common to the whole earth and vague, just like their quarters too, which do not take place in places that are in a quadrant or semicircle from the place of the conjunction, but in different places. Still, [it is necessary] to compare a consideration of these [revolutions] to the particular revolutions of the natives, [to see] to what extent a particular [revolution] is subordinated to a universal one; and the Sun and the Moon are primary universal causes, and are as it were the father and mother of sublunar effects, always acting universally with their own forces and in their own syzygies in whatever sublunar [region], according to its disposition, either merely elementary, or even influential from the radical impression.

But it is true that neither response weakens the objection concerning the virtue of the mundane revolutions of the Sun and the synodic revolutions of the Moon; and it is Microcosmic man who is subject to his own revolutions, both of the Sun and of the Moon, as is demonstrated in detail in Chapters 7, 8, and 9. [Hence], it seems that one must conclude that [in order to arrive] at a more certain and accurate understanding of the future accidents of the native, the genethliacal revolutions of the Sun and the Moon should be divided into quarters, and the figures of the quarters should be judged with regard to their own beginnings, which are the genethliacal figure [itself] and the figures of the genethliacal revolutions of the Sun and the Moon; for from that it can more evidently be conjectured what things in the quarters of the Sun and the Moon will bring forth the accidents signified by the nativity and the revolutions. And this method of judging on particular times has certainly a true foundation in nature and one that is conformable to the primary principles of science, namely the efficacious determination of the places of the Sun and the Moon, and their aspects, and the celestial state, in which the Sun and the Moon come to these places in [the course of] their own transit, which, from that state, is more or less efficacious. Also, it is not useless to erect figures for the good [places] signified in the nativity, especially by the luminaries; at the moment of time in which they are found in their own radical trines or sextiles. But because the

---

[1] This chapter is entitled "How many Astrological Aspects are there, and What is the Quantity of Distance of each of them; Then, which are Simple and which are Mixed." The passage to which Morin refers reads "Consequently, twelve aspects, no more and no less, are made by that division of the circle [into 12 signs], because the individual points of division are powerful in virtue from the above said [signs]; and therefore it is contrary to reason to reject any one of them, since the individual [signs] are equal in this respect, because they have a natural origin; and there are no points that divide the circle into 8 or 16 parts, which is merely fictitious and arbitrary. [Here, Morin rejects the 45° and 22.5° aspects and their multiples.}... Moreover, it is remarkable in nature that these 12 places in the *primum caelum,* determined to the characteristics of whatever planet, are active in accordance with the nature of that planet, its celestial state and its determination in the figure."

places of the squares and the opposition are more effective than the others; for that reason, figures erected at [the time] of transit through those places will be those deserving of principal consideration, [but] with the others not neglected.

Furthermore, the figures of the quarters, the trines, and such like should plainly be erected in the same manner as the revolutions of the Moon. Moreover, since very accurate tables of the luminaries for this purpose have been lacking hitherto, we judged that we should refrain from [offering] examples, lest erroneous figures should be swallowed down by us, perchance [seeming to argue] against a doctrine established on the best principles, [but] cautioning that just as revolutions do not act against the presages of the nativity, neither do the quarters act against the things signified by their revolutions. Moreover, a revolution of the Moon corresponding to the [previous] revolution of the Sun can produce effects signified by both, [even] in a quarter of a revolution of the Sun that is not in agreement [with those effects], and particularly in a quarter of that revolution of the Moon that does correspond; for the stronger cause always conquers the weaker one, and two [causes] prevail over one.

And yet, if anyone wishes to be content with the figures of the revolutions of the Sun and the Moon, which are prior to and more powerful than the figures of the quarters, just as the [bodily] place of a planet is more powerful than the place of its aspect, and the force of these has most evidently been proved to be superior, I think that the former will produce less confusion and more verity in making judgments. But from this it follows that at least the individual revolutions of the Moon should be examined, unless the directions of the annual revolution have specially decreed certain revolutions of the Moon as being more in agreement with the effects of those directions, both in their celestial state and in their time; for then the other revolutions of the Moon will not need to be examined, at least in regard to those effects. For it is certain that concourses of the revolution of the Sun and Moon that are in agreement will be the most efficacious causes of the future effects for a man, especially when the radical figure and its directions agree, as will be mentioned below.

But Cardan, *Book on Revolutions*, Chapter 4, having erected a revolution of the Moon in each individual month to the place that it occupied in the revolution of the Sun, then erects figures of the quarters for the individual weeks, when the Moon has come to the squares and opposition of that place. And after this in fact, he erects a figure for each individual days of a quarter with the degree in the ascendant that was the ASC degree of that quarter. Finally, he observes the place of the significator or the promissor, namely in what hour it comes by its diurnal motion to the ASC or the MC or the cusp of the 7th. And he already judges about the effects in that year from the figure of the revolution of the Sun, according as they are similar or dissimilar to the signification of the radical figure and the radical directions; [and] the effects of a month from the figure of the revolution of the Moon, accordingly as it agrees with the radix and the revolution of the Sun; [and] the effects of a week, accordingly as the figure of the quarter is in agreement with the radix and the revolutions of the Sun and Moon. [And he judges] about a day from the figure [drawn for that] day; and about an hour from the position of the place of the significator or the promissor in the horizon or in the meridian. But the revolution of the Moon by Cardan's method was rejected by us above; about the rest, for predicting the effects for a day and for an hour, we shall treat of that [subject] below and in the next book.

Chapter XII.

Whether Revolutions without the Concurrence of Directions can have any Effect on the Native.

It must be known that to elucidate this question is [a matter] of no small importance: a revolution is in the nature of an efficient cause of the future things happening to the native, which [holds] a middle place between the radical figure (to which the directions belong) and the transits of the planets, which will be treated in their own proper place. For the influx of the radical figure and its directions is, at the moment of the nativity, something that is only a potential with respect to the future things happening [as indicated] by the nativity. But transits are only the active causes that produce the effects through their own action. But the revolution is partly active and partly potential: active, it is true, to the extent that by its own influx it actuates the potential of the radical constitution or a direction, for neither the radical constitution nor a direction acts without a corresponding revolution; but potential, to the extent that that figure or constitution of a revolution is whatever is universal and potential in the whole year, but which is reduced into an actuality by the transits of the planets. For since all the effects [promised by] the radical constitution do not happen on the very day of the nativity, but they come forth successively through [the action of] the revolutions and directions during the whole [span of] life, so not all the effects of the revolutions of the Sun and those of the Moon happen on the very day of the revolution, but through corresponding annual or monthly directions, and then they burst forth through the corresponding transits of the planets during the year or month as will be explained below.

With these things understood, it seems that it should be stated: First, that a radical direction accomplishes nothing that is contrary to that which is signified in the radical figure, although it can excite vain attempts, especially when accompanied by a corresponding revolution. For it is plain from experience that if the radical figure has strongly denied a martial nature and matrimony, or wealth, or children, no radical direction can bestow any of these, as has already been said elsewhere. Otherwise, it would not be possible to have any faith in the radical signification, and thus there would be no science of astrology, contrary to experience. see Book 22, Section 4, Chapter 2.

Second, that a radical direction that is in agreement with the radical figure, does nothing without a corresponding revolution. For since that direction pertains to the radical figure, and the force of both the former and the latter is only a potential for future accidents, it is necessary that it be reduced to actuality by something that is actual, which will be a close revolution, which is intermediate between the radical directions and the transits of the planets. For it does not proceed from one extreme to the other, but rather through the middle; and neither the form nor a particular act that is [indicated] by transits is introduced without previous dispositions, which the revolutions themselves accomplish, along with their own directions as has been said frequently in this chapter. Therefore, transits alone are not sufficient to reduce the potential of a radical direction to actuality, and much less so the potential of the geniture, at least in notable changes [in the life]; even though, Cardan, *Book on Revolutions*, Chapter 7,[1] at the end, asserts that "A transition[2] from the geniture to the day without [the concurrence of] the year is not denied, if there was a valid signification of the day." Here, he contradicts himself in that same chapter,

---

[1] The text says "8," but the passage cited is actually at the end of the 7th chapter.

[2] The Latin word is *transitum,* which Morin may have taken to mean 'transit', but *it* does not mean that here; instead it refers to passing from a consideration of the geniture to a consideration of the day.

when he says, "it is impossible that anyone could know the day more than the year."[1] And therefore, when any radical direction is completed, and its signification does not agree, or (what is more) the annual revolution is strongly contrary [to that signification], the signified effect will be delayed until a corresponding revolution occurs in one or two years following, provided that [another] radical direction contrary to that same significator does not intervene, which would suppress the previous [direction]; but whenever the effect of that previous direction will be hastened by a corresponding revolution of the Sun, the time of [the action of] the direction [will be] at least one year earlier. Moreover, if the revolution of the Sun is not strongly contradictory to the signification of the direction, or if it is in agreement for even a little while, then the signification will be enabled to come forth by a strong and corresponding revolution of the Moon, especially if the radical direction was a direction of the Moon herself, or to her, or to her aspects of a corresponding nature.

Third. One of the revolutions is primary, and the others are secondary. If it is primary, it is the radical figure itself, which is in truth the first revolution of the native, both solar and lunar. Since, therefore, the similarity of this revolution to the radical figure is very great, indeed it is identical; because of this, the effect of the radical figure itself is strongly signified, and it will be soon, solely from a corresponding transit of the planets it will be produced, even in the native's first year, provided that the native's age is capable of [experiencing] that effect, such as an illness, a fall from a height, death, removal into another province, and such like, sometimes with a concurrent secondary revolution of the Moon. Moreover, secondary revolutions are all those other than the radical figure and that follow after it. In which, because a sufficient similarity is lacking and something otherwise happens; consequently, even though a secondary revolution is allotted a great similarity to the radical figure for some type of accident, nevertheless, transits in accord with this type [of accident] will scarcely cause changes or effects without radical directions; otherwise, no faith could be had in rectifications of nativities by radical directions for accidents that have already occurred, which, however, are found to be very certain, but it would be sufficient for a previous accident to know the similarity of the revolution to the radix, which similarity can be obtained with the ASC of the radical figure, even unchanged by many degrees. Add that the time of a revolution cannot be known from the precisely unknown time of a nativity; nor, consequently, its abovesaid similarity. Nevertheless, with the figure of the nativity exactly established, either by observation of the hour [of birth] or by rectification with the aid of directions, a revolution that is in agreement with the natal figure, will not be lacking in its effect, even without corresponding radical revolutions, which in individual years do not occur at the same time as revolutions conformable to the radical figure. It will, therefore, produce effects from directions conformable to the years or months or transits occurring at the same time for a notable effect, or [if] differently, for a moderate effect.

From what has just been said, therefore, it can be concluded that neither the radical figure nor the radical directions can accomplish anything along the line of future changes without conformable revolutions, either of the Sun or the Moon. But conversely, a secondary revolution, even though it is similar to the radical figure, will hardly perfect anything that is noteworthy without conformable radical directions, although it can cause vain attempts or something preliminary to a future effect or some minor changes, in accordance with its major or minor similarity to the radical figure and the strength of the

---

[1] In Chapter 7, Cardan seems to be saying that normally the signification of the day is subsidiary to the quarter of the month, and that to the revolution of the month, and that to the revolution of the year, and that to the geniture itself, but that there are exceptional cases in which the signification of the day (or the month) is particularly strong and in concordance with the geniture itself, and that in such a case they can be independent of the signification of the revolution of the year.

significators. Also, something notable can indeed be caused by two immediate revolutions of the Sun and the Moon that strongly signify it.[1]

But when the radical figure, a radical direction, and a revolution of the Sun come together in signification and in time, without doubt the effect of that direction occurs and is perfected in that very year, unless something more powerful obstructs it, like the will in free actions.

You will object that if radical directions are only something that is potential with respect to future accidents, it would follow that in the year of the accident there is no actual influx, and that consequently every actual influx for an accident in that year would be from revolutions or from transits. But this cannot be said [to be true], since revolutions and transits at the most do not operate without radical directions, because it is most evident that the directions themselves also have an actual influx and that accidents effectively concur with it, for otherwise accidents would not effectively occur from those directions, which must be thought absurd. Therefore, they are not just something potential.

I reply that we have said above that radical directions at the moment of the nativity were only something potential with respect to future accidents [resulting] from them, just as an infant is only something potential with respect to its own future offspring, and the force of the seed in a grain of wheat is something potential with respect to producing a head of wheat. But in Book 22, Section 3, chapter 2, we have said that the force or efficacy of a radical direction, through the revolutions of the *caelum* from [the time of] the nativity, matures in that native and passes from a remote potential to one at hand to produce its own effect. In which case it only needs to be excited and reduced to that very action by a conformable revolution of the Sun. Just like a grain put into the earth, the force of its seed is excited by that same Sun, and its is reduced to the action of generating a head of wheat; and something similar must be understood about the force of a direction. Having settled that, it is plain that the revolution is always something intermediate between the radical directions and the transits, in the nature of an efficient cause of future accidents.

Chapter XIII.

In Which the Accompaniment of Radical Directions by Revolutions of the Sun is Proved by Many Examples.

The doctrine of Revolutions is of such importance that it needs to be illustrated by examples for greater certainty, which I will not object to do as a favor to students, having explained radical directions in this chapter, which accompany suitable revolutions of the Sun.[2]

And so, Gustavus Adolphus, the king of Sweden, was killed in battle in the year 1632 because of a

---

[1] By "immediate revolutions," he evidently means "by a solar revolution and an immediately following lunar revolution."

[2] This chapter contains many directions calculated by Morin. I have not attempted to verify his calculations.

direction of the MC to the square of Saturn badly afflicted in the 8th, to the square of an unfortunate Jupiter in the 2nd, and to the body of Mars in the 12th. In fact, the MC is first and per se the significator of actions and their success, whether in good or evil, which very often is death itself, especially in duels and battles entered into, as can be confirmed by many other examples; but the concourse of the three abovesaid promissors [indicating] a violent death, which the nativity signified, was so strongly deadly that it seemed that an inevitable fate was at hand.

Right ascension of the sinister square of Saturn with latitude	232°44'
Right ascension of the Midheaven	195°22'
Difference	37°22'

Which, converted by Naibod's Table, equal the time of death. the right ascension of Mars was 233°05', emceing [the preceding arc] by 21'; and the right ascension of the dexter square of Jupiter was 232°00', deficient by 44'; and therefore, these three directions occurred in the same year.

The death of Cardinal Richelieu happened due to a direction of the ASC, the primary significator of life, to the opposition of Jupiter, which was in the 8th house in exile and with a violent fixed star. And this [man] was the killer of many through the whole of Europe, made horrid with iron, flames, blood, famine, pestilence, and corpses, [and] imprecating the same [evils] against the Cardinal, as those that once upon a time Brutus, contemplating the stars by night after the disaster at Philippi, imprecated against Antony,[1] according to Apion:

May Jupiter strike down the one who is the cause of all these evils!

Oblique ascension of the opposition of Jupiter at Paris	275°57'
Oblique ascension of the ASC	220°30'
Difference	55°27'

Which according to Naibod equals 56 years and 101 days; moreover, he fell into an illness from which he never recovered in the summer of 1642, that is 56 years and 331 days after his birth, and he died on the 4th of December 1642, having passed through 57 years and 86 days, with very bad revolutions of both the Sun and the Moon; due to which, the total effect of the direction was retarded by the greatest care [that he had received] from physicians and surgeons.

The very noble Mr. Tronson, for his merits to the king and to France, was honored with two dignities by King Louis XIII between April and August of the year 1617. and the direction of the MC to the Sun, ruler of the 10th, caused this, and then to the Moon, Jupiter, and Venus in the tenth.

---

[1] A reference to the decisive battle at Philippi, Macedonia, in 42 B.C., in which Octavos and Marc Antony defeated Brutus and Cassias. The reference to Apion may refer to tee Roman historian Appianus (2nd century).

Right ascension of the Sun	160°20′
Right ascension of the MC	120°04′
Difference, or arc of direction corresponding to the time	40°16′

But a little while after, namely on 19 February 1618, he married the most noble Claudia de Sève, outstanding in her appearance, mental qualities, virtues, and dowry; at which time the Sun, ruler of the 10th and the Moon (who ruled the MC), was directed to the sinister sextile of the Moon herself; moreover, the Sun is also the ruler of Venus, who ruled the ASC. And both the Sun and the Moon had the authority of exaltation in the 7th.[1] Moreover, I had predicted the day of his marriage to Mr. Tronson himself almost a year before he had decided to get married.

This same very noble Mr. Tronson, on the 2nd of August 1626, was expelled from the court and despoiled of his own dignities by the wicked arts of Cardinal Richelieu. And at that time, the Sun, ruler of the 10th, had come by direction to the square of Mars; and Saturn, ruler of the 4th [and] powerful in the 12th, had come to the opposition of the Moon in the ecliptic, who ruled the MC; and Saturn and Mars were inimical to the 10th, and consequently to honors and dignities.

Oblique ascension of the square to Mars in the ecliptic	203°14′
Oblique ascension of the Sun	154°53′
Arc of direction	48°21′
Converted time of the accident	49°10′

Oblique ascension of the Moon's opp. in the ecliptic	324°40′
Oblique ascension of Saturn	275°14′
Arc of direction	49°26′

That same most noble man died on the 8th of December 1642 from a double tertian [fever], which had degenerated into a quartan [fever]. And that happened because of the direction of the ASC to the square of the Sun.

Oblique ascension of the Sun's square	274°23′
Oblique ascension of the ASC	210°04′
Arc of direction	64°19′
Time of his illness	65°06′

---

[1] The Sun, because Aries was on the cusp of the 7th, and the Moon, because the first half of Taurus was in the 7th.

In the year prior to this, he had been sick with a tertian fever, and the revolution was very bad, but he recovered. But in the succeeding revolution of the year 1642, still a bad one, the deadly effect occurred from the two revolutions and the direction—it began in one [revolution] and was completed in the other.

Constable Lesdiguières died in the month of September 1626 from the direction of the Moon to her own sinister square in the ecliptic; for the Moon was the principal apheta because she was the ruler of the 1st. And there followed a quincunx to Saturn, ruler of the 8th.

The Moon's pole was	14°04′
Oblique ascension of the Moon's sinister square	70°13′
Oblique ascension of the Moon	348°10′
Arc of direction	82°03′
Converted time of the illness	82°14′

Moreover, Mars, in the revolution of the Sun, was almost partilely in the place of the direction [and] also square Saturn, ruler of the 8th house.

Which in truth resembles my accidents, besides the quartan fever, with which I was seized in the eighth year from my nativity, which arose from the direction of the Sun to Saturn; then a great, spontaneous, and unlucky trip to Paris in the month of October 1603, from the direction of Jupiter, ruler of the 9th, to the dexter square of Mars with latitude. I was very dangerously wounded because of a woman on the 9th of July 1605 on account of the direction of the ASC to the sinister square of Venus without latitude. Since Venus, ruler of the 1st, and therefore the significator of moral nature and life [itself], was applying to a conjunction of the Sun, ruler of the 5th, and then Jupiter, ruler of the 8th. And the squares to the Sun and Jupiter followed the square to Venus, for whose state, see the revolutions of the Sun and the Moon.

Oblique ascension of the square of Venus at Villefranche	36°43′
Oblique ascension of the ASC	14°36′
Arc of direction	22°07′
Converted time of the accident	22°03′
Arc of direction to the square of Venus with latitude	22°31′
Arc of direction of Mars to the sinister square of the ASC in that same year	22°00′

In the year 1612 on the 30th of May, I fell into a long and dangerous illness during the great eclipse of the Sun,[1] at which time Jupiter and the Moon, the significators of illnesses and death were directed to the ASC. Moreover, the ASC was at 9 Gemini, in which the eclipse took place; and along with the ill-

---

[1] This was a total solar eclipse in 10 Gemini, whose path of totality passed through northern Scandinavia. It is No. 6688 in Theodor, Bitter von Oppolzer's *Canon of Eclipses* (New York: Dover Publications, 1962).

ness a lengthy journey took place, on account of Jupiter's being ruler of the 9th.

Oblique ascension of the ASC under the pole of Jupiter and the Moon	15°57′
Oblique ascension of Jupiter and the Moon to be subtracted	346°37′
Arc of direction	29°20′
Converted time	28°51′
Or the oblique ascension of the 9th degree of Gemini at Villefranche	43°17′
Oblique ascension of the ASC	14°36′
Arc of direction	28°41′

In the year 1613 on the 9th of May, I was made a Doctor of Medicine by the directions of the MC to the partile semi-sextile of its ruler Saturn, which was then also directed to the Part of Fortune; and then by the directions of Jupiter and the Moon to the ASC. For, since Jupiter and the Moon, powerful in the 4th and in the place of Mars, which rules the ASC, were conjoined to the Sun and Saturn, ruler of the MC. Therefore, not only were they significators of illnesses, but also of honors. Add that they were also directed at the same time to the sextile of Mercury with latitude.

Oblique ascension of the ASC under the pole of Jupiter and the Moon	15°53′
Oblique ascension of Jupiter and the Moon to be subtracted	346°35′
Arc of direction	29°18′
Converted time	29°46′
Arc of direction of Jupiter and the Moon to the sinister sextile of Mercury	30°09′

In the revolution of the Sun, Jupiter and the Moon were in mutual antiscions, the radical ASC was in the MC of the revolution, and Mercury was on the cusp of the 7th applying to a trine of Mars, ruler of the MC; therefore, everything was in agreement.

In the year 1614, I came to Paris out of fatal necessity, and I was made Ordinary Physician to the Most Reverend Claude Dormio, Bishop of Boulogne or of Thérouanne, who compelled me to take up the study of astrology, although I was reluctant to do so, [and] whom I trusted very much. And then the Sun came to the ASC by direction. For the Sun, Moon, Saturn, and Venus in the domicile of Jupiter, ruler of the 9th, and those conjoined to Saturn, also ruler of the 9th, and this was in the 12th house, which is cadent, by their own directions to the ASC, brought me illnesses and journeys and dangers, as well as various periods of servitude.

Oblique ascension of the ASC under the pole of the Sun	16°10′
Oblique ascension of the Sun, to be subtracted	345°01′
Arc of direction	31°09′
Converted time	31°12′

In the year 1615, I undertook a great journey into Hungary, and I fell into various huge dangers to my life in waters, disputes, duels, [and] extravagance; and in that same year the ASC was directed to the square of Saturn in the ecliptic, and Venus to the ASC. See the revolution of the Sun [for that year].

Oblique ascension of the sinister square of Saturn at Villefranche	46°09′
Oblique ascension of the ASC, to be subtracted	14°36′
Arc of direction	31°33′
Converted time of the danger in the Rhine	31°54′
Arc of direction of Venus to the ASC	31°34′

In the year 1616 in the month of April, I was seized by a great and malign illness, at which time the ASC had come by direction to the sinister square of Saturn with latitude. Saturn itself and the Sun were transiting the radical ASC, and Venus was transiting the [radical] places of Saturn and the Moon.

Oblique ascension of the square of Saturn at Villefranche	48°07′
Oblique ascension of the ASC, to be subtracted	14°36′
Arc of direction	33°31′
Converted time	32°42′

In the year 1621 in the month of October, I made a long journey on horseback and was received by the Duke of Luxembourg,[1] the brother of Constable De Luynes,[2] as Ordinary Physician. And at that time, the Sun had come by direction to the dexter sextile of Mars in the ecliptic; and Jupiter, ruler of the Sun, had come to the Part of Fortune.

Oblique ascension of the sextile of Mars under the pole of the Sun	23°04′
Oblique ascension of the Sun, to be subtracted	345°01′
Arc of direction	38°03′
Converted time	38°05′
Arc of direction of Jupiter to the Part of Fortune	37°55′

---

[1] Léon d'Albert de Luynes, Duke of Luxembourg (d. 1630).

[2] Charles d'Albert, Duke of Luynes (d. 1621).

In the year 1629 in the month of August, I was given the dignity of Regius Professor of Mathematics, and I received it on the 4th day of September. Moreover, this happened from the direction of the MC, significator of professions and dignities, to Mercury, ruler of the 2nd house.

Right ascension of Mercury	330°50′
Right ascension of the MC, to be subtracted	284°36′
Arc of direction	46°14′
Converted time	45°47′

In the year 1634 on the 30th of March, I publicly demonstrated the science of longitudes and published it at the end of the following July.[1] And its approvals by the more famous astronomers of Europe that had been sent to me in 1635 were published by me at the beginning of the year 1636.[2] In truth, by then, the fame of my name had been generally spread throughout the whole of Europe. This, moreover, was signified by the illustrious direction of the MC to the Sun, which did not bring me dignity and notable good fortune, but only celebrity for my name and a secret enmity of great potency.

Right ascension of the Sun	336°14′
Right ascension of the MC, to be subtracted	284°36′
Arc of direction	51°38′
Time of the demonstration	50°22′
Time of the publication of *The Science of Longitudes*	50°42′
Time of approval and fame	51°38′
Time of publishing its approval	52°14′

All these outstanding and notable things were [caused] by that direction of the MC, the significator of actions and undertakings, to the Sun in the 12th house.

In the year 1642 on the 2nd of November, a long and lingering fever happened to me with a stupendous evacuation of bile; [and this was] from the direction of the ASC to Mars in the ecliptic. for in the year 1637, in which the direction of the ASC to Mars with latitude was completed, many violent misfortunes happened to me, also with danger to my life—from the bite of a dog, from a quarrel with my neighbor's absolutely worthless porter, who drunkenly attacked me on account of the dog, [and] from the entrance of soldiers into my own home on the instigation of whores; and in the annual revolution, Mars was in the 6th degree of Aries, square its own radical place, ruler of the 6th house, opposed to Jupiter, ruler of the 7th, in the 5th; moreover, Venus and Saturn, powerful in the 5th, were conjoined in the 8th in square to Mars. All of which was in marvelous agreement.

---

[1] *Longitudinum terrestrium nec son coelestium nova et hactenus optata scientia...* {The New and Hitherto Hoped For Science of Terrestrial as well as Celestial Longitudes...] (Paris: J. Libert, 1634.).

[2] *Lettres escrites au S' Morin par les plus célèbres eistpenomes de France, approuvant son invention des longitudes...* [Letters written to Mr. Morin by the most famous astronomers of Prance, approving his invention of longitudes...} (Paris: The Author, 1635.)

Oblique ascension of Mars at Villefranche	72°44′
Oblique ascension of the ASC	14°36′
Arc of direction	58°08′
Time of the accident on 2 November	58°49′

In the year 1644, I undertook a request in the Royal Council for my remuneration for my invention of the science of longitudes and for the restitution of astronomy.[1] And I had other quarrels with Boulliau[2] and with a neighbor of low condition. Moreover, these [events] were stirred up by the directions of the MC, the significator of actions, to Saturn in the 12th, claiming the right of its exaltation on the cusp of the 7th,[3] which has to do with quarrels; the direction of Mars, ruler of the ASC and the 7th, [and] having the right of its exaltation in the MC, to the opposition of the Sun, which direction spurred my mind on to litigation against the injustice of Cardinal Richelieu; and the direction of Saturn to the square of the Moon in the ecliptic, which instigated my actions against low and plebeian men.

Right ascension of Saturn	344°30′
Right ascension of the MC, to be subtracted	284°36′
Arc of direction	59°54′
Time of the beginning of the annual revolution	60°07′
Arc of direction of Saturn to the square of the Moon	60°03′
Arc of direction of Mars to the opposition of the Sun	60°48′

From which it is not surprising that I was involved in all sorts of quarrels in that year.

In the year 1645 on the 8th of April, I was awarded by the Royal Council a pension of 2,000 livres above an ecclesiastical benefice, with [a lump sum of] 1,000 livres from the Treasury. At that time, three directions were in force that were conformable to this, namely Mars to the opposition of the Sun to the opposition of Jupiter, ruler of the 9th; and Mars was on the cusp of the 2nd and Jupiter was in the ASC of the annual revolution; and finally, the Part of Fortune to the trine of the Moon in the ecliptic.

Arc of direction of Mars to the opposition of the Sun, as above	60°48′
Arc of direction of Mars to the opposition of Jupiter	61°27′
Arc of direction of the Part of Fortune to the sinister trine of the Moon	61°16′
Time of the beginning of the annual revolution	61°07′

Many other notable things happened to me, but especially some bad ones, with [all of] which the directions and revolutions are in marvelous agreement. But that which has been put above is sufficient to

---

[1] This is a reference to Morin's book *Astronomia jam a fundamentis integre et exacts restituta...* [Astronomy, now Restored Wholly and Exactly from its Fundamentals...] (Paris: The Author 1640.)

[2] Ismael Boulliau (1605-1694), French priest and astronomer, was also an ardent amateur astrologer (according to a private communication from Prof. Robert A. Hatch of the University of Florida to the present writer).

[3] He means that Saturn is a sort of co-ruler of the 7th because Libra, Saturn's sign of exaltation, is on the cusp of the 7th.

prove how powerfully the stars future events to men, and how difficult it is to avoid them, except by renouncing and [their own inclinations] absolutely. For the more someone is bound by many ties to the world, the more closely he is subject to the 7 planets, the governors of the world.

And now we have come to the revolutions of the Blessed Father Charles de Condren. He, therefore, in the 21st year of his age, which began in the month of December 1608, decided to lead a religious life. At which time, two directions were in force for about a year, namely Jupiter, the ruler of the ASC in the 9th, to Mars in the 10th; and the MC to the sextile of the Sun, ruler of the ninth; and then a very notable direction of the ASC, the principal significator of inclinations, to the Sun, ruler of the 9th in the 1st.

Oblique ascension of the Sun under the pole of the nativity	293°58′
Oblique ascension of the ASC, to be subtracted	274°00′
Arc of direction	19°58′
Time of the beginning of the 21st revolution	19°43′
Arc of direction of the MC to the dexter sextile of the Sun	18°47′
Arc of direction of Jupiter to Mars	18°47′

After having completed his 24th year, from the reading of Rusbroch and Thauler[1] on the whole and perfect [life] (as he himself told me), he had decided to resign himself to God, [and] he was initiated into the orders of the sub-deaconate and [then] the deaconate. With this devotion being naturally excited (God forbid, that we should deny the *supernatural* motion from God) by the direction of the Sun, ruler of the 9th in the 1st, to the sinister trine of Jupiter, ruler of the ASC in the 9th, a direction that was very potent for such an effect.

Oblique ascension of the sinister trine of Jupiter under the pole of the Sun with latitude	315°22′
Oblique ascension of the Sun	292°02′
Arc of direction	23°20′
Time of completion of the 24th revolution	23°39′

In his 26th year, i.e. on the 17th of September 1614, he was made a priest, which, although it could be a continuation of the effects of the direction of the Sun to the trine of Jupiter, nevertheless, at the beginning of his 26th year, Mercury, ruler of the 9th, and Jupiter in the 9th arrived by direction at the antiscion of the Part of Fortune, whose ruler, Mars, is in the house of professions and dignities.

Oblique ascension of the antiscion of the Part of Fortune under the pole of Mercury	335°22′
Oblique ascension of Mercury, to be subtracted	311°04′

---

[1] I suppose the reference is to the two Christian mystics, Jan van Ruysbroeck (1294-1381) and Johannes Tauter (c. 1300-1361), the latter of whom was the author of a book of sermons (printed 1498, 1522, and 1543). Van Ruysbroeck's writings were undoubtedly also available.

Arc of direction	24°20′ [sic!]
Time of the beginning of the 26th year	24°38′

In his 29th year, the Blessed Father devoted himself to the Congregation of Oratory of Jesus, and this was caused by the direction of Mars, ruler of the Part of Fortune, in the 10th to Venus, ruler of the MC; with Mars and Venus in mutual reception by domicile, and Venus conjunct the Part of Fortune.

Oblique ascension of Venus under the pole of Mars	217°46′
Oblique ascension of Mars	190°10′
Arc of direction	27°36′
Time of the beginning of his 29th year	27°36′

When his 41st year was almost completed, i.e. in November 1629, he was elected General of his order, namely of the Congregations of Oratory of Jesus in France, following the demise of the most eminent Cardinal Bérulle in the month of October. And at that time the MC by direction had come to the sinister sextile of Jupiter, ruler of the ASC, in the 9th house, Jupiter to Venus, ruler of the MC, in the ecliptic, and the ASC to Mercury in the ecliptic, the ruler of Jupiter and the 9th.

Right ascension of the sextile of Jupiter in the ecliptic	224°54′
Right ascension of the MC, to be subtracted	184°00′
Arc of direction	40°54′
Time of the election	40°20′
Arc of direction of the MC to the sextile of Jupiter with latitude	41°09′
Arc of direction of Jupiter to Venus in the ecliptic	41°07′
Arc of direction of the ASC to Mercury in the ecliptic	40°45′

Finally, in the beginning of his 53rd year, the holy man died of a fever. This accident was in fact made with the revolution of the Sun, a direction of the Sun, ruler of the 8th, in the 1st; consequently, the apheta and at the same time the anaereta, to the sinister square of the Moon, ruler of the 8th, in its fall in the 12th, and consequently a very pernicious significator or illnesses and death. I also predicted the day of his death.

Oblique ascension of the Moon's square in the ecliptic and under the pole of the Sun, 47°30′	343°55′
Oblique ascension of the Sun	292°02′
Arc of direction	51°53′
Time of death	51°17′
Arc of direction of the Sun to the square of the Moon with latitude	50°53′

I could confirm the doctrine set forth above with many other examples, if I were not deterred by the tedium of the calculation; and anyone who wants to can test its verity with other examples. Incidentally, however, the reader should be warned that in the foregoing calculations an error of several minutes can be found, either in the altitude of the pole above the circles of position or in the ascensions; [and] because the tables of the planets, even the Rudolphine Tables that I follow, are not yet accurate, I have not attempted to obtain the greatest precision in all of the [examples] on account of the tedium of the calculations; but the error cannot exceed a half degree, which is sufficient to prove the doctrine. Perhaps, with more accurate tables, everything would agree more accurately, or even with calculations carried to greater precision.

You will object. In the abovesaid directions, we have sometimes used the time of the end of a revolution, but at other times the beginning, during which revolution some accident occurred. But that is contrary to [the usual procedure for] the rectification of the true time of nativities, which assumes an arc of direction equal to the converted time of the accident, so that the direction would indicate not only the year of the accident but also the day. And this is logical, because a direction can indicate not just the year but also the part of it.

I reply. A direction per se does of course indicate the year and the part of the year or the day; but because it does not operate without conformable revolutions and transits, its effect is advanced or retarded by these. And this does not obstruct the rectification of the time of the geniture, for no geniture can be rectified by means of one direction that would indicate the day of a single accident, but many are required. And the precise times indicated by directions are adjusted to the true time of the nativity, so that they will deviate from it by no more nor less than an equal amount, but among these [directions] that [time] is as it were in the middle; which is an important secret that should not be spurned.

Chapter XIV.

In What Way Revolutions Act; and What Must be Noted both Generally and in Particular about the Times of Their Actions

The celestial constitutions of revolutions in a way that makes a new impression on the native through its likeness to the radical figure or directions, by means of which the potential force of the radical figure itself or its directions is reduced to an action—if not a final and particular one (which coincides especially with the transits of the planets through the conformable place of the geniture), at least a middling and special one. And the native himself is actively or passively excited, moved, and disposed very closely to conformable effects of a predicted similarity in that year. Moreover, this is proved from the fact that since the radical figure and the directions are only something potential with respect to the native's future accidents, this potential cause will be ineffective and vain if something actual corresponding to it is lacking, by which it can be reduced to an action; something that renders the native closely receptive to each of those influxes; moreover, revolutions are that actual cause. Moreover, I have said that the native is receptive to the influx, because seven things are found, among others, that prevent the native's being susceptible to the influxes of the stars, namely death, illness, imprisonment, confinement, exile, travel, [and] servitude; of which, with one of them in existence at the time of a presignified event, and with the two of them incompatible, such as imprisonment with presignified travel, travel will be prevented, at least freedom to travel, unless his release from prison occurs. And we do not think that free will ought to be taken into account here, which in unrestricted effects, as we have said elsewhere, can break and ward off even the most powerful influxes of the stars.

Therefore, absent the just mentioned impediments or a strongly signified release from them, a revolution, through its close disposition to the native, reduces into actuality whatever the radical figure by reason of its signification has in common through similarity with that revolution; only the time of the effect presignified in the radical figure falls in the year of that revolution or thereabouts, which calculation of the directions makes known. Wherefore, having erected the figure of the revolution, attention must be given to which directions fall into the year of that revolution, especially those that are recent or current, which are allotted their own effects. For to those that will be similar to the revolution, i.e. that have signified similar things, they will produce their own effects, provided that the radical figure is in agreement; that is, provided that it does not signify long life or celibacy when the revolution and the direction presages death or marriage, for then in place of death, only illness, and in place of marriage, useless suits or fruitless love affairs will be signified by the direction and the revolution. Just as happened to me from a direction of the MC to Venus, ruler of the 7th, which only caused preparations for matrimony that were in vain, because Venus combust in the 12th with Saturn presaged celibacy for me; which state was at least the cause sine qua non; I, [therefore], devoted myself contentedly to the reformation of the celestial sciences, for such a task demanded [the attention of] the whole man.

But from this [consideration], the reason can be deduced why all years, even for a man confined or incarcerated, are dissimilar in their events. For this results from the fact that all the revolutions are dissimilar among themselves, as are the directions of the 7 planets and the 12 cusps of the geniture in individual years; whence it happens that on account of the abovesaid similarity of signification, the revolution of this year may actuate this thing of those presignified in the geniture, and the revolution of the next year something else; and so, consequently, by reason of the [then current] status or disposition of the native.

Furthermore, this similarity of signification can happen in a five-fold manner. First, that in both the figure of the geniture and that of the revolution, the *caelum* and the planets are all arranged in the same manner; and this to be sure is the greatest similarity that is possible, but one that rarely occurs. Second, that the *caelum* is indeed arranged in the same manner, but the planets are not, or on the contrary, the planets are [so arranged], but the *caelum* is not. Third, that many planets are returned to their own radical places. Fourth, that with the places of the planets transposed in the revolution, they do at least come to the places in the geniture, they do at least come to the places of the geniture, by reason of which they signify the same things as the geniture or the directions. Fifth, that having made a judgment from the revolution and the geniture, with regard to the celestial and terrestrial state of the planets, the same particular effect is signified by each figure, or the same one by a direction and the revolution; but from the preceding, the dissimilarities of the revolutions are sufficiently indicated.

With regard to the times of the effects, the following should always be noted. First, what are the natures of the planets that are the significator and the promissor. Planets indeed of a slow nature [are] Mars, Jupiter, and Saturn; both in the radix and in a revolution they will give their effects more slowly; the swifter planets, such as the Moon and Mercury, more quickly; that is, the latter anticipate, but the former retard the true time of effects; but the moderate planets, such as the Sun and Venus, have a middle mode [of action]. This, moreover, should be understood to be when other things are equal, and with other causes absent that might accelerate the effects of the slow ones, or retard those of the faster ones. Second, what is the manner or quality of motion of the planets? For increasing in their course and direct, they accelerate the end of their effects; but diminishing in their course and retrograde, they will finish slowly what they began quickly; [while] the one that is increased in motion and direct quickly perfect what it began quickly. But the superior [planets] increased in motion and direct will quickly perfect what they began slowly; and those diminished in their motion and retrograde will slowly perfect what they began slowly. Third, what is the position of the planet with respect to the Sun; for [the planet] oriental to the Sun gives its effects more quickly, the [planet that is] occidental more slowly. Fourth, what is the planet's placement in the figure. For in the angles, especially in the 1st and 10th houses, more quickly; in cadent houses, more slowly; and in succedent [houses] they operate in a middle manner. And these things should be taken into consideration both in nativities and in revolutions; for if the planet that is being directed was, both in the nativity and in the revolution, increased [in its motion], direct, oriental, and angular, and the same thing is true of the promissor, the velocity of the effect will then be strongly signified; but slowness or hindrances if they are in the contrary mode; and in a mixed mode, the thing will be done in accordance with [the condition] of the most powerful [planet].

As for the indications of particular times, these are designated first and per se by the directions that agree with the radix; these designate the years of the effects. Second, from the revolutions of the Sun, which indeed do not indicate the years of the effects per se and by their own virtue, but [rather] through their own similarity to the direction and the radical figure. Third, from the revolutions of the Moon, to the extent also that they agree with the revolution of the Sun, the radical direction, and the radix, by reason of their similarity. For these are so subordinated in acting, that nothing that occurs later can act contrary to prior or superior [indications]. That is, a lunar revolution can [accomplish] nothing contrary to the revolution of the Sun; and the latter [can accomplish] nothing contrary to the radical direction; and the direction [can accomplish] nothing contrary to the figure of the geniture; for posterior [indicators] only assume their force of acting from the similarity of their signification to the prior [indicators]. Consequently, Cardan says rightly, in his *Book on Revolutions*, Chapter 8, "The consideration of the month is more difficult than that of the year." Indeed, because in defining the month of an accident, not only the figure of the month, also those of the year and the nativity must be considered; and so it is impossible to know the *month* of an accident better than the year. Moreover, this is proved from the fact that radical directions sometimes retard their own effects by one or two years, due to the lack of a conformable revolution of the Sun, which extent of time cannot be said to happen in the case of revolutions of the Moon; also, several of them are in agreement with the radical direction. but they do not act [due to] the direction alone, even when the radical figure is in agreement, which certainly is an indication that these [lunar revolutions] alone are not sufficient to actuate the potential of a radical direction; consequently, they are subordinate in acting to the revolutions of the Sun.

Moreover, even if some particular revolution of the Moon is able to actuate something [signified] by the radix and the revolution of the Sun, by reason of its similarity [to them], nevertheless, any important effect signified by a radical direction, to which the revolution of the Sun is favorable, will burst out from a revolution of the Moon that will signify that effect more strongly, unless more conformable and efficacious transits fall into [the time of] a weaker revolution of the Moon, which precedes the stronger one; and if the revolution of the Sun signified [the effect] more weakly, it will be necessary for its force to be supplemented by the revolution of the Moon; that is to say, something signified weakly by the revolution of the Sun can be made effective by a stronger revolution of the Moon.

And with these [considerations] the subject of the action of the stars, as of that of a man, must be taken in hand, namely whether and to what extent it either corresponds to their proper and accidental dispositions, or it struggles against the action of the celestial bodies. And the judgment of the wise astrologer ought to be concerned with all of this.

Chapter XV.

Whether Their Own Directions Should be Assigned to Revolutions of the Sun and the Moon, and in What Way and the Measure of Time

The directions of the geniture, which I call *radical* directions, [are formed] in the same manner; and they have the same, common measure [of time] for all of the significators, i.e. for the cusps and all of the planets, as is proved in defining the years of their effects, namely the mean diurnal [motion] in right ascension of the Sun,[1] which is 59′08″, which equals one year in the radical directions of individual significators, as was stated in Book 22, Section 3, Chapter 5. But in addition to these radical directions, it might be asked, whether revolutions also have their own proper directions, by means of which the days destined [to experience certain] effects might be discovered; and what is the measure of time for them?

Cardan, in his *Book on Revolutions*, Chapter 13, says: "Many principal parts are directed in annual revolutions by giving to the individual degrees one day or a little more. And although this may seem to rest upon reason, on account of the Sun's motion; nevertheless, this thing may not agree with experience." And yet, this method is recommended by Alchabitius and many others. And this is its principle: the year of 365 days and 6 hours is divided by 360 degrees of the equator, and 1 day 0 hours and 11 minutes [of time] correspond to 1 degree, which can be doubled for 2 degrees, tripled for 3 degrees, etc., in the Table of Annual Directions placed below, the use of which, according to those astrologers, [is] that the distance from the significator to the promissor in the revolution should be taken in the ecliptic without regard to latitude or circle of position, or ascensions; and that distance is sought in the table of degrees placed below; for the days are put on the right, numbered from the beginning of the revolution with the hours and minutes in adjoining [columns], [and] they will be the precise time of a future accident [resulting] from such a direction. As, for example, if the distance was 80 degrees, there are had to their right 81 days 4 hours and 0 minutes for the corresponding accurate time counted from the beginning of the revolution. But if there are minutes added to the degrees, the second table for minutes must be used. We have, therefore, put these tables [below] with the converse of the first.

And the days from the beginning of the revolution up to the day when some accident happens are numbered vice versa; and the number of degrees corresponding in the table to the number of days is added to the ASC, or to the MC, or to the degree of any other significator, and that will show the place in the ecliptic to which the significator in the annual revolution will come on that day.

---

[1] Modern astronomers would say that it is the Sun's mean motion in *longitude*. This is the measure of time mentioned by Valentin Naibod (1527-1593), which is usually called "Naibod's Measure."

[in the Latin headings of the tables, Grad. = Degrees, Dies = Days, and Minuta = Minutes]

Tables of Directions for Revolutions of the Sun.

First   *Second or Converse*   *Third or Minutes of Degrees*

Grad.	Dies	Ho.	Mi.	Dies	Grad.	Mi.
1	1	0	22	1	0	59
2	2	0	42	2	1	58
3	3	1	3	3	2	58
4	4	1	24	4	3	57
5	5	1	45	5	4	56
6	6	2	6	6	5	55
7	7	2	27	7	6	54
8	8	2	48	8	7	53
9	9	3	9	9	8	53
10	10	3	30	10	9	51
20	20	7	0	20	19	43
30	30	10	30	30	29	35
40	40	14	0	40	39	27
50	50	17	30	50	49	18
60	60	21	0	60	59	11
70	71	0	30	70	69	2
80	81	4	0	80	78	54
90	91	7	30	90	88	46
100	101	11	0	100	98	37
200	202	22	0	200	197	17
300	304	9	0	300	295	53
360	365	6	0	365	360	0

Minuta Gr.	Dies	Hora	Minuta
1	0	0	24
2	0	0	49
3	0	1	13
4	0	1	37
5	0	2	2
6	0	2	26
7	0	2	50
8	0	3	15
9	0	3	39
10	0	4	4
20	0	8	7
30	0	12	11
40	0	16	14
50	0	20	18
60	1	0	21

Besides, those who approve of this kind of direction have demonstrated more laziness than expertise. For it is not surprising that I have sometimes found it to be false, just as Cardan has. For if radical directions by equal degrees are false, and they are only true when they are [made] by right ascensions or oblique ascensions in circles of position, not having neglected the latitude of the planets and their aspects, why should not the same thing be said [to be true] of the directions of revolutions, since the stars act uniformly, and the ways of [making] predictions ought to be natural, and not fictitious, which is what that method of equal degrees is?

And so, Cardan, in his *Book on Revolutions*, Chapter 13, [speaking of] finding the days of the effects during the annual revolution, has devised another form of directions with the aid of the three tables shown below. "The Moon," he says, "returns to the conjunction of the Sun in 29 days 12 hours and 46 minutes according to Ptolemy; therefore, in that period of time it is elongated from the Sun by 12 degrees 11 minutes and 26 seconds per day [until] it makes one revolution of the firmament.[1] Therefore, the force of the whole circle that the Moon traverses in elongating itself from the Sun in 29 days 12 hours and 46 minutes is [in each space of] 12 degrees 11 minutes and 26 seconds. Therefore, just as the

---

[1] Actually, Ptolemy, *Syntaxis iv. 3,* has 29:31,50,08,20 days or 29 days 12 hours 44 minutes 3 seconds. Dividing this into 360° gives 12; 11,26,41,20... degrees for the Moon's daily elongation from the Sun.

whole circle of the Sun is given to each degree of the Sun (i.e., to its mean daily motion), so will we give a circuit of the Moon in 29 days 12 hours and 46 minutes to each "degree" of the Moon (i.e., the mean daily elongation of the Moon from the Sun); and in accordance with this [rule], we have made this table."

Tabula directionum secundum Lunam. Ex Cardano.

Grad.	Dies	Ho.	Mi.
1	2	10	8
2	4	20	16
3	7	6	24
4	9	16	32
5	12	2	40
6	14	12	48
7	16	22	56
8	19	9	4
9	21	19	12
10	24	5	20
20	48	10	40
30	72	16	0
40	96	21	20
50	121	2	40
60	145	8	0
70	169	13	20
80	193	18	40
90	218	0	0
100	242	5	20
200	484	10	40
300	726	15	0

Tabula Mensium ac Dierum Anni.

Menses	Communes Dies	Bissextiles Dies	
Januarius	31	31	31
Februarius	59	60	28
Martius	90	91	31
Aprilis	120	121	30
Majus	151	152	31
Junius	181	182	30
Julius	212	213	31
Augustus	243	244	31
September	273	274	30
October	304	305	31
Novemb.	334	335	30
December	365	366	31

Table of Lunar Directions from Cardan   **Table of Months and Days of the Year**

Moreover, in making this table the synodic lunar month, i.e. 29 days 12 hours 46 minutes, reduced into minutes and seconds of the day, which are 106315 seconds,[1] is divided by the daily elongation of the Moon from the Sun, which is 12 degrees 11 minutes 16 seconds. And so 2 days 25 minutes 21 seconds, i.e. 2 days 10 hours 8 minutes, is given to 1 degree, twice that to 2 degrees, thrice that to 3 degrees, and so on.

---

[1] This number results from converting 29 days 12 hours 46 minutes into $29°31'55''$ and then converting that into seconds of arc. The 2 days 25 minutes 21 seconds are actually 2:25,21 days in sezgesimal notation, which is equivalent to 2 days 10 hours 8 minutes and 24 seconds. There are some small errors to the calculations.

And so he uses that table of directions in [connection with] revolutions of the Sun. First, he takes for example the significator of life in the figure of a revolution, namely the ASC, the Sun, and the Moon. Second, he finds the anaereta or the terminator of life in the nativity or in the revolution of the Sun, and, in the usual manner of Regiomontanus, he directs the significator of life to the anaereta by ascensions of the circle of position of the apheta, and, having found the arc of direction, he looks for that [number] in the first column of the *Table of Directions for the Moon* shown above, through many ingresses if it was needed; and on the right are the [corresponding] days, hours, and minutes, in which number [of days] from the beginning of the revolution of the Sun, the effect will occur on that day on which the counting leaves off. And if to that time is added the time elapsed from the beginning of January, which can be taken from the *Table of Months and Days of the Year* also shown above, he will have the time of the accident counted from the beginning of January.

Moreover, so that Cardan can be made more certain of that effect and day, he considers another table of the synodic months of the Moon, which he calls the *Table of the Elongation of the Moon from the Sun*; and he looks to see whether or not the time of the accident counted from the beginning of the revolution of the Sun is the same in the number of days as the time of any of those months put in the table. And in either case he adds the nearest lesser time shown in the table to the time of the accident counted from the beginning of the revolution, and he looks through the table of months placed above to find into which day, hour, and minute from the beginning of January that time falls; at which time, he erects a figure of the revolution of the month for the "distance of the Moon" (as he calls), [and] according as that figure is related to the [figure of] the revolution of the Sun, and the transits of the Moon are made to the places of that figure, on the day of the accident found [by the above procedure], it indicates whether or not the accident will take place on that same day. Cardan, moreover, says that this method is more certain and valid for the [native's] life, and he tries to confirm it with examples, which to discuss and refute would be too tedious. But we shall add his table of the elongation of the Moon.

Table of the Elongation of the Moon From the Sun

Menses	Dies	Ho	Mi
1	29	12	46
2	59	1	32
3	88	14	18
4	118	3	4
5	147	15	50
6	177	4	36
7	206	17	22
8	236	6	8
9	265	18	54
10	295	7	40
11	324	20	26
12	354	9	12
13	383	21	58

Besides, we have rejected Cardan's method for three reasons. The first is, that when he says that just as for each part of the [motion of the] Sun, i.e. the daily motion of the Sun, the whole circle is given, i.e. the whole period of the Sun or one year, for directions of the nativity; so, for each part of the [motion of the] Moon, i.e. for its mean daily elongation from the Sun, or 12 degrees 11 minutes 26 seconds, we shall give 29 days 12 hours 46 minutes, [i.e.] the circuit or synodic period of the Moon, he confuses the measures of the directions of the geniture, then of the revolutions of the Sun and the Moon, if in fact the daily [motion] of the Moon is only applied to the month and its parts, [but] not to the year and its parts. But Cardan uses the daily synodic motion of the Moon for his measure of the arc of direction in the annual revolutions or those of the Sun.

Second. Because by dividing the whole circle by the mean daily synodic [motion] of the Moon, [the length of] the synodic month itself is obtained, or 29 days 12 hours 46 minutes. But by dividing the month itself by that daily [motion], as Cardan does to construct his table, a [period of] time is obtained that corresponds to each degree, put next to it in the table, supposing that in the month itself only 12 degrees 11 minutes 26 seconds are traversed; but this hypothesis is false; therefore, what truth could Cardan deduce from it?

Third. By that table of directions that he applies to the annual revolutions of the Sun, a significator can only complete the circle in 872 days, and not in an annual revolution, which will be exposed below as an absurdity. Therefore, this method of Cardan should be dismissed.[1]

But, so that we may discuss and resolve the question of this chapter, [which is] certainly of the greatest importance, it should be noted that the figure of the nativity indicates the state of the entire life of the native from birth itself up to death; the figure of a revolution of the Sun indicates the native's annual state; and the periodic figure of a revolution of the Moon indicates the native's monthly state. Moreover, in each revolution the *caelum* is determined with respect to the native, not only in actuality by reason of a new disposition, which the *caelum* itself then imprints upon the native, but also in potential by reason of his future actions during that [revolution], just as in the nativity. For the whole force of the annual revolution of the Sun is not allotted its effect on the very day of the revolution, but with the succession of time during the year. So with the monthly revolution of the Moon for the month. Therefore, that potential that is in these must be reduced to actuality, either by directions of the revolution, or by transits of the planets over conformable places of the geniture and of the revolutions of the Sun and the Moon, or through both of these [occurring] at the same time. And, as a matter of fact, if the accident arriving on a certain day is supposed to be [indicated] by the stars, [then] there ought to be some actual celestial causes that would have produced it on that very day; and these should be more or less notable according as the accident itself was more or less notable. Here indeed, he should have been mindful of those things that were said at the end of the last chapter of Section 3, Book 22, about the potential and actual virtue of the celestial causes [arranged] in the order of the subordination by anteceding [causes].

But now, as for that which pertains to directions: in the first place. This should be held for certain, that if they are to be admitted into revolutions, a significator must in each revolution, either of the Sun

---

[1] From the fact that Morin has cited Cardan's method at some length, even including his tables of directions, we may assume that Cardan's method was being used by astrologers in Morin's time. Morin dismisses it on theoretical grounds, but whether he ever experimented with it to determine whether or not it is valid is uncertain. In any event. Cardan was too prominent an astrological authority to ignore. But it is perhaps worth noting that Morin (in another place) also dismissed the methods of his younger contemporary Placidus on theoretical grounds.

or of the Moon, traverse the whole zodiac by directions, and thus to be annually and monthly revolved by directions, which is against [the opinion of] Cardan in Aphorism 84 of Segment 1 [of his *Seven Segments of Astronomical Aphorisms*].[1] And this is right, because since many revolution succeed each other [in turn], their directions should be confounded as little as possible, but [instead] each revolution should be explained and activated by its own revolutions, not indeed by those of another revolution. Moreover, this cannot be done in any other way than if in the annual revolutions of the Sun the mean daily motion of the Sun is made the measure of each day of that year; and in the periodical monthly revolution of the Moon its mean daily periodical [motion] is made the measure of each day of the month for the individual significators. And the same thing should be judged [to be appropriate] for the periodical revolutions of Saturn, Jupiter, Mars, Venus, and Mercury. Moreover, the directions of the nativity are not bound to a circle that is exactly completed, since the life of the native, which was once more extensive, but is now less than the time in which a significator could be thought to run through the whole zodiac in radical directions, in which the mean daily [motion] of the Sun is the measure of one year.[2] And so, for directions of the revolutions of the Sun, we shall employ placed first in this chapter; but for the revolutions of the Moon, we shall use those that are shown below, not to be sure [using] equal degrees as the old [astrologers] did, but [rather] this mode for revolutions of the Sun.

Direct any significator to whatever promissor by the method of Regiomontanus, explained by us in connection with the directions of the natal figure; and, having found the arc of direction, look for it by multiple entry[3] if need be in the first table of directions for revolutions of the Sun; for on the right [of the degree number] are the [corresponding] days, numbered from the beginning of the revolution of the Sun, so that it may be known on which day of the year that direction may be completed. Vice versa, the days may be counted from the beginning of the revolution up to the day in which any particular accident happens; and the number of degrees corresponding to the number of days in the table is added to the right ascension or the oblique ascension of the significator. Finally, the sum [of these figures] is looked up in the table of right or oblique ascensions for the altitude of the pole above the circle of position of the significator. And the place in the ecliptic to which the significator has come on that day in the annual revolution will be known. Furthermore, the monthly directions for the revolutions of the Moon should be made in the same manner from the tables of directions; and examples of both will be furnished in the next chapter.

And you will note that the directions of revolutions are just as real as the directions of the geniture and that these are twofold, namely natural and artificial, just as we have stated in Book 22, Section 1, Chapter 1, so also these. And the actuality of natural things consists of the motion of the *primum mobile*, on the day of the nativity or of the revolution which is actual, and from which they have their own rising, as was stated in that same place. Furthermore, you will note that unless the revolutions of the Sun and the Moon are erected for the place in which the native is found at the beginning of the revolution, there will generally be an serious error in specifying the days [of occurrence] of the accidents by means

---

[1] Segment 1, Aphorism 84 says "The revolutions of the Moon do act complete an entire circle in one year, but neither do the degrees of the zodiacal circle go through the whole circle during the life of a man," This is followed by three abbreviated tables similar to those cited by Morin.

[2] This is a reference to the extended life spans of some of Biblical patriarchs, during which the natal charts would have completed one or more complete revolutions of the zodiac.

[3] He means that if you need to find the equivalent for, say 169 degrees, you need to take out the figures for 9 degrees, 60 degrees, and 100 degrees and add them together.

of the directions, especially the annual directions; because the ascendants of the revolutions [erected] in the place of the nativity and the place of the revolution may differ among themselves by many degrees.

Prima.

Grad.	Di.	Ho.	Mi.	S.
1	0	1	49	10
2	0	3	38	20
3	0	5	27	30
4	0	7	16	40
5	0	9	6	50
6	0	10	55	0
7	0	12	44	10
8	0	14	33	20
9	0	16	22	30
10	0	18	13	0
20	1	12	26	0
30	2	6	39	0
40	3	0	52	0
50	3	19	5	0
60	4	13	18	0
70	5	7	31	0
80	6	1	44	0
90	6	19	57	0
100	7	14	10	0
200	15	4	20	0
300	22	18	30	0
360	27	7	48	0

Secunda vel conversa.

Di.	Grad.	Mi.	Sec.
1	13	10	55
2	26	21	50
3	39	31	45
4	52	42	20
5	65	52	55
6	79	3	30
7	92	14	5
8	105	24	40
9	118	35	15
10	131	45	50
20	263	31	40

Tertia pro Hora.

Ho.	Grad.	Mi.	Sec.
1	0	32	56
2	1	5	55
3	1	38	49
4	2	11	46
5	2	44	42
6	3	17	39
7	3	50	35
8	4	23	32
9	4	56	28
10	5	29	25
11	6	2	21
12	6	35	18

First *Second or Converse*
Third for the Hour

Moreover, the use of the first table [above] is that the arc of direction is looked up in the column of degrees, with multiple entries if this is required. And to the right the time from the beginning of the revolution of the Moon will be shown. The method is the same for the second and third table for the days and hours. Furthermore, the same thing should be judged [to be appropriate] for the directions of revolutions as was said [to be appropriate] for radical directions at the end of Chapter 12. Certainly because they are something that is potential, needing a cause that is purely actual, by which they may be reduced to actuality; which causes are conformable transits of the planets. For even though the directions of the revolutions may indicate the day of an effect by [a consideration of] the proportion of the daily [motion] of the Sun or the Moon to the whole circle for a year or a month (since the radical directions are supposed to indicate not only the year but also [by proportion] the day of an accident in the rectification of nativities), still, in the case of radical directions, the year of the accident may be retarded if there is no conformable revolution of the Sun; and even if there is, the day indicated by that direction may be retarded or accelerated if there is no conformable transit of the planets, but [in this case only] a little later or a little earlier; and the same thing must be said about the directions of the revolutions of the sun and the Moon.

Two things can be objected to here. First, that if the annual directions in a revolution of the Sun do indicate the day of an accident, then the revolutions of the Moon and all the more the monthly directions will be superfluous to that; consequently both the latter and the former are useless.

But I reply. The same thing can be said about the radical directions that indicate the day of their own effect, if they do not produce [that effect] without a conformable revolution and conformable transits, as [indeed] experience confirms. Similarly, therefore, an annual direction that is conformable in signification to a radical one, even though it may indicate the day of the year on which that accident will be produced, yet that day needs to be confirmed, either by a conformable monthly revolution and its directions, or by conformable transits, or by both. And yet it is not necessary for the production of the effect that annual and monthly revolutions concur and the directions and transits of these, since not even that can be done except rarely; but it suffices if the principal factors concur, and especially the radical direction, the annual revolution, and transits that agree at the same time. For experience proves that this concurrence is very efficacious, especially if a conformable annual direction accompanies them. Moreover, since the periodic revolutions of the Moon are perceived to be of no small virtue, it can be said by anyone that a revolution of the Sun conformable to a radical direction only indicates the year of the accident, [while a lunar] revolution in that year that is more conformable indicates the month, and conformable transits the day, without any directions of the revolutions. But those directions of the revolution, both annual and monthly, are also of exceptional virtue, as will appear from the examples below. Therefore, they should be utilised in judgment, and finally the transits of the planets through the appropriate places of the figures. Still, it should be noted that the most conformable revolution of the Moon during the whole year with the most conformable transits is not necessary, but it suffices that at least the two prior causes are in agreement, especially when the subject is already disposed to the effect, as a decrepit man to a lethal illness.

It may be objected secondly. That if the radical directions should point to the day of the effect, [and also] the figures of the revolutions, and their directions, and the transits of the planets to the places of three figures, namely of the radix and the revolutions of the Sun and the Moon, which are numerous in the individual figures, then certainly no accident will happen on the day of which many causes do not occur that are not credibly powerful to produce such an effect, and perhaps [even] more to obstruct it. Indeed, stronger causes of an accident very often occur on those days on which it does not take place, which certainly argues that this science is of no small uselessness.

I reply first. In general predictions of [the native's] life, few things should be noted, and the general ones from the radical figure alone. In predictions of [the events of individual] years, more; namely, because an annual prediction is made from a revolution of the Sun, but it only signifies these things through its relationship with the figure of the geniture; consequently, both of them must be taken jointly and compared to [make] an annual prediction. But in monthly and daily predictions, more things must be looked at, both the general [indications] from the figure of the nativity and the figures of the revolutions, and the particular [indications] from the directions and transits, which depend upon those prior causes. For, just as for ascending towards general and universal things, understanding becomes simpler, so, descending towards particulars and individual things is more complex, namely because the later figures [only] speak in accordance with the earlier ones, by reason of the place of the planets, not contrary [to them]. Hence, the reason is plain why it is more difficult to know the day of an accident [than it is to know] the month, and more difficult to know the month than the year, since indeed the knowledge of the day presupposes the knowledge of the month, and that presupposes the knowledge of the year.

I reply secondly. If the laws of prediction that have been given so far are observed, the inconvenience that is object to will not occur. That is, if the concurrent causes are not chosen carelessly, but only those conformable to the effect signified by the radical direction. For such are few, and a sufficient concourse of them is not [so] frequent that it may fall on individual days or even months, from which the worthlessness of the previous objection is revealed.

Finally, it should be noted that both the directions of the nativity and those of the revolutions are most powerful to indicate the time of the beginning of or the preparation for the effects. But the transits are most powerful to determine at what time an effect, such as marriage, receipt of dignity, illness, death, and such like, will burst forth. But since as transits conformable to the effects are likely to be present on many days, [and even] if they were absent, effects are also occasionally caused by conformable conjunctions of the planets; and, even though those seen in the *caelum* are operating universally throughout the whole world, nevertheless because they are acting in accordance with the dispositions of their individual positions and with relation to their own situation with respect to the horizon, for that reason a position disposed with a conformable revolution can occasionally be affected by conjunctions, namely with the inciting disposition of a position, in the absence of conformable transits.[1] But when the effect is sudden, such as when someone falls down or is drowned or is killed by robbers, then either a direction and a transit agree on the day of the accident, or the direction only gives a general indication of the year or the month, but a transit indicates the very day. And here also, take careful notice of the annual and monthly directions, because it is from the celestial state both of the significator or its ruler and of the promissor, at the time when their direction is completed, that you can judge more certainly about that.

Chapter XVI.

In Which the Verity of Revolutionary Directions is Proved by Many Examples in Revolutions of the Sun and the Moon.

After the above chapter, we have admitted directions in the revolutions of the Sun and the Moon, made through right ascensions or oblique ascensions, like radical directions; and we have set forth tables for measuring the arc of direction, so that since the force and certitude of these is proved by experiences to be detected at the particular times of their effects, some examples seem to be appropriate here. Warning that the significators of these directions are always either the ASC or the MC or the place of

---

[1] Here, I have translated the Latin word *passum*, which means 'step', 'pace', or 'track', as 'position'. Morin seems to be saying that if two planets that are significators in the nativity or in the current revolution come into conjunction, they may occasionally indicate the time of an effect.

some planet in the figure of the revolution whose directions are being made; but especially those of the Sun and the Moon; but the promittors are the places either of that revolution or of another preceding figure; but more frequently, those of the nativity and of the revolution itself.

Besides, it must be noted that if in a radical direction the year of the effect it signifies is retarded or accelerated, on account of a necessary concourse of a revolution of the Sun, which is not always present at the precise time of a radical direction. And, with a given concourse of both causes in the same year, the day of the effect is retarded or accelerated, on account of the necessary concourse of either a compatible transit or some other concurrent celestial cause; the same thing should certainly be judged to be the case in revolutionary directions, which are not different from radical directions other than in their potential; moreover, we speak of another concurrent celestial cause, because compatible transits of the planets through the places of the radical or revolutionary figures do not always occur on the days of the effects or significant changes; even though this does rarely happen on rare occasions. For which reason, in the effects that are from the stars, it is necessary that other concurrent celestial causes be given, which are able to reduce [the indications] of figures and directions of the nativity and of revolutions from a potential to an actual [state]. Moreover, these are compatible transits of the planets through the places of directions, especially those of the nativity at the day or particular time of the accident; and the most powerful are the conjunctions of the planets in those same places (as happened to me on 30 May 1612, from the conjunction of the luminaries with a notable solar eclipse on the degree of the direction of the radical ASC); then too, other mutual conjunctions of planets that are mutually compatible, but especially [if they are] in compatible houses. As for example if there was both a direction and a revolution compatible for death, and the ruler of the ASC is conjoined in the 1st or the 8th with the ruler of the 12th or the 8th, especially if it is a malefic, or they are opposed[1] from the 2nd and the 8th (as happened at the beginning of the illness from which the most noble Mr. Tronson died) or squared from the 12th or 8th of the radix; then they will be able to bring death, or a [severe] illness, or some danger to life, on account of the cause set forth at the end of Chapter 15,[2] and so with the rest.

But whatever effects on men do not occur in the aforesaid cases, are solely from their own free will or solely from some sublunar causes, or from both [acting] together. For in fact, either (1) everything that happens to the native from natural causes is effected by the stars alone; or (2) by the free will of that native alone; or (3) solely by other sublunary causes; (4) or else there are some by unmixed individual [causes]; or (5) in short, everything or some things [at least] by a combination of the individual [causes] among themselves.[3] The first of these [cases] cannot be said [to be true], for it introduces [the idea of] fatal necessity, which suppresses the enjoyment of freedom [of will], and it makes God and Nature to be themselves the authors of evil, and it is contrary to experience, by which many things are proved to occur for which there is no celestial cause, unless perhaps some fictitious cause can be assigned. Similarly, the second [case] cannot be said [to be true], and that is because when someone is killed unexpectedly, his free will in itself contributes nothing to that effect; and whoever suffers from many things against his own will, and does not do what he would like to do. Then, because it is proven by many most evident experiences that the stars arrogate to themselves a conspicuous force in many things of great moment that are accustomed to happen to men, which reason is also contrary to the third case.

---

[1] Reading *opponantur* 'opposed' rather than *apponantur* 'put in'.

[2] Where Morin stated that directions tend to mark the beginning or preparation of an event, while transits may mark the very day of its manifestation or completion.

[3] To make the discussion clearer to the reader, I have numbered the five alternatives.

But the fourth [case] can be said [to be true]; for some things are effected by the stars alone, as when someone alone experiences a fatal fall or a drowning unexpectedly with no one else causing it; some things from free will alone, which, since it is inherently superior to the influx of the stars, can of itself determine and act contrary to their influx or without them; and some things too [occur] from other solitary sublunar causes, such as an illness from too much cold, heat, dryness, or humidity of the air; or the suppression of an illness that is threatened by the stars by a purging medicament; or when many thousands of men are slain in some battle, for which individuals the stars were not threatening death on that day. And finally, the fifth [cause] must be said [to be true] and it is the more frequent. For the stars incline the native towards virtues and faults, and his free will towards the former or the latter, so that for the most part it complies with the influx or inclination, especially when other sublunar causes also concur, even though the [native's] will must be viewed as an intermediate as it were between the influxes of the stars and the sublunar causes; and although the will itself is the master of [the native's] own actions, and it cannot be compelled in those things which are derived from itself or by the stars or by sublunar causes, and certainly not by Demons, it can, nevertheless, be inclined, excited, attracted, and tempted towards them by the former and the latter, and can yield to them; but only freely and in accordance with his own judgment. And therefore, in free effects at least, the stars are sometimes frustrated from [producing] their own effect; and more things can happen by command of the will contrary to the decrees of the stars according to Aphorism 5 of Ptolemy's *Centiloquy* and to St. Thomas [Aquinas], saying that "A wise man will rule the stars."[1] Indeed, against the motions of other sublunar causes and the temptations of a demon. Indeed, other sublunar causes too, which by Ptolemy are called fate secondary or inferior in nature, often resist the superior fate or the celestial influences, the effect of which is suppressed [when the native is] in prison, in exile, in confinement, in illness, and the other circumstances mentioned previously. If, therefore, the will along with the other sublunar causes jointly oppose the celestial causes, the effects of the latter will be much more effectively repressed. But if, on the contrary, the celestial causes along with the sublunar ones acting simultaneously act against the will of the native through his natural physical desire, as for example [when] a Venusian influx [coincides] with the presence of a whore, or a Martian influx with the presence of an enemy, etc., then in fact the native will scarcely evade it without supernatural assistance, and the will, debilitated by the sin or by its urging and prone to evil, will succumb. And the same thing must be judged about virtues.

We are stating these things in advance, lest anyone should think that all accidents are due to the stars, and so that he may know to what extent the force of the stars extends itself. Then, so that he may understand that, with the native disposed [to something] through revolutions and compatible directions, if a current celestial cause is lacking,[2] which can actuate the potential of the directions and revolutions, it can still be actuated by solely[3] sublunar causes, either freely or necessarily acting then concurrently. For, experiencing an arrangement through strong directions and revolutions, it easily passes into action from a light also current compatible cause, either celestial or sublunar, and either influential or elemental, as happens to those who are disposed to nasal catarrhs if they shall have exposed themselves to even a little heat of the Sun or moistness of the Moon, they suffer from catarrhs then. Therefore, it must be particularly noted at what time the native is more disposed from concordant directions and revolutions, for then the effects are imminent.

---

[1] The Greek text of the *Karpós (Centlloquy)* translated literally says, "The knowledgeable man can avoid many effects of the stars, when he is acquainted with their nature and has prepared himself beforehand for the occurrence of those effects."

[2] He means if there is no concurrent transit.

[3] Reading *solis* 'solely' rather than *Solis* 'of the Sun'.

Finally, it should be known that the day of an event from directions must be most certainly sought from the directions of the revolution of the Sun. And having probably found this, the figure of the revolution of the Moon in which that day falls must be erected; and if from many significators of that same thing in the revolution of the Sun, many days are indicated, revolutions of the Moon must be erected for each of them, so that the stronger one may be chosen, these are in fact subordinated to the figure and directions of the Sun, just as that is to the figure and directions of the radix. By which means the labor of erecting 13 revolutions of the Moon will be avoided; besides, the danger of being deceived by some [particular] revolution of the Moon, seeing that the event falls in only one of them, which can nevertheless be distinguished from the many. And yet, if the revolution of the Sun is not found to be compatible with a direction and with the radical figure, the directions of that revolution will be sought out in vain. And the same thing must be said about a revolution of the Moon that is not at all compatible, after a compatible direction has been given in a compatible solar revolution; but now we may take up some examples or experiences. Giving warning incidentally that even in these revolutions and directions we may omit the latitudes of the planets on account of the velocity of these same directions; still, it would be better not to omit them, so that the days of the events, or even the hours, might be established more certainly.

In the revolution of the Sun of Gustavus Adolphus, the king of Sweden, begun in the year 1631, during which he was killed on 16 November 1632, it would be good to know which directions were hostile to his life.

From the beginning of that revolution to the end of the year 1631 there are 12 days and 6 hours, to which if there are added 305 days from the beginning of January to the end of October in the bisextile year 1632; and in addition, 15 days and 21 hours from the end of October or the beginning of November up to the 9th hour of the morning of the 6th day of November on which he was killed make 333 complete days and 3 hours. Which time from the second and third tables of directions previously given for directions of the Sun; having made multiple entries in those tables for the numbers that they contain, the value is 328°35′. If these are added to the Oblique Ascension of the ASC in the revolution of the Sun, [which is] 273°41′, they make 242°06′, to which correspond 14 degrees of Scorpio under the pole of the figure of that revolution; then that was therefore the direction of the ASC, the primary significator of life in the sign Scorpio, into which there fell in the radix the place of Mars, the square of Saturn from the 8th, and the square of Jupiter, the ruler of the radical ASC from the 2nd; then the direction of the radical MC, and also the place of Saturn and the square of Mars in the revolution. Therefore, the direction of the ASC of the solar revolution was already falling into a very bad sign and was very badly afflicted and exactly square the radical Venus, ruler of the MC.

Furthermore, taking 90 degrees from 241 degrees, the remainder is 152°16′, to which comes the direction of the MC of the revolution, which is the last degree of Leo, in which sign are found the place of Saturn, the square of Mars, and the opposition of Jupiter in the radix, as well as the square of Saturn and the place of Mars in the revolution of the Sun, which this direction would have passed over in only two days. And consequently, the direction of the MC, the primary significator of actions and undertakings, was also in a very bad place. Moreover, [consider] the Sun, the ruler of the 8th, in the 1st of the radix and the revolution; [its] direction was in the 2nd degree of Sagittarius, near the ASC, which was occupied by the violent fixed star, Cor Scorpii.[1]

---

[1] Antares or αScorpii, which was at 4°37′ Sagittarius.

Similarly, in the revolution of the Moon during which that king was killed; from the beginning of that revolution, which was begun on 24 October 1632 at 0:04 [PM] up to the hour of his death amounted to 22 days and 21 hours, which, from the second and third tables for the revolutions of the Moon, were equivalent to 301°25′. Which, if they are added to the Oblique Ascension of the ASC of the revolution of the Moon 299°20′, make 240°45′, with which, in the pole of the figure of the revolution of the Moon, 14 Scorpio corresponds; therefore, the direction of this ASC was in the same very bad place where the direction of the ASC of the solar revolution was. Furthermore, when 90 degrees are taken away from 240°45′, there remain 150°45′ for the Right Ascension to which comes the direction of the MC and the Sun, the ruler of the 8th of both the radix and the revolution, which is 28 Leo, partile square to Saturn, falling in this revolution in the 8th house. Therefore the direction of the ASC and the MC of both revolutions come together marvelously and meet in very bad and lethal places of the figures. And some of the directions do not yet operate, but others will march past the true places of the anaeretic promittors; but [still] others operate exactly on the very day of death. And yet all of them are within the orb of virtue of the anaeretics, which will also be made plain in some other subsequent examples; and this suffices in these directions on account of the cause adduced at the beginning of the chapter. For the actual celestial cause coming on top of them on the day of his death, namely the transit of the planets, which we shall explain in its own proper place, has produced the effects.

But on the other hand, he may desire to know on what day of the revolution of the Moon the MC may come by direction to the 28th degree of Leo square Saturn in the 8th. From the RA of 28 Leo, viz. 150°11′ subtract the RA of the MC 209°20′, and 300°51′ remains for the arc of direction, which, from the first and third tables of directions for revolutions of the Moon, is equivalent to 22 days and 20 hours, at which time, counted from the beginning of the revolution of the Moon, that king was slain; and so with the others. And by the method of directing already given, we may set forth some other examples more briefly for the reader, leaving the examination of the calculation from the previously given tables.

In the revolution of the Sun of Cardinal Richelieu for the year 1642, in which he died on the 4th of December around noon. From the beginning of the revolution to [the time of] his death there are 85 days and 7 hours; and on that day his ASC came to 12 Scorpio, nearly opposite Mars, ruler of the 8th. But the Sun, ruler of the 12th in the 1st, and therefore the significator of illness and life, is directed to the 20th degree of Scorpio, and so it lacked 4 days of [being exactly] opposite Mars; moreover, this was 4 days past the place in the figure that was most dangerous for his life

But from the revolution of the Moon, begun on the 29th of November at 9:58 PM, there were 3 days and 14 hours to the time of his death. And the ASC came then by direction to 25 Scorpio, the radical place of Mercury, ruler of the 8th house, and opposite the Moon and Saturn in the revolution of the Sun, when in 10 hours before his death it had also come to the opposition of Saturn and the Moon conjoined in the 8th of the revolution of the Moon; and these should be carefully noted.

In the revolution of the Sun of the most noble Mr. Tronson in the year 1625, during which he was expelled from the court and stripped of his dignities on the 2nd of August 1626. From the beginning of the revolution up to the accident there were 334 days and 6 hours. And the MC is directed to the 12th degree of Taurus, nearly square the radical Moon, ruler of the MC of the radix and the 10th of the revolution.

But from the revolution of the Moon that began in the year 1626 on the 24th of July at 10:20 AM up to the time of the accident there were 9 days 1 hour and 40 minutes. And the direction of the MC had come to 10 Scorpio, almost to another radical square of the Moon, and to a square of the Moon itself, the Sun, and Mars [that were] conjunct in the revolution of the Moon, which the direction of the MC was passing through in agreement on that very day, with the Sun and the Moon ruling the 10th house; therefore, both directions of the MC are in strong agreement on such a misfortune.

In the revolution of the Sun in the year 1642, during which Mr. Tronson died on the 8th of December around 9 AM. From the beginning of the revolution to the accident there are 98 days 3 hours and 16 minutes. And the ASC had come to 28 Sagittarius, which was the place of the radical Saturn and the square of that same Saturn in the revolution.

But from the revolution of the Moon that began on the 13th of November at 11:58 PM up to the hour of his death there were 23 days and 9 hours. And the ASC had come to 22 Cancer, the opposition of the radical Mars, which was square the ASC in the nativity, and in this revolution it was the ruler of the 8th in the 8th of the revolution of the Sun.

In the revolution of the Sun in the year 1626, during which Constable Lesdiguières died on the following 28th of September, from the beginning of the revolution to his death there were 170 days. And on the day of his death, the ASC had come to 8 Sagittarius, almost in sinister square to Saturn, ruler of the 8th in that revolution, with a square to Mars following.

But from the revolution of the Moon, which began on the 6th of September at 10 AM, up to the day of his death [there were] 22 days. And on that day, the ASC had come to 11 Virgo, nearly the place of the Sun in this revolution and of Saturn in the revolution of the Sun, with Saturn and Mars following, conjoined to the Sun, whose places the ASC the ASC was also transiting by direction on that day. Both directions were, therefore, lethal.

We have already looked at my directions, at least at the lunar ones and at the solar ones corresponding to them, which I have put above. Therefore, in the revolution of the Sun of the year 1605, during which I was pierced with two very dangerous wounds on the 9th of July around 8 in the evening. From the beginning of the revolution up to the time of the accident, there were 136 days 4 hours and 38 minutes. And the ASC had then come to 8 Sagittarius [and] a violent fixed star on the cusp of the 8th of the radix, and to the dexter square of my cluster of planets in the 12th house, but especially to the Sun, Jupiter, and Saturn, rulers of the 5th, 8th, and 10th. Moreover, the Sun, ruler of the ASC and the 12th had come to the sinister square of the radical Moon.

But from the revolution of the Moon, begun on the 5th of July at 6:07 PM, during which the accident occurred, there are 4 days and 1 hour to the hour of the wounds. And then the direction of Jupiter, ruler of the ASC, had come to 15 Aries; consequently, on that day it was passing through squares to Mars, Venus, Mercury, and the Sun, which were in the 7th house, which is [the house] of open enemies. Moreover, the direction of the MC, the significator of actions, of which, and also of the 5th, the ruler Venus was in the 7th partilely conjunct Mars in the radical place of Mars, [that direction, I say] had come to 11 Sagittarius in the radical 8th and was square the radical Saturn, through which house Saturn was then transiting; and it was in the ASC of the revolution of the Moon, to which it was square. All these things, therefore, united [to indicate] death or at least very dangerous wounds.

In the revolution of the Sun of the year 1612, during which on the 30th of May, from a violent game in the heat of the Sun and from social drinking, I fell into a great, long, and most dangerous illness; from the beginning of the revolution to the accident, there are 96 days and 3 hours. And then the direction of the ASC had come to 16 Leo, almost to the place of Jupiter retrograde in the domicile of the Sun and in the 5th of the revolution. Jupiter itself was ruler of the 12th and the 8th, which agreed very well with the effect.

But in the revolution of the Moon, which began on the 23rd of May at 11:16 PM, from its beginning to the beginning of the illness, there are 6 days 12 hours and 44 minutes. And then the direction had come to 10 Gemini, the cusp of the 5th and the sinister square of my cluster of planets, but especially to Saturn, indeed to the square of Saturn and the Moon of this revolution, which that direction was transiting on that same day. And a great solar eclipse occurred on the place of the direction, both of this ASC and of the radical ASC.

In the revolution of the Sun, during which I received my Doctorate of Medicine on the 9th of May in the year 1613; from the beginning of the revolution there were completed 47 days 20 hours and 41 minutes. And then the direction of the ASC had come to 7 Libra opposite the Moon and square the radical Mars, which rules the Moon and the MC of this revolution. But the MC itself had come to 8 Cancer partilely [conjunct] the place of the radical Mars and in sinister trine to my cluster of planets; and Mars was ruler of the radical ASC and is found in the MC of this revolution; which [indications] are very worthy of being noted.

But in the revolution of the Moon which began on the 16th of April at 11:37 AM, there are to the 9th of May, i.e. the completed 8th day, 22 days 0 hours and 23 minutes. And then the direction of the ASC had come to 1 Gemini partile square Venus in the radix, which was the ruler of the Part of Fortune, with following squares to the Sun, Jupiter, Saturn, and the Moon; but the Lot[1] had come to 25 Pisces, which in this revolution was occupied by Saturn, ruler of the radical MC.

In the revolution of the Sun of the year 1615, during which on the 7th day of July at 10 PM, I experienced a huge danger to my life while swimming in the Rhine. From the beginning of the revolution to the accident there are 133 complete days and 20 hours. And then the direction of the ASC had come to 29 Gemini, almost opposite the Moon, ruler of the 8th, and badly afflicted in the 1st house. But in the revolution of the Moon that began on the 27th of June at 1:10 AM, there are 9 days 20 hours and 50 minutes [from the beginning of the revolution] to the hour of the accident. And the direction of the ASC had come to 23 Sagittarius, nearly opposite the Sun, ruler of the 12th and Mars, which ruled the 8th, and almost in trine to Saturn in the 8th. Moreover, the direction of the MC, the significator of actions, had come to 26 Libra opposite Saturn, ruler of the 5th, in the 8th, where it is found in the domicile and aspect of Mars, and almost on the ASC of the radix.

In that same revolution of the Sun, I experienced the danger of a lethal fall on the 1st of January 1616 at about 2 PM. From the beginning of the revolution to the hour of the accident, there were 311 days 13 hours and 16 minutes. And the direction of the ASC had come to 10 Scorpio, nearly trine Saturn in the radix.

---

[1] That is, the Part of Fortune in the chart of the lunar revolution.

But in the revolution of the Moon that began on the 25th of December at 5:16 PM, there are to the hour of the accident 5 days 20 hours and 44 minutes. And the ASC had come to 16 Virgo, opposite the radical Saturn and Moon, [and] in the 6th of the radix, with Saturn, ruler of the 8th, in the 10th of this revolution in the domicile and square of Mars; and the Moon was in the 9th. But the direction of the MC had come to 12 Gemini, a partile sinister square to that same Saturn in the radix; moreover, these things were particularly in accord with a lethal fall. And since this danger had been caused for me by a fortune-teller,[1] who, on the day before, had very badly tormented my friends with her arts; it must be said that if the Devil is serving fortune-tellers, he sometimes uses the concourse of the stars in [connection with] his own actions, he had waited until the next day for an opportunity from the stars that was convenient for my destruction, if the great goodness of God had not miraculously released me [from his power].

In the revolution of the Sun of the year 1629, during which the Most Serene Queen Mother Marie de' Medici wanted to and took the trouble to have conferred upon me the dignity of Regius Professor of Mathematics, there were 127 days counted from the beginning of the revolution up to the 30th of June, on which I undertook that matter, and through the Most Excellent Cardinal Bérulle I sought that dignity from the Queen. And at that time the direction of the MC had come to 14 Cancer, in sinister trine to the radical Saturn and the Moon; and the Moon in this revolution was ruler of the ASC in the 9th and in the radical place of Mercury with Mercury itself [in the revolution]; moreover, the Sun was directed to the 10th degree of Cancer, in sinister trine to Saturn, ruler of the MC, and to the place of Mars, ruler of the ASC in the radix, and that degree was rising in the figure of the revolution.

But in the revolution of the Moon, begun on the 13th of June at 0:54 PM, there are 17 days to the 30th of June. And then the direction of the MC had come to 17 Aquarius, namely to a trine of Venus, ruler of the ASC, to Mercury, ruler of the Sun, to the Sun itself and to Venus [all of them] conjoined; also, [it was in trine] to Saturn, ruler of the MC of the radix, which was exalted in the 1st of this revolution; and also in a partile quincunx to the Moon, ruler of the MC [of the revolution]. Therefore, all of these things were outstanding [in their signification] for undertaking [things] with good prospects for success. And certainly the thing was undertaken and promoted very fortunately with success; look at this figure of the revolution of the Moon.

---

[1] Morin evidently felt that the fortune-teller had placed an effective curse on him and his friends.

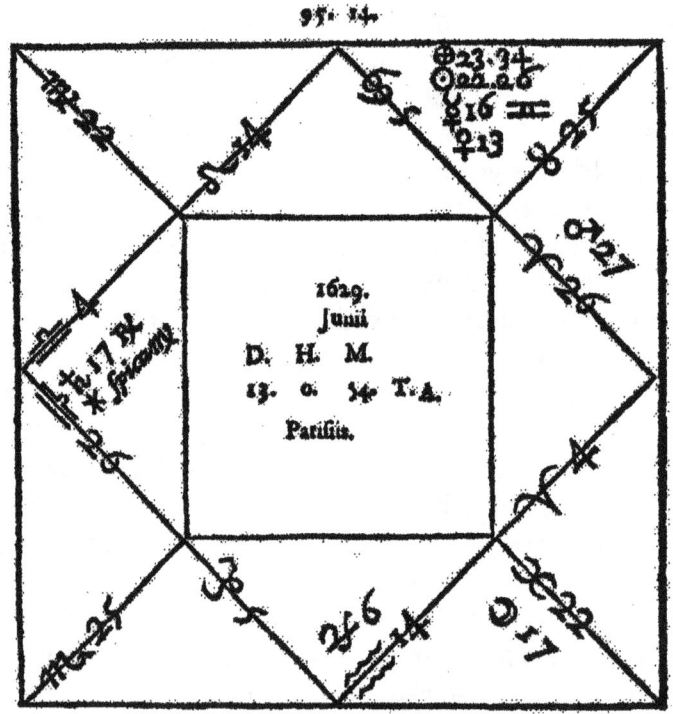

Morin Lunar Revolution
Paris
13 June 1629 0:54 PM

In this revolution, Venus[1] rules the ASC, which it aspects by trine; and the Moon rules the MC, which it also aspects by trine; and both of them are free from the malefics and in the houses of joy and science; consequently, by the favor and assistance of the Queen and the rulers, they were presaging good fortune and joy in scientific dignities for me. Then too, with the assistance of Ecclesiastical Magnates, because of the Sun, Mercury, and Venus in the 9th in trine to Jupiter, ruler of the Moon, which is in the 4th. Especially because Saturn, ruler of the MC of the radix and ruler of Jupiter in the revolution, is exalted in the 1st in his own radical antiscion and conjunct Spica,[2] in trine to the Sun, Mercury, and Venus, then also in trine to Jupiter; moreover, the Moon is in square to the Sun, Mercury, and Venus, which is auspicious. And Mars, ruler of the radical ASC, is in that ASC, strong, in sextile to the Sun and the Part of Fortune in conjunction in the 9th. All of these things, therefore are strongly fortunate for dignity. And consequently the success was very fortunate.

Moreover, in the next revolution, which began on the 10th of July at 7:48 PM, there are 23 days [from the beginning of the revolution] to the 3rd of August, on which day I received the certificate of Professor from the King. And the direction of the MC had come to 19 Virgo, trine Mars, ruler of the MC and the place of the Part of Fortune, in opposition to the Moon.

In the revolution of the Sun of the year 1634, during which, on the 1st of March at 1 PM, I undertook

---

[1] The Latin text has the symbol for Mercury, but Venus is the ruler of the rising sign Libra.

[2] Spica or α Virginis was in 18 Libra 40.

the arduous and illustrious task of publicly demonstrating the science of longitudes that I had invented; there are from the beginning of that revolution to the hour of my action 35 whole days. And at that time, the direction of the MC, significator of actions and undertakings, had come to 1 Cancer in partile sinister trine to Venus in the radix, the ruler of the Part of Fortune in the 1st, with following trines to the Sun, Jupiter, and Saturn, ruler of the MC, and Mars ruler of the ASC in the radical figure. And this direction was a very outstanding one and most conformable to such an undertaking, fortunately and gloriously completed.

But in the revolution of the Moon begun on the 27th of March at 3:20 PM, there are 2 days 20 hours and 40 minutes up to the hour of my action. And the direction of the MC had come to 4 Cancer, partile trine the Sun and Jupiter in the radix, and in platic trine to the rest of the planets; in which nothing more fortunate and conformable to the direction of the MC could be hoped for in the revolution of the Sun, especially because that direction was also to the partile square of Mercury, ruler of the 10th, where Jupiter was in this revolution, with Mercury applying to the exalted Sun.

In the revolution of the Sun of the year 1642, in which I was seized by a dangerous illness on the 2nd of November, on that very day the Sun was directed to 27 Scorpio, dexter square to Jupiter, ruler of the 8th and of Saturn; and the radical ASC was found in the 9th house of the revolution, and it was directed to Mars in the revolution, i.e. to the opposition of the radical Mars.

But in the revolution of the Moon, she was applying partilely to Saturn on the very day of the illness, and consequently was directed to it.

In the revolution of the Sun of the year 1645, during which a pension of 2,000 livres was granted to me [by action] in the Royal Council on the 8th of April, there are, from the beginning of the revolution to the 8th of April, 44 days 2 hours and 33 minutes; and at that time the direction of the ASC had come to 10 Cancer, in close trine to the radical Saturn, ruler of the MC of the radix and of the revolution, and also close to the radical place of Mars, ruler of the ASC of the radix; moreover, the MC had come to 10 Pisces, close to the radical place of that same Saturn and trine the radical Mars; so that this direction was to the cluster of planets, but the former direction was to the trine.

But in the revolution of the Moon that began on the 26th of March at 9:42 AM, there are, [from its beginning] to the day of the accident, 12 days 2 hours and 18 minutes. And the direction of the MC had come to 8 Leo, trine the Sun in the 11th house of that revolution; moreover, the Sun by direction had come to 16 Virgo, opposite the Moon [in the radix], and in turn the Moon [had come by direction] to 3 Virgo, opposite the Sun and Jupiter in the radix.

Finally, [we shall look] in the revolution begun on the 15th of December of the year 1640 at 9:50 PM, during which the Blessed Father Charles de Condren died on the 6th of January 1641 at about 6 AM. From the beginning of the revolution up to the day of his demise, there are 20 days 14 hours and 10 minutes. And at that time the direction of the ASC had come to 17 Virgo, the place of the radical Jupiter, which was the ruler of the 8th in that revolution, with a following square to the Sun, ruler of the 8th of the radix and the 12th of the revolution, then to the opposition of Mars, ruler of the 8th in the 8th of the revolution and ruler of the 12th of the radix. Moreover, the direction of the Sun had come in the revolution to Jupiter in its fall and ruler of the 8th; and the direction of the Moon had come to 23 Aquarius, square the radical Saturn and nearly square its place in the revolution.

But in the revolution of the Moon that began on the 11th of December at 6:50 AM,[1] there are 20 whole days to the day of his death. And the direction of the ASC had come to 26 Virgo, square the radical Sun [that was] the apheta in the radix and in this revolution, and partilely opposite Mars in this revolution, the ruler of the 12th, and of the Moon in the 12th, which was [co-]ruler of the 8th along with the Sun. Therefore, all these things were indicating death.

What need is there for more [examples]? In all the figures that I have tested, the force of the revolutions of the Sun and the Moon has seemed so evident to me, and also the way [of calculating] directions pertaining to them that I have discovered and set forth above, and from what has been put above it is so manifest, that, since it cannot be denied by the sharper astrologers, and since I am already worn out by the tedium of calculation, I shall here make an end of talking about these things.

Still, it seems that we should omit here [to say] that no directions are assigned to the figures of the quarters of either the year or the month, since from the examples we have given above it is sufficiently obvious that the directions of revolutions, either of the Sun or of the Moon are in force during the entire solar or lunar period, and not only in the first quarter of that period; and consequently that they exclude others in that period; otherwise, if some particular quarter should have its own directions, they would not be in force during the whole period that belongs to the figure of the revolution, or else a continuous confusion would be admitted into [the application of] directions. Whence, it is plain that the figures of the quarters should only to be viewed as the state of the *caelum* for a more efficacious transit of the Sun and the Moon through the places of their aspects.

Besides which incidentally, I give warning that [the reader] should take note and then be convinced of how false and erroneous is that new doctrine of Didacus Prittus Pelusiensis[2] in his *Astrological Theses*,[3] in which he has not only rejected circles of position in erecting figures and directing significators[4] but in addition he has rejected both the annual and monthly revolutions,[5] which he takes absolutely no account of in his judgments. He promises [to publish] demonstrations of his doctrine, which are expected [by us] to be, not demonstrations of truth (as I easily deduce from his *Theses*), but [rather] as demonstrations of his own hallucinations, which, if I am not mistaken, having been made wiser, he will suppress.

---

[1] But this revolution was badly miscalculated. See Morin's figure on p. 86 above and my remarks in Note 1 on that page; also, my recalculated chart on p. 87.

[2] Placidus de Titis (1603-1668), Professor of Mathematics at the University of Pavia 1657-1668. He was a member of the Olivetan Order and an astrological consultant to the Archduke Leopold William of Austria (1614-1662).

[3] Probably Morin refers to Placidus's *Quaestionum physiomothematicarm libri tres* 'Three Books of Physiomathematical Questions' (Milan, 1650). I have not seen the original but only the English translation (of the 1657) edition by John Cooper entitled *Primum Mobile* (London: Davis and Dickson, 1814), which opens with 70 Theses in its first book. The latter part of Cooper's translation is of a section entitled "Thirty Remarkable Nativities to prove the truth of things by examples..." This section was perhaps not present in the 1650 edition; in which case Morin would not have seen it, since he died in 1656.

[4] *Primum Mobile,* Canon XII "Under circles of position...later authors direct their moderators and constitute the intervals of the houses. But how frivolous and remote from natural truth this opinion is, may be seen in my *Celestial Philosophy,* where it is largely and plainly demonstrated..." Placidus rejected the Regiomontanus system of primary directions, which uses circles of position, and replaced it with the Placidus system of primary directions, which uses proportional semi-arcs (as Ptolemy had recommended).

[5] *Thirty Remarkable Nativities,* "To the Reader," paragraph 14, "The revolution, as taught by some, I have not seen, though in reality they may possess some virtue...therefore, let any one, if he pleases, observe them, but at the same time, let him not place so great a value on them, as some authors do..."

Chapter XVII.

The Ruler of the Revolution.

After having erected the figure of a celestial constitution, whether it is a universal one, as in mundane revolutions of the Sun or eclipses, or whether it is a particular one, as in the nativities of men and their revolutions, astrologers are first of all accustomed to inquire which of the planets is the ruler of this constitution, i.e. which of them is more powerful than the others. Truly, they inquire about this and define it in various ways; but since there ought to be one and the same rule for all, namely that the stars act uniformly; and Ptolemy seems to have thought that way in Book 2, Chapters 6 & 11, of the *Quadripartite*,[1] where, in the constitutions of revolutions of the Sun and of eclipses he prescribes that the ruler of the figure ought to be chosen in the same way, although he made no mention of the ruler of the geniture and its revolutions. For the stars do not act one way in universal constitutions and another way in particular ones, but in the latter they are determined only to a particular, namely the native, but in the former they are determined to anything that is universal, namely a region or a city; and whether they affect the subject according as elemental or influential actions of the stars, or whether it is subjected to both and is capable of experiencing both. For what is received is received in a manner appropriate to the recipient.

Moreover, it seems to us that some distinction should be made here between the ruler of the year and the ruler of a revolution. The ruler of the year is chosen in two ways by many astrologers, who are also spewing out, at least for the most part, the nonsense of the Arabs and the other orientals, for arcane secrets of science that should only be handed down to the sons of science, namely the universal and the particular [rulers].

The universal is given out by Ptolemy in Book 4, Chapter 11, from a comparison of the planets according to their order with respect to us looking into the sky, with the ages of men, also looked at according to their own natural order. And he says that the first four years of the native, or his infancy, are generally subject to the Moon and ruled by it, because it is the planet first in order [of distance] with respect to us. The ten years following, or youth, are ruled by Mercury following the Moon in that order of the planets; the eight years following, or adolescence, are governed by Venus, the following 19 by the Sun, the following 15 by Mars, the following 12 by Jupiter, and the rest of life by Saturn. But Ptolemy gave no reasons for his own distribution of years, that are consistent and are based upon a true foundation, nor yet does his commentator Cardan. Since the planets move in ellipses, and not in epicycles as Ptolemy supposed, then certainly their revolutions in their own orbits are set free by their absolutely elliptic motion in the super-fluid Ether. Besides, of the rulerships, or the governance of childhood, Venus and not Mercury would agree, for Venus's orbit happens to be second to ours and Mercury third ascending upwards, because they revolve around the Sun, and Mercury is closer to the Sun than Venus, which had not become known to Ptolemy and those who followed him in his system of the world. Finally, that distribution and its reasons would have been absolutely absurd [even] in the time of the first men, who lived for many centuries,[2] and were still young when they had completed their first century of life. Therefore, it should also be judged to be fictitious now, at least by reason of the distribution of years, since the planets have changed neither their own forces, nor their own periods of motion, nor their own

---

[1] The *Tetrabiblos*, ii. 6 & 10, in Robbins's edition and translation.

[2] He refers to the long life spans attributed to Methuselah and others in the Bible. See p. 111, note 2, above.

modes of action. Add [to this the fact] that it cannot be accommodated to the ages of brute beasts and [the lifespan] of plants.[1] And yet as far as body and life are affected by the stars and they have their own different ages, even as men do; and others, such as stags, crows, whales, and the oak tree; and others very short; and others middling, as is known to anyone.

Nevertheless, there certainly exists among them different ages of the native that are analogous to the different natures of the planets, namely youth to the Moon, on account of the excess of moisture; adolescence to Mercury, on account of the motion and culture of mental ability; youth to Venus, on account of the desire for sexual pleasure and procreation; first virility to the Sun, on account of the ambition for honors that arises then; second virility to Mars, on account of work; first old age to Jupiter, on account of prudence [derived] from the things experienced, and also from judgment; and finally, that part of old age that embraces the remainder of the life, to Saturn, on account of the coldness of age, the slowness of motion, solitude, sicknesses, etc. And it must be considered similarly with regard to the ages of brute animals and plants.[2] But this analogy of rulerships became known only generally, by which the planets act upon individual subjects in accordance with their own dispositions, and therefore easier and more efficacious on those similar to themselves; whence, a decrepit man is more apt to be affected by the influx of Saturn than by that of Venus. And the individual planets act in the individual ages according as these are apt to be affected by them.

Wherefore I also think that that artificial division of the year into seven parts made by the Arabs must be rejected—that governance of the individual "sevenths" by the individual planets, that they have called "rulers of the sevenths" or *Alfridaries*, [and] prefixing another planet as ruler of the individual years of the sevenths, which they have said to be a partner to the Alfridary. For besides that the order of the planets is not preserved, as I said above in opposition to Ptolemy; this division is also lacking in a natural foundation, however Cardan (with Origanus[3] referring to it and giving it his approval) in Genitures 34 and 39 makes them out to be of great import, and he asserts that he has found them by experiment and reason.[4] For what he offers as proof of these is nothing other than the analogy of the planets and the ages [of man] that we mentioned above; and consequently the rulership is entirely general [in nature], concerning which Cardan reasons badly. And therefore it need only be said that it is an ingenious figment of the imagination invented and expounded by the Arabs, who were extremely well provided with such [ideas], and badly approved by Cardan.[5] For if, as he will have it, the Alfridary of children is from the 28th year up to the 42nd, in which [period] Mars and Jupiter are dominant, why will it not rather be from the 14th year to the 28th over which Venus and the Sun preside—which planets correspond more to the generation [of children] than do Mars and Jupiter? Indeed, why will it not be

---

[1] Reading *plantarum* 'of plants' rather than *Planetarum* 'of planets'.

[2] Again reading 'plants' rather than 'Planets'.

[3] David Origanus (1558-1628).

[4] I don't know what Morin is referring to by this statement. In *The Book of Examples of One Hundred Genitures,* Cardan says at the very end of his commentary on Geniture 34 This also took place in the Alflidary of Venus, a planet weaker in the whole geniture." In the commentary on Geniture 39, he says nothing about Alfridaries. Perhaps Morin is citing some remark by Origanus, based on a statement by Cardan in another place.

[5] As noted previously, Morin, like other astrologers of his time, was evidently unaware that most of the features of Arabian astrology were simply copied from Greek astrology, which was much broader than the cut-down version given by Ptolemy, Morin's low opinion of Alfridaries may be justified by their ineffectiveness (if indeed he had tried them and found them to be ineffective), but they cannot logically be dismissed simply by saying that they were an Arab invention.

similar from the 77th year to the 91st, over which those same planets Mars and Jupiter preside?

Having said these things about the universal as well as the particular ruler of the year, we may now come to the ruler of the revolution, which is the planet that is more powerful in the figure of the revolution, and that one of the stars which, because of its uniformity in acting, ought to be the ruler of the revolution without any further consideration.

It may therefore seem that in the nativity whichever planet is the more powerful from its rulership, exaltation, triplicity, or aspect in the principal places of the geniture, which are [those of] the Sun, the Moon, the ASC, the MC, and the Part of Fortune, that one will be the primary ruler of the revolution. But in revolutions of the Sun, the principal place must logically be that of the Sun, and in revolutions of the Moon that of the Moon. Because if two or three planets are found with approximately equal power, that one should be selected which will prevail because of its celestial and terrestrial state, that is, the one that is in its own proper essential dignities, oriental to the Sun, swift, direct, with strong or multiple aspect to the others, but especially to the Sun or the Moon in their individual revolutions, and also [placed] in the principal angles of the figure; for thus configured, it will act more efficaciously—but especially if in the genethliacal figure there occurs in that year any new and strong direction to the body or aspect of such a planet, and the status of that same planet in the revolution agrees with [the nature of] the direction, for then it will be very strong in that year, at least with regard to those things that are signified by the direction. But if, other things being equal, one of these planets is in its own proper dignities, but another is in an angle in the first or the tenth house, even if it is in exile or in its fall, that one should nevertheless be selected, since it is stronger by its terrestrial state or determination, by which it has a most powerful effect. For the native, both in his nativity and in a revolution can be equally subject to a malefic ruler of the figure or to a benefic ruler, and equally well affected or badly affected by that ruler according to it nature and state. But another planet that is inferior [in state] but near in power, may be taken to be a secondary ruler of the revolution.

And because the ASC presides over the body, life, habits, and mental ability, but the MC over undertakings, actions, and profession, on which almost all other [facets of life] depend to some extent, therefore the rulers of these angles must be particularly noticed, and after them the Sun in its revolution, and the Moon in a revolution of the Moon. For although the Sun and the Moon are not considered by us with the universal significations attributed to them by the ancients, but only in so far as they are determined in a figure, as is the case with Saturn, Jupiter, Mars, Venus, and Mercury, yet both in a nativity and in its revolutions their places[1] must be looked at when selecting the ruler, because they are primary planets primarily arranged around the earth,[2] and [consequently] of primary power among the planets, as experience proves; to one of which, namely the Sun, the governance of years is attributed by nature, and to the Moon the months, but not to any of the other planets, which are merely satellites of the Sun acting as agents in the sublunar world.

Finally, in selecting the ruler, a planet powerful by domicile will have to be preferred to one powerful by exaltation, and to one only powerful by being in its triplicity. And furthermore, a planet in the

---

[1] That is, those of the Sun and the Moon.

[2] Remember that Morin held to the theory that the earth was the center of the solar system, not the Sun; hence, both the Sun and the Moon are primary "planets" that circle about the earth, while the others circle about the Sun and are therefore not primary.

first house will have to be preferred to its absent ruler, because the presence of a planet is more powerful than the rulership of an absent one, although the force of the present planet does not absolutely exclude or stop the force of the absent ruler, but it merely prevails over it. And finally, that planet will have to be preferred that aspects the place it rules, to one not aspecting it, especially if it rules by domicile;[1] also, the one that is above the earth will have to be preferred to the one below the earth.

And these individual [remarks] about the selection of the ruler of a revolution of the Sun or of the Moon have a valid foundation in nature by reason and experience, which cannot be said for the figments of the Arabs and the Indians that we have rejected, who, for the most part devoid of any knowledge of the true causes, have thought up so many false ones, so that there was no effect for which they could not render either a true or fictitious reason. And so, playing with the numbers of the signs, the planets, the degrees of the ecliptic, with the days of the year and of the month, and of the hours of the day, and likewise with their order or series, they have greatly depraved this divine science with plainly chimerical causes, no few of which Hermes recommends in *The Revolutions of Nativities*, Book 2, Chapter 1, that are not at all worthy of our refutation, because our time should scarcely be taken up with such nonsense.

Besides, it can be asked, why the Sun is not always and solely the ruler of the year, since the year is only [derived] from the Sun, and the annual revolution is a revolution of the Sun, which is the most powerful of the planets?

I answer that although the Sun acts on its own, still it acts according to the nature of the sign that it occupies, and the nature and state of its ruler, just as we have said elsewhere. Since, therefore, in [the case of] a revolution of the Sun, it is especially sought what it is going to accomplish, therefore especial attention must be given to its rulership on account of that cause; and it[2] must be taken to be the ruler in the year, also it must be preferred to any other; not to be sure for the effects of the whole figure or the year, unless it also rules the places of the Moon, the ASC, the MC, and the Part of Fortune, or the major part of these, but only for the effects signified by the Sun. And since the status of that ruler is varied in the individual years, and it may sometimes be favorable, but other times unfavorable, then consequently its ruler and its status will have to be carefully noted, not only in a nativity, but also in the individual revolutions. But when the Sun in the radix shall have been found in Leo, its own domicile, then because it is subject to no other planet, it will be the primary and very powerful ruler of its own revolutions. And the same thing similarly should be thought [to be true] for revolutions of the Moon.

---

[1] The Latin text has *praesertim si dominio praesit* 'especially if it rules over the rulership', which does not seem to make sense. I have, therefore, translated *dominio* as 'by domicile', instead of 'rulership', but this may not be correct.

[2] That is, the ruler of the Sun's sign, which will always be the same but in a different state in each revolution.

Chapter XVIII.

The Universal Laws of Judgments on Solar and Lunar Revolutions of Nativities.

Although from what was said in all of Book 21 about the determinations of the celestial bodies and then especially what was said in Chapts. 6 and 7 of the present book, it should be plain enough how revolutions should be judged, at least in a general way; nevertheless, because the universal laws of judgments are common to genitures and revolutions, the doctrine of revolutions also possesses some laws of its own, both universal and particular; therefore, it seems to us that the universal laws ought to be given here, lest anything should be lacking in a theoretical doctrine of such importance; and we shall give the particular laws in our [book] *Astrological Prediction*, if God grants us the time to compose it.[1] Therefore, the principle ones of the universal laws follow, from which the lesser principal laws can easily be discovered by a skillful astrologer.

1. In a revolution, nothing should be predicted—at least nothing significant—unless it is signified by the radix or by its directions at the time of the revolution. For if the Sun in the 10th of the radix is directed to the trine of Jupiter well disposed (which is a distinguished and fortunate direction per se), but in the revolution of the year indicated by the direction, the Sun is in the 12th square Saturn or Mars without any fortunate aspect of Jupiter, which is also badly afflicted, the direction will produce nothing, and only ineffective attempts for honours will occur along with impediments, and perhaps also misfortune in connection with honours; and so with the rest. But generally one ought to look in every revolution, both of the Sun and of the Moon, how the planets on that day are related to the places of the geniture. For, if favourably related [they indicate] good, if unfavourably related, evil in the affected type of accident of life, wealth, honours, etc., having taken into account the determination of the planets themselves, both radical and revolutional.

2. Similarity of signification of a revolution with the geniture brings forth the things signified in the geniture. But dissimilarity suppresses or retards them, or fulfills them in a minimal fashion or corrupts them. And therefore whatever is performed by a revolution must certainly be presignified in the nativity. But whatever is presignified in the nativity for any particular year, is not performed by the revolution of that year in the absence of similarity to the thing predicted, which actuates the potential of the geniture and its directions in the things signified. Therefore Cardan rightly warns that nothing should ever be pronounced about radical directions without having inspected the revolution of the year indicated by the direction—but in fact also the one immediately preceding or following; otherwise, even the best astrologer will be deceived.

3. The more the figure of the revolution, whether solar or lunar, is similar to the radical position of the signs and planets, the more efficaciously it will bring forth the significations of the geniture, whether good or evil, and especially those that will be signified by a similar direction. For that similarity is not always favourable and a promise of some great good, as Origanus and many others suppose, but it only signifies the same things as the figure of the geniture, whether good or evil. Otherwise the planets would not act in accordance with their determinations; and a malefic influx in a nativity would be corrected by one similarly malefic, or it would be completely changed, which is inconsistent with experience and nature. But this greater similarity (at least in the position of the signs) can be acquired or

---

[1] This work was unfortunately never written, as Morin died not long after finishing the *Astrologia Gallica*.

vitiated by the native's travelling to appropriate places of the earth for the time of the revolution, and especially for that of the Sun, as was already said in Chapt. 4. And this is a secret of the science that should by no means be despised. And in particular those revolutions should be watched for in which the same degree of the ecliptic is found in the Ascendant as was in the Ascendant of the radix; for then each planet rules the same houses in the revolution as it ruled in the radix, which does not usually happen without [producing] some notable effect signified by the nativity, since the force of signification of the signs will also be doubled, at least in the place of the nativity and thereabouts.

4. A thing strongly signified by the nativity or by a radical direction can be reduced to actuality or perfected by a weak solar revolution of the same signification; and therefore much more readily by a strong one. But it will not be perfected by a weak lunar revolution. And vice versa, a thing weakly signified by the nativity or one of its directions can be brought forth into actuality by a strong solar revolution of the same signification, but hardly by a strong lunar revolution. But a thing weakly signified in the nativity will hardly be brought into actuality by a weak solar revolution of the same signification, and it will not be done at all by a weak lunar revolution, because a strong resistance of secondary fate, i.e., a strong contrary disposition (if it is present) of sublunar causes passively or actively joining in an effect, wards off a weak celestial influx. Therefore, in all things signified in a particular year, the disposition of the secondary fate must be carefully attended to. And the natives must be questioned about those things, so that where their undertakings, actions, and experiences lie may be discovered; and from this [information] a more sagacious prediction can be made after having considered the virtue of the revolution.

5. When the Ascendants of the radix and the revolution are opposed, it is evil and disturbing, and worse still when the degrees [themselves] are opposed, especially in the case of a solar revolution. For, since the revolution either brings forth or inhibits the effect of the nativity, and it can only bring it forth from a similarity of the figures, it is plain that this contrariety of position, both of the Sun and of the whole *caelum*, will inhibit the radical influx and prevent it from bursting forth into action, but especially into good action, and will only bring forward ineffective efforts in connection with the good things signified by the directions in that year, with many contrarieties, damages, anxieties, sicknesses, and dangers to life. And the reason is because the signs are then determined to significations contrary to the radix. For just as bad changes and harm happen in the Great World, or in universal nature, when the sign Leo of solar nature is determined to the contrary saturnine nature by Saturn's movement into Leo, and Saturn's virtue is also corrupted there, so also when the planets and signs in revolutions, and especially in transits, are determined to significations contrary to their radical ones, or the planets themselves are disposed in a contrary manner, bad changes and misfortunes must be expected in the Microcosm, or the native. But if Jupiter or Venus is in the 1st [house] of the revolution, without rulership in the 8th or 12th of the radix or the revolution, the evil things in the essential significations of the 1st house indicated by this contrariety will be removed or mitigated, and some happiness and joy will also happen in connection with marriage, lawsuits, and contracts, especially if the 7th of the radix is well disposed and the directions are in accord—namely because each house of the radix can [also] signify for its opposite. But if any evil is signified by the geniture and its directions in that year, especially in connection with illnesses, lawsuits, and open enemies, and the 7th of the radix is badly disposed, and there are bad planets in the 1st of the revolution, those evils will happen in that year. And the same thing should be thought in the case of opposed signs culminating[1] in the radix and the revolution, and also in the case of the other cusps.

---

[1] That is, on the cusp of the 10th house.

6. If the Ascendant of the revolution is trine the radical Ascendant, it is good for the significations of the 1st house; if it is square, it is evil. But one must not pronounce about the good or evil of the significations of the first house simply from these [aspect indications] alone, but the state of both Ascendants and also the state of the planets in the revolution must be looked at, and especially the state of the rulers of the Ascendants of the radix and the revolution, along with the direction of the radical Ascendant and its ruler. And one must think about the Midheavens of the radix and the revolution in the same way.

7. The sign ascending in the revolution, in which some planet is posited in the radix, and especially the place of that planet on the Ascendant of the revolution, affects the native in the things signified by the 1st [house] according to the nature, state, and determination of that planet in the radix and the revolution. And the same thing is true of the Midheaven of the revolution and the other cusps. And if in the solar revolution the Ascendant is the place of the radical Saturn, or of Mars in the 8th, or of the ruler of the 8th, [the native] will have to be on guard against death in that month in which the Ascendant of the lunar revolution is the same, or in that quarter in which it is the same, and with the rest in agreement.

8. Each sign's effect signified by the geniture happens in connection with the significations of the house of the figure that that sign occupies in the revolution, especially if the radical directions are in agreement. And thus the sign of the 1st [house] of the radix in the 12th or the 8th of the revolution threatens illnesses, imprisonment, enemies, death, or dangers to life if the radix and its directions agree; in the 11th it presages friends; in the 10th, undertakings, actions, dignities, etc. The sign of the 2nd of the radix in the 7th of the revolution [indicates] wealth from marriage, lawsuits, and contracts, or expenses and losses in connection with these same things in accordance with the state of the 7th and its ruler, both in the radix and in the revolution. For the signification of good or evil state of the 7th of the revolution does not overturn the signification of the state of the 7th of the radix or act against it [as was explained] in Chapt. 7. And the reasoning is the same in the rest.

9. Any planet in the revolution can act in accordance with the nature of the house that it occupied in the radix, yet it acts more evidently according to the nature of the house that it occupies in the revolution, whether it is a solar or a lunar revolution. This is proved from the Sun itself, which in all its own revolutions is in the same house of the radix, although it will vary its effects in individual years—indeed, that which is radically signified by the Sun from the house of the [natal] figure will be specified and determined to the signification of the house that the Sun occupies in the revolution; and it will be proved similarly by the Moon in its revolutions. Therefore, if Mars from the 2nd [house] of the radix comes to the 5th of the revolution, it will signify prodigality or outlays for pleasure in that year. But on the contrary, if Jupiter from the 5th of the radix comes to the 2nd of the revolution, it will presage increases in wealth from children or lovers[1] or games and pleasures. But although the same thing could be said of the ruler of the 2nd of the radix in the 5th of the revolution or the reverse, yet, because the presence of a planet is stronger than its rulership when absent, if in the nativity the ruler of the 2nd is in the 5th, but in the revolution it is in the 12th, one will have to say that [the native] will become ill as result of pleasures, or that he will be incarcerated because of them or from outlays on them,[2] and thus the significations of the three houses 2, 5, and 12 are combined. But it is not always necessary to combine the significations of all the houses. And the reasoning is the same in the rest. Nevertheless, it must be noted that in revolutions the determinations of the planets by reason of bodily position and rulership in the figure of the rev-

---

[1] Reading *amasiis* 'lovers' instead of *amesiis*.

[2] That is, from going into debt from expenditures on pleasures.

olution must be combined in accordance with the doctrine of Book 21, Sect. 2, but always with respect to the determinations of the same planets in the radical figure also thus combined. And this is to combine the radical combinations with those of the revolution, because whoever does this more sagaciously will judge more certainly.

10. In the case of any planet in the figure of the revolution, one must first turn his attention to which house of the radix it falls in, and after that to which house of the revolution. For the radical figure precedes the figure of the revolution in time, in virtue, and in universality. And therefore one must first look at how these planets are related to the figure of the radix, rather than how they are related to the figure of the revolution. And this is proved by the fact that if Saturn is the anaereta in the radix and in the revolution it comes to the Ascendant of the radix, it threatens the native with danger to his life no matter in which house of the revolution that Ascendant is. But that house can decree the type of danger, e.g., if the Ascendant comes to the 5th of the revolution, the danger will be from pleasures or from their cause, because there it takes a new determination to pleasures. But if the radical Ascendant and Saturn in it comes to the 8th of the revolution, sudden or violent death is signified or some great unforeseen danger to life on account of the doubled anaeretic force of Saturn and the doubled aphetic force of the subordinated Ascendant. And consequently, the following things must be looked at for each planet in the revolution. First, what is its nature. Second, what is its celestial state in the radix. Third, what is it determined to in the radix by body and by rulership. Fourth, which house of the radical figure does its [position] in the revolution fall into. Fifth, what is its celestial state in the revolution. Sixth, what is it determined to in the revolution by body and by rulership. Seventh, how can the radical and revolutional determinations be combined with regard to their conformity, contrariety, or dissimilarities. For the greatest secret of revolutions lies in these [considerations] before [all] the rest.

11. Any planet will fulfill its own radical significations in any year mainly in accordance with the house that it occupies in the revolution. And therefore one must judge about its effects from each of its determinations—the radical, namely, and the revolutional—arising from its celestial and terrestrial state in each figure. And it must be seen from what and into what it may be changed from the radix to the revolution by reason of sign, house, ruler, and configuration. Noting that its radical determination is specified [as to type] and determined by its signification in the revolution. And therefore the ruler of the 1st [house] of the radix, or the planet that is in the 1st of the radix, if it comes to the 5th of the revolution, and especially Venus,[1] will incline to pleasures; if it comes to the 10th, and especially Jupiter, it will cause ambition for honours; and the reasoning is the same with the others.

12. A planet migrating from one house of the radix to another house of the revolution does not have a simple and absolute influx on its significations as it does in the radix, but a mixed one and dependent upon the significations of its radical house. And one must always look in both places, insofar as it pertains or refers primarily and per se to the native and not to other persons. And therefore Schöner and others are mistaken when they assert that a planet migrating from the 11th of the radix to the 8th of the revolution signifies the death of the native's friends. For the 8th house in the native's particular, or radical, figure is not the house of death of the native's friends or for everybody in general, but it is only the house of death of the native himself, as we have explained elsewhere. And consequently such a planet is

---

[1] That is, 'and especially [if it is] Venus'. However, only the planet's symbol is given in the Latin text, so it could also be translated 'and especially to Venus', but I incline to the former interpretation. (And similarly for Jupiter in the latter part of the sentence.)

determined to the native's death, and it will rather signify death for him or danger to his life from a friend. But in universal constitutions[1] the 8th house is the house of death in general. And it will be better to say that if a planet in the 11th of the radix comes in a revolution to the 6th of the radix, which is the 8th from the 11th of the radix, some friend of the native will die, especially if that planet is evilly disposed in the revolution. In this regard, a planet migrating from the 11th of the radix into the 8th of the revolution does not signify the same thing as a planet migrating from the 8th of the radix into the 11th of the revolution. For the former signifies that a friend concurs per se in the native's death, especially if it is a malefic planet, but the latter signifies that it happens to a friend that accidentally and without any intent he is the cause of the native's death. But it can also signify escape from death through the favour or assistance of a friend. Similarly, a planet from the 11th of the radix coming to the 7th of the revolution turns a friend into an open enemy, or it stirs up lawsuits because of friends, or it gives a spouse through the efforts of friends, or it settles lawsuits. But a planet from the 7th of the radix coming to the 11th of the revolution turns an open enemy into a friend, or it settles lawsuits with the aid of a friend. But the nature of the planet must always be noted, and in these examples how it is related to each Ascendant, and especially to the radical Ascendant. Furthermore, that which is said here about a planet in the 7th can also be said about the ruler of the 7th.

13. A planet in a revolution is returned either only to the sign or only to the house that it occupied in the figure of the radix, or to both of them at the same time, or to neither. If it is only returned to the sign, it will produce an effect signified by the radix in accordance with the house that it occupies in the revolution. If only to a similar house, it will produce its own radical effect from the house by reason of the sign and its ruler in the revolution, also by reason of the radical house that that sign occupied, and both of these cases are strong on account of the doubled force of the planet, either from the sign or from the house. But if it comes to the sign and house at the same time, this case is the strongest of all and will very often produce effects from unexpected sources, which makes the influx even more admirable. But if a planet returns to neither [sign nor house], it must be seen whether it returns to its own opposition by sign or by house, which is very bad, but less so if it only returns to the opposition of the latter. And if it comes to its own trine, it will bring forth its own fortunate radical significations; but if to its own square, the reverse. And the nature and celestial and terrestrial state of the planet must be taken into account in each figure. But if the planet does not come to any of its own radical aspects, it will generally be weak in regard to its own radical significations, although it can do something else.

14. A planet in the revolution coming to the radical place of another combines the radical significations of both planets, and these are specified or determined by the signification of the house of the revolution in which the place [of the planets] is. However, it must be noted which of these planets is in the stronger place there, then whether they are friends or enemies by nature and by radical determination, i.e., whether they presage similar or contrary things in the radix. But a planet in a revolution coming to the radical aspect of another, whether good or evil, is affected—being made fortunate or unfortunate—in those things that it signifies in the revolution by reason of both of its determinations, viz. the radical and the revolutional, by that aspect in accordance with its type and the nature of the aspecting planet and the latter's radical determination. And consequently, if the ruler of the radical Ascendant comes in the revolution to the 12th house in square to Saturn, ruler of the 8th of the radix, a lethal illness or one with danger to life will be portended by this. And if Venus [comes] from the 7th of the radix to the 5th of the revolution in trine to Jupiter, ruler of the Ascendant of the radix, [the birth of children from his

---

[1] The charts erected in mundane astrology.

wife will be signified for a married native. And thus with other [combinations].

15. If a planet in the radix that is in evil aspect to another comes in the revolution to the evil radical aspect of that same planet, and there is no reception between them by house or by exaltation, it will be very evil, but less so if there is reception; but if it comes to a good radical aspect of the same planet without reception, it signifies no good from this, [but] with reception, a little good, in which one can hardly trust. But if a planet in the radix in benefic aspect to another comes in the revolution to a malefic radical aspect of the same planet with mutual reception, a great good [accomplished] by contrary means is signified if the determination is to good; [but] if there is no reception, evil will happen, no matter what the determination of the planets is.

16. If planets conjoined in the radix are conjoined anew in the figure of the revolution or similarly configured, they will bring forth the radical effects, whether good or evil, that are signified by their radical connection, [but] in accordance with the significations of the houses of the revolution that they occupy. [But] if they are configured dissimilarly, i.e., if they are in trine in the nativity, and they aspect each other by square or opposition in the revolution, or the other way around, and if there is no reception by house or exaltation between them, the change to a trine will produce nothing, but the change to a square will produce harm. But if there is reception between them, especially mutual reception, the change to a trine will be potent for good, and the change to a square will hardly produce any harm.

17. If the celestial state of a planet is the same in the geniture and the revolution, as if in each figure it is in its own domicile or exaltation, or it is direct, swift, oriental of the Sun, occidental of the Moon, free from the rays,[1] in fortunate aspect with other planets, diurnal by day above the earth, etc., it will be very effective in bestowing its own radical significations in that year, especially if its direction and determination in the revolution are in agreement. But if the state is entirely contrary, it is very evil and disturbing for those same significations, especially if the change should be made from a benefic state in the radix to a malefic state in the revolution. But [if it is] partly similar and partly contrary, it insinuates that [the effect) must be declared according to the part that prevails.

18. A planet determined to the same signification in both the radix and the revolution will undoubtedly produce it in that year if its direction is in agreement or there is something else of similar or concordant signification. [But] without a direction, it will either do nothing or little.

19. If two planets are determined to the same thing[2] or something similar in the radix, and in the revolution they come together or are in concordant aspect and in concordant places of the figure, they will also produce their effect for certain in that year, as [was said] above.

20. For any planet, it must be seen in both the radix and the revolution whether it is subject to the same ruler or to different rulers. For if the latter happens, the prediction about its effects will be more obscure and confused; and one will have to pay attention to whether the different rulers are mutually friendly or inimical by their nature, connection, and determination in the revolution, and one must judge according to that.

---

[1] That is, not under the Sunbeams.

[2] Reading *ad idem* 'to the same thing' instead of *ad diem* 'to the day'.

21. In solar revolutions, one must chiefly look at the Sun itself and those things that it signified in the radix, for because its virtue is greater than that of the others, it will always do something in each year in accordance with its own radical determination, even without any new solar directions. This is plain in my case, as I have the Sun in the 12th with Jupiter, the Moon, and Saturn, and I have always had great opposition in all my undertakings, either by magnates, or by the lords whom I served, or by public affairs, such as wars, the plague, new laws, the state of the royal court, or such like. And the same thing must be said about the Moon in lunar revolutions. And one will have to be fearful when Saturn by its own proper motion transits the Moon's sign or the opposite sign in lunar revolutions because of the conjunction or opposition of Saturn, especially if it is partile, also on the day of the revolution. And if Saturn is the significator of illness or death and the Moon is the significator of life, one will have to be very fearful of illnesses or death in that month, especially if there is a concordant radical direction. And the reasoning is the same with the rest. Besides, in solar and lunar revolutions, those things that concur with the radical directions of the luminaries must be more diligently attended to than the rest; for if they agree in their signification, they will undoubtedly produce their effect.

22. Whoever has many planets in the same house of his geniture will experience many things throughout his whole life in connection with the things signified by that house. Because each year those planets act in the revolution in accordance with their radical determination; and therefore, whether [instigated] by one of them or by another, something of the things signified by that house will always happen. This is plain in my case, as I have Venus, the Sun, Jupiter, Saturn, and the Moon in the 12th, and there is never lacking a year in which there are not some things from among those signified by that house that must be endured or overcome.

23. In a solar revolution, see how the significator and the promittor of the new direction are related to each other, especially in the case of a strong direction that falls in that year or close by and has not yet produced its effect. For if the significator is in the place of the promittor or comes to its good or evil aspect (according to the goodness or malice of that direction), and the promittor is there by body or by concordant aspect, it will complete the effect of the direction in that year. But if the promittor is absent by body or by ray, the direction will be less effective. But it will also be very effective if the planet that is the promittor in the revolution is in its own radical place, and the significator is concordant in its ray with the direction; then, if each of them returns to its own radical place without an aspect, one must also see first whether they are allotted a determination in the revolution that is similar to their radical determination or its direction.

24. In the case of the ruler of the year, or of the solar revolution, one must generally judge from its nature, then from its state, both celestial and terrestrial, in each figure. But in particular, the ruler of the year benefic and strong in each chart will in general bring forth the fortunate things signified for that year, but especially those that it signifies by reason of each figure and its own direction. In this regard it mitigates the evils of the revolution, especially if it sees the significators of evil in the revolution by a friendly ray, or if it rules them. But the ruler of the year in each chart malefic by nature or by determination and unfortunate will bring forth all the misfortunes of that year, but especially those that it signified by reason of its own determination in each figure; and it will impede all the good things in the revolution, especially if it sees the significators of good things by a hostile ray. And the same judgment must be made about the ruler of the month, or the ruler of the lunar revolution.

25. If the ruler of the revolution, either solar or lunar, is combust, it threatens evil in those things that

it signifies in both charts, and in hidden things, either in being acted upon or in suffering, and especially from [the action of] magnates.

26. If the ruler of the revolution, either solar or lunar, is also the ruler of the geniture, it will be very strong either for good or for evil. The same thing must be said about the ruler of the lunar revolution if it is also the ruler of the solar revolution.

27. If the ruler of the revolution comes to the place or the radical aspect of another planet, it will have to be judged by Law 14 [above], but the influx of the ruler of the revolution will be more effective.

28. In every revolution, one must pay particular individual attention both to the rulers of the Ascendant and the rulers of the Midheaven, then to the Sun and the Moon, namely by taking note of the nature and determination of the individual rulers in each figure, to what radical places they return, and what their state is in the revolution, and especially which planet they apply to, and how, and what they are determined to.

29. If any house of the radical figure that signifies good is well disposed and is also well disposed in the revolution, and not [affected] by planets determined in the radix to a contrary signification, the significations of that house will be advantageous in that year; but if it is evilly disposed in the revolution, especially by planets determined in the radix to a contrary signification, and they are malefics, the significations of that house will be evil. But on the contrary, if a house of the radical figure that signifies evil is also evilly disposed in the revolution, the evil significations of that house will happen; but if it is well disposed, the evils will not happen, or they will be mitigated.

30. The agreement or disagreement of two revolutions of the Sun following one after the other must be noted not only universally but particularly, both as regards [the charts] themselves and also the radical directions. For universally, a bad [revolution] succeeding universally to another bad one certainly threatens misfortune universally. But particularly, one indicative of illness succeeding another one indicative of illness certainly portends illnesses, especially if the directions are in agreement. For what one could not do, or could only begin, the other one will perfect. And the reasoning is the same in the case of other particular significations.

31. One must not judge any revolution without having inspected the radical figure and its directions for the year of the revolution. However, in every revolution pay careful attention to that which it principally signifies, for it will principally bring that forth if it is signified strongly. And the greater part of the contents of the above laws are made plain in the examples given previously.

Chapter XIX.

Compendiously Embracing General Things that must be Looked at in Revolutions, with a Directory of Judgment.

Here we have compressed into a few words those things that are said at greater length in the chapters above. Therefore, note first: Whether in the figure of the revolution, either of the Sun or of the Moon, the *caelum* is disposed as it is in the radix, and whether the Ascendants are opposed or in trine or square, and into which houses of the revolution the signs of the houses of the radix are removed.

Second. Note whether the cusps of the revolutional figure are the places or radical aspects of the planets, then of which [planets] by nature, determination, and state, also to which rulers they are subject by nature and to what kind of rulers they are subject by state and determination in the revolution.

Third. For each planet in the revolution, note which house of the radix it is in and especially which houses it rules. Then, note what it presages from these positions and from its own celestial state in the radix.

Fourth. Note whether it has returned to its own radical place or to any aspect of it. And to the place or aspect of any other radical planet, and how these are related among themselves by connection and determination in each figure.

Fifth. Note from which house of the radix it departs and to which house of the revolution it comes and which it rules, and in which house of the revolution its radical house is located and how it is disposed in the revolution.

Sixth. Note to which ruler it is subject and how it is related to it, both in the radix and in the revolution.

Seventh. Note whether its celestial state in the revolution is the same as its state in the radix or contrary to it and how much or in what respects.

Eighth. Note whether it is allotted the same determination in the revolution as it has in the radix or one similar to it. And this should particularly be noted in the case of significators and promittors of directions completed within the current year.

Ninth. Note whether the same house in each figure, such as the 10th or the 8th, presages the same things or at least something related, or whether they presage contrary things.

Tenth. Note whether the directions favour or are contrary to the things signified by the revolution, both in their kind and type.

Eleventh. Gather the significations of each planet from its nature and its celestial state and determination in the figure of the radix and keep this collection [of information], made accurately and once for all, for [use in] judging the individual revolutions. And do the same with the figure of the annual revolu-

137

tion. Then, see in what respects the radical and revolutional significations agree and disagree among themselves and with the significations of the direction of the planet if any new direction is completed then; and judge about the effects of that planet in the revolution in accordance with the combination of these significators; and take this for a secret [of astrology].

Twelfth. From those directions agreeing in the same kind or type of effect in both the radical figure and in the annual revolution, select the one in the revolution that agrees and is most concordant with the radical direction; and at its time inspect the revolution of the Moon, and if it is also in agreement, the effect will happen in that month, and on that day on which that lunar revolution supplies a concordant direction, especially [when accompanied] by a concordant transit. But perhaps it will be safer to erect all the individual lunar revolutions of the year, so that the more concordant one can be selected, especially if an effect of great importance is expected. And from these considerations it is plain that astrological judgment is very difficult, especially when the types of effects and their accurate times are to be described. And for this purpose not only is an outstanding perspicuity and sagacity of intellect required, but also good luck, which God alone, or a Good Spirit, of the natal stars bestow by some impulse of nature. But it is also plain that the solar revolution must be judged first, rather than erecting [all] the lunar revolutions, since only those that are conformable to the solar revolution are investigated, so far as this is conformable to the radical signification and its direction. For if the solar revolution does not agree with the signification of the radix and its direction, the lunar revolutions will hardly produce anything at all, unless the effect is strongly signified by the radix and its direction and a similar lunar revolution, i.e., one which also signifies the same thing strongly.

Chapter XX.

A Caution of no Small Importance that Must be Observed in Judging Revolutions.

Lest the mind of the astrologer be terrified by the multitude of directions established both in solar revolutions for the Ascendant, the Midheaven, and all the planets to the places of the radical figure and of the solar revolution, and in lunar revolutions to the places of the radix and to those of the revolutions, both of the Sun and of the Moon itself, it must be known that the greater part of these produces no effect or at least no significant effect in a particular year, but only some of them. For the number of significant effects that can happen in a year is not so many as the number of directions that can occur from the solar and lunar revolutions (as I shall omit the revolutions of the other planets that are only satellites of the Sun to their own radical places, which I think are useless or superfluous, and at least of minor efficacy and less universal in signification than the revolutions of the Sun and the Moon), and they cannot produce great or significant events; perhaps they serve to produce the daily minor [events] to which we pay little attention; and this is much more certain than the fictitious planetary hours from which some falsely think they can predict daily accidents,[1] even down to the hour. So that, if all the abovesaid directions are set up and the days on which they fall are sought out, all the things, both significant and trivial, may be known that are going to happen throughout the whole year from [the action of] the astrological

---

[1] Accidents in the astrological sense, i.e., occurrences.

influences, unless [some] secondary fate or human will should oppose them. For since it is established by certain experience that significant effects are produced by the greater and more powerful causes, why can't the trivial effects be produced by minor and weaker causes in accordance with their own determination in the figure? Certainly no valid reason can be offered in opposition. And therefore, if anyone has calculated all these directions from the beginning of a year and has arranged the days of the year on which the individual directions fall in order and according to their succession, he will have for almost every day, or at least very often, the means whereby he may marvel at the stupendous forces of the stars. But these minutiae are in fact concealed from men, but not from Demons. And because the Director does not concern himself with details, as it is commonly said, nor do men consult astrologers on account of them, but only for accidents of major importance, whether unexpected or undertaken deliberately, relating to life, dignities, marriage, journeys, etc., the astrologer should therefore see in a particular year which effects are signified by the radical directions in that year that are more significant in type or in kind, and whether the solar revolution confirms that signification. For when he has done this he will arrive at the effects for that year. And therefore in a solar revolution one should see which directions are more concordant in type or kind with accidents of a certain sort, for effects of that sort are produced by these. As, if a sickness is signified by a direction of the radical Ascendant to the square of Mars, the directions of the Ascendant of the revolution to the body or the bad aspects of Mars, in the radix as well as in the revolution, should be made, or also those to Saturn or to the Sun and the Moon, especially if they are in bad houses of the radix or the revolution, or if they rule them. For the Ascendant of the revolution is determined to the life of the native in that year as the Ascendant of the radical figure is for his whole time of life; and among these directions, let the stronger one be selected, i.e., the one that is more concordant and closet to the terminus of the radical direction, for the principal effect will be produced by this one. And so, having found the day of the year on which that direction falls, one should see whether it falls in [the period of] a concordant lunar revolution. For when this is the case, the effect will be produced in that month by a concordant direction of the lunar revolution, and especially by a direction of its Ascendant, especially when a concordant transit occurs [at the same time]. And the same thing will have to be done for the rest of the effects of greater importance signified by the radix and its directions, and in this way the immense labor of [calculating] all the directions will be avoided, to which the recognition of particular effects [otherwise] compels us. But vice versa, if on some day anything unusual or new should happen, first having noted its type, by means of which it is referred to one of the twelve houses of the figure, and having made the directions in the solar revolution and the lunar revolution appropriate to that time, one will detect by what cause it was produced, which by the way the transits do not furnish. But if anyone wants to know on what day the *caelum* may influence him in some way in connection with his health or his life, he will find this out as follows. First, let him direct the radical Ascendant and its ruler for that day, i.e., let him see where their direction comes to on that day. Second, let him direct similarly the Ascendant of the annual revolution and its ruler for that day. Third, let him direct similarly the Ascendant of the lunar revolution in whose [period] that day falls and its ruler; and the places to which the directions of the revolution come should be looked at, not just in the figures of the revolutions but particularly in the figure of the radix. Fourth, one should look in the ephemerides to see which transits the planets may make in the figures of the revolutions, and especially in the figure of the radix. And according to these [precepts] he will judge far more certainly than he has been accustomed to do hitherto. Noting, however, that planets in the 1st, 8th, and 12th and those that are the rulers of these houses also signify by accident in connection with health and life; therefore, their directions must be inspected as said above if you want nothing to be lacking [that would lead] to a more certain judgment. And the same thing will have to be done for [predicting] actions and dignities by directions of the Midheaven and its rulers in the figures of the radix and the revolutions, etc. to a day on which the native wants to undertake something outstanding or difficult. However, two things must be noted here. First, that sometimes an effect that is also noteworthy happens without any radical direction, by the solar revolution concordant to that effect and powerful and its concordant direction to the places of the radix and of the solar revolution, with a lunar revolution concordant with them, and its direction, along with appropriate transits, not opposing but rather agreeing with the radical figure. Second, not all the abovesaid causes must be subordinated to themselves for a particular effect, even a significant one, viz. the radix, its concordant direction, a solar revolution and its concordant directions, a lunar revolution and its concordant directions, nor concordant transits. But *some* of the subordinated causes will suffice with a radical figure that signifies the effect at least in kind. Thus in fact, nothing (at least influentially) happens that is alien to the radical figure, but transits—as actual causes of the effects—are very effective in producing them. But what has already been said about this is sufficient.

End of Book 23.

APPENDIX 1

The time used in all of the charts in Book 23 is Local Apparent Time (LAT). To assist the reader who may want to recalculate some of the charts, I have prepared a table of the Equation of Time for the year 1625. That year is approximately in the middle of the time period spanned by the charts. The Equation of Time changes slowly from year to year, but the table shown below is sufficiently accurate for dates within 75 years or more before or after 1625.

The argument of the table is the true longitude of the Sun. To find the value of the Equation of Time locate the solar longitude that is just before the longitude of the Sun and the one just after; these are at 5 degree intervals. Interpolate these two values to get the value for an intermediate longitude. Once found, the Equation of Time can be rounded off to the nearest whole minute.

Table of the Equation of Time for the Year 1625

Sun	Eq.T	Sun	Eq.T	Sun	Eq.T	Sun	Eq.T
0	+7.7	90	+0.9	180	-7.7	270	-0.9
5	+6.1	95	+2.0	185	-9.4	275	+1.6
10	+4.5	100	+3.0	190	-11.0	280	+4.0
15	+2.9	105	+4.0	195	-12.4	285	+6.3
20	+1.4	110	+4.8	200	-13.7	290	+8.4
25	-0.0	115	+5.3	205	-14.7	295	+10.2
30	-1.3	120	+5.6	210	-15.4	300	+11.8
35	-2.3	125	+5.7	215	-15.9	305	+13.1
40	-3.2	130	+5.5	220	-16.1	310	+14.1
45	-3.8	135	+5.0	225	-15.9	315	+14.7
50	-4.2	140	+4.3	230	-15.4	320	+15.0
55	-4.3	145	+3.3	235	-14.5	325	+14.9
60	-4.1	150	+2.1	240	-13.3	330	+14.6
65	-3.7	155	+0.7	245	-11.8	335	+13.9
70	-3.1	160	-0.8	250	-10.0	340	+13.0
75	-2.3	165	-2.5	255	-7.9	345	+11.9
80	-1.3	170	-4.2	260	-5.7	350	+10.6
85	-0.2	175	-5.9	265	-3.3	355	+9.2
90	+0.9	180	-7.7	270	-0.9	360	+7.7

```
LMT = LAT + Equation of Time
LAT = LMT - Equation of time
```

Suppose for example that the Sun in a chart is in 23 Scorpio 19. This is equivalent to 233°19′ or 233.3° to the nearest tenth of a degree. Looking in the table, we find for 230° that the Equation of Time has the value -15.4, and for 235° the value is -14.5. The difference is 0.9 and it is decreasing. We want 3.3/5 or 0.67 of that difference; it will be 0.67 X 0.9 or 0.6. so we subtract that amount from the figure

141

for 230°, and we have -15.4 reduced by 0.6 or -14.8. That is the value in minutes and tenths of a minute. We can round it off, and we will say that the approximate value of the Equation of Time is 15 minutes. Then, if the stated time was 6:05 AM LAT, the equivalent LMT will be 6:05 AM -0:15 or 5:50 AM LMT.

Index of Persons

Albumasar (Abû Ma'shar), *astrologer*, 7n.4&5
Alchabitius (al-Qabîsî), *astrologer*, 24n.3,106
Alphonso X, King of Spain, 7n.2
Ancients (*see* Old Astrologers)
Ancre, Concino Concini, Marquess of, *Marshal of France*, 32,34
Anne of Austria, *Queen and later Regent of France*, 85
Apion (*probably* Appianus), *historian*, 94
Arabian Astrologers, 7n.4,125,126,128
Argol (Andrea Argoli), *mathematician and astrologer*, 69
Austria, Leopold William, Archduke of, 124n.2
Babylonians, 8
Baldwin, Richard S., *translator*, ix,147
Bavaria, Maximilian I the Great, Elector & Duke of, 28
Beaugrand, *commissioner*, 49,146
Bérulle, Pierre de, Cardinal, 48,63,81
Biblical Patriarchs, 111n.2
Bouché-Leclercq, Auguste, *historian*, 7n.5
Boulenger, *commissioner*, 49,146
Boulliau, Ismael, *astronomer*, 54,100
Brahe, Tycho, *astronomer*, 4n.1&2,7,13,67n.1
Brutus, 94
Cassius, 94n.1
Cardan, Jerome, 6,13,24-27,46,66-69,88-91,92n.1,105-111,125-127,129,146
Chavigny, Léon Bouthillier, Count of 30
Cinq-Mars, Henri Coiffier d'Effiat, Marquess of, *royal favorite*, 31
Commissioners, 49,53,83
Condé, Henry II, Prince of, 35,56
Condren, Charles de, *preacher*, 57-65,81,85-87,101-102,123
Cooper, John, *translator*, 124n.3
Copernicus, Nicolas, *astronomer*, 7n.2
Courtiers 34
Davis & Dixon, *publishers*, 124n.3
De Marsillac, 33
Demons, 161,139
De Thou, François Auguste, *royal librarian*, 31
Devil, 58,121
Didacus Prittus Pelusiensis (*see* Placidus de Titis)
Dormio, Claude, Bishop, 97
Duvair, Guillaume, *politico*, 40
Ecclesiastical Magnates, 122
Egyptians, 8,89
Ferdinand II, *emperor*, 27

Forgách, Ferencz, Cardinal, 45
Foreign magnates, *unidentified*, 45
Fortune-teller, *unidentified*, 43,121
Garollo, G., *biographer*, 30n.2
God, 4,5n.1,10,42,44,49,54,57-58,62,65,76,79,81,101,115,121,129,138
Good Spirit, 138
Green, H.S., *astrologer*, 146
Greek astrologers, 6n.2
Guardian Angel 81
Gustavus Adolphus, King of Sweden, ix,27-29,70-72,93,117-118
Halbronn, Jacques, *astrologer and editor*, 146
Hatch, Robert A., *professor*, 100n.2
Henry IV, King of France, 32n.4,48n.1
Hérigone, *commissioner*, 49,146
Hermes the Philosopher (*actually*, Albumasar), 7,128
Hieroz, Jean, *astrologer and translator*, 147
Holden, James Herschel, *translator*, ix-xi,114,147
Horton, Susan, *patron*, iii
Indians, 8,128
Kepler, Johann, *astronomer*, 12,14n.1,27n.3,26,54n.1,56n.4
Kings of Europe, 49
Lachatre, Maurice, *historian*, 32n.4,34n.1
La Rochefoucauld, François, Cardinal, 81
Le Brun, J., *publisher*, 146
Lesdiguières, François de Bonne, Duke of, 37-38
Libert, J., *publisher*, 50n.1,99n.1,146
L'Hôpital-Vitry (*see* Vitry)
Longomontanus, *astronomerand mathematician* 12
Louis XIII, King of France, 30-35,47,48n.1,56n.1,81,94,122
Luynes, Charles d'Albert, Duke of, *Constable of France*, 33,47,98
Luxembourg, Charlotte-Margaret, Duchess of, 47n.2
Luxembourg, Léon d'Albert de Luynes, Duke of, 47-48,98
Magini, Giovanni Antonio, *mathematicand and astrologer* 12
Magnates of the Court, 49,54,56
Marc Antony, 94
Marie de' Medici, Queen of France, 33n.4,48-49,81,85,121-122
Medieval Astrologers, 6n.2
Ménard, P., *publisher*, 146
Merchants, *unidentified*, 43
Merchant of Cologne, *unidentified*, 43
Methuselah, *patriarch*, 125n.2
Morin, Jean Baptiste, iv,v,viii,ix, *and as the subject of many charts and in many footnotes*
Mydorge, *commissioner*, 49,146
Naibod, Valentine, *mathematician*, 26n.2,94,106n.1
Nestor, King of Pylos, 37n.3
Octavius (*later, the emperor Augustus*), 94n.1

Old Astrologers, 111,127
Oppolzer, Theodor, Ritter von, *astronomer*,57n.1,96n.1
Origanus (David Tost), *mathematician and astrologer*, 20,126
Orléans, Jean Baptiste Gaston, Duke of, *brother of Louis XIII*, 56
Pappenheim, Gottfried Heinrich, Count of, *field marshal*, 28n.6
Pascal (*not* Blaise Pascal), *commissioner*, 49
Perray, *assassin*, 34n.1
Persians, 8
Pingree, David, *editor*, 7n.5
Placidus de Titis, *mathematician*, ix,110n.1,124
Ptolemy, Claudius, 4n.1,6,27,88,116,125
Queen of France, (*see* Marie de' Medici *and* Anne of Austria)
Queen's Council, 85
Regiomontanus (Johann Müller), 24n.3,49n.2,109,111,124n.4
Reinhold, Erasmus, *astronomer*, 7n.2
Retz, *publisher*, 147
Richelieu, Cardinal, ix,29-32,34-35,37,49-50,53-54,62,72-73,83,94,100,118,123
Robbers, 44,114
Robbins, F.E., *editor & translator*, 6n.1
Royal Council, 53-56,84,100
Ruland, Johann, M.D., 45
Ruland, Martin, M.D., *imperial physician*, 45
Ruysbroeck, Jan van, *mystic*, 101
Saint-Saire, Henry de Boulainviller, Count of, *scholar and astrologer*, 32n.1
Selva, Henri, *astrologer and translator*, 147
Seni, Giovanni Battista, *astrologer*, 27n.3
Sève, Claudia de, *see* Tronson, *Claudia de Sève*
Stadius, Johann, *mathematician*, 3,7
Swiss Students, *unidentified*, 40-41
Tauler, Johannes, *mystic*, 101
Teubner, B.G., *publisher*, 7n.5
Thomas Aquinas, Saint, 65,116
Tilly, John Tserclaes, Count of, *general*, 28
Tronson, Claudia de Sève, *wife of Louis Tronson*, 37,95
Tronson, Louis, *government official*, 32-37,73-74,94-96
Vlacq, Adrian, *publisher*, 147
Villennes, Nicolas Bourdin, Marquess of, *astrologer*, 146
Vitry, Nicolas de l'Hôpital, Duke of, *Captain of the Royal Guard*, 34n.1
Wallenstein, Albert of, Duke of Friedland, *general*, ix,27
Wolf, Hieronymus, *editor*, 7n.5
Woman, a famous, *unidentified* 38,76

BIBLIOGRAPHY

Original Works

Green, H.S.
A Thousand and One Notable Nativities. London: Modern Astrology, 1915?. 2nd ed. rev.
The Book of Notable Nativities. Chicago: The Aries Press, 1943. repr. in facs. of the 2nd ed.

Holden, James Herschel
A History of Horoscopic Astrology. Tempe, Az.: A.F.A., Inc., 1996. xv,359 pp. 21 cm. diagrs. tables

Lachatre, Maurice
Histoire des Papes/Rois, Reines, Empereurs/à travers les siècles. Paris: Librairie du Progrès, c. 1875. 2nd ed. 3 vols. illus. 4to.

Morin, Jean Baptiste
Longitudinum terrestrium nec non coelestium nova et hactenus optata scientia... [The New and Hitherto Hoped for Science of Terrestrial and Celestial Longitudes...] Paris: J. Libert, 1634. 4to. 164 pp.
Lettres escrites au Sr Morin par les plus célèbres astronomes de France, approuvant son invention des longitudes, contre la dernière sentence rendue sur ce subject par les sieurs Mydorge, Beaugrand, Boulenger et Hérigone, commissaires députez pour en juger... [Letters Written to Mr. Morin by the Most
Famous Astronomers of France, Approving his Invention of Longitudes, Against the Unfair Decision Rendered on That Subject by Messers Mydorge, Beaugrand, Boulenger And Hérigone, Commissioners Deputized to Judge it...] Paris: The Author, 1635. 8vo. 55 pp.
Astronomia jam a fundamentis integre et exacte restituta, complectens ix partes hactenus optatae scientiae longitudinum coelestium nec non terrestrium... [Astronomy now Wholly and Exactly Restored from its Fundamentals, comprising IX Parts of the Hitherto Hoped for Science of Celestial and Terrestrial Longitudes...] Paris: The Author, 1649. 4to 361 pp.
Tabulae Rudolphinae ad meridianum Uraniburgi supputatae a Joanne Baptista Morino, ... ad accuratum et facile compendium redactae. [The Rudolphine Tables, Calculated by Jean Baptiste Morin for the Meridian of Uraniborg, ... Reduced to an accurate and easy compendium] Paris: J. Le Brun, 1650. 4to. 117 pp. tables
Remarques astrologiques de Jean-Baptiste Morin, ... sur le commentaire du Centiloque de Ptolémée mise en lumière par Messire Nicolas de Bourdin, ... [The Astrological Remarks of Jean Baptiste Morin, ... on the Commentary on Ptolemy's *Centiloquy* Published by My Lord Nicolas de Bourdin...] Paris: P. Ménard, 1657. 4to. 168 pp.
Remarques astrologiques/de Jean-Baptiste Morin... sur le Commentaire du Centiloque de Ptoloémée ou la seconde partie de l'*Uranie* de Messire Nicolas de Bourdin, marquis de Villennes, etc. ed. by Jacques Halbronn [with a valuable introduction, notes, and a bibliography of Morin's works] Paris: Retz, 1976. repr. of the 1st ed. 303 pp. 20 cm. portr. facs. tables. biblio.
Astrologia Gallica. [French Astrology] The Hague: Adrian Vlacq, 1661. folio. Pref., 784 pp. portr. diagrs. tables

Translations and Commentaries

Morin, Jean Baptiste

La Théorie des Déterminations Astrologiques de Morin de Villefranche conduisant à une Méthode rationelle our l'Interprétation du Thême Astrologique. [Morin of Villefranche's Theory of Astrological Determinations, Leading to a Rational Method for the Interpretation of the Astrological Chart] [an abridged translation into French by Henri Selva (*pseudonym*) of the *Astrologia Gallica*, Book 21] Paris: Bodin, 1902. vi, 218 pp. 2 plates Ma vie devant les astres/ Collationné dans l'Astrologia Gallica (1661)/ et traduit par

Jean Hieroz.... [My Life Before the Stars/ Collated from the Astrologia Gallica (1661)/ and translated (into French) by Jean Hieroz] [Morin's own explanation of the events of his life, as indicated by directions of the radix, solar and lunar returns, transits and elections] Nice: Éditions Cahiers Astrologiques, 1943. paper 87 pp. diagrs. tables

The Morinus System of Horoscope Interpretation/Astrologia Gallica/ Book Twenty One. trans. from the Latin by Richard S. Baldwin Washington: A.F.A., 1974. paper [i-v],109,[1] 23 cm.

Astrologia Gallica Book/ Twenty-Two/ Directions. [with excerpts from Books 2, 13, 15, 17, 18, 20, 23, 24, and Jerome Cardan's works] trans. from the Latin by James Herschel Holden Tempe, Az.: A.F.A. Inc., 1994. paper xv, 292 pp. diagrs. Tables

Astrologia Gallica Book/ Twenty-Four/ Progressions and Transits. trans. from the Latin by James Herschel Holden Tempe, Az.: A.F.A. Inc., 2004 paper viii, 66 pp. Diagrs. Table 21 cm. [in preparation]

"Jean Baptise Morin's Comments on House Division in his *Remarques Astrologiques*" (House Division III) trans. from the French by James H. Holden Journal of Research of the AFA 6, Nos. 1&2 (1991):19-35 Tempe, Az.: A.F.A., Inc., 1982-

Astrosynthesis. The Rational System of Horoscope Interpretation according to Morin de Villefranche, translated (from Selva's version) by Lucy Little New York: Zoltan Mason Emerald Books, 1974. 192pp. 23 cm.

www.ingramcontent.com/pod-product-compliance
Lightning Source LLC
Chambersburg PA
CBHW080341170426
43194CB00014B/2648